S0-EOI-392

THE CONSTITUTIONS OF POLAND AND OF THE UNITED STATES
kinships and genealogy

by

JOSEPH KASPAREK-OBST

THE AMERICAN INSTITUTE OF
POLISH CULTURE
MIAMI, FLORIDA
1980

The Polish Heritage Series
Editorial Board
chairman: prof. Zdzisław P. Wesołowski

Other Publications in the
POLISH HERITAGE SERIES

TRUE HEROES OF JAMESTOWN by Arthur Waldo
SELECTED TALES by Henryk Sienkiewicz
JAGIELLONIAN POLAND by Paweł Jasienica
THE CONSTITUTIONS OF POLAND AND
THE UNITED STATES by Joseph Kasparek-Obst

Copyright® 1980
The American Institute of Polish Culture
1000 Brickell Avenue
Miami, Florida 33131
Library of Congress Catalog Card Number 80-65959

THE AMERICAN INSTITUTE
OF POLISH CULTURE
1440 79th ST. CAUSEWAY, SUITE 117
MIAMI, FLORIDA 33141

For Sylvia

ACKNOWLEDGEMENTS

My son Christopher's research assistance was an important contribution to this work. I also want to express my thanks to my wife Sylvia for her understanding and patience; and to those who gave me support: my daughter Hania LaBorn by her words of encouragement and her son Joseph and my son's daughter Monica by being there.

California, 1980   J.K.O.

CONTENTS

Foreword	1

PART I: KINSHIPS

1	America to the end of the eighteenth century	3
2	Poland to the end of the eighteenth century	27
3	Poland: 1791-94	57
4	Poland: 1794-1831	69
5	Poland: 1831-1921	79
6	Poland: 1921 -	97

PART II: GENEALOGY

7	The United States as cultural product	121
8	Poland as cultural product	133
9	The ideas of the Polish Second Reformation abroad	159
10	The Socinian contribution to west European thought	183
11	Poland: collapse and resurrection of thought	197
12	The Second Reformation and America	213
13	Conclusions	225
Notes		251
Bibliography		275
Index		285

FOREWORD

As the eight-century-old Polish Republic was entering into its hundred-twenty-three-year eclipse as a political entity, on the other side of the ocean there was springing to independent life a young people, the bulk of them settled there for no more than a few generations. A joint consideration of these two historical events, an attempt to associate in any fashion countries spatially so distant from one another — particularly while having before one's eyes our contemporary economic-political map of the world — is likely to induce a sense of ludicrous mis-juxtaposition. Accordingly it is helpful to bear in mind that the relative situations of these two countries in the world today are not those of the period when the Polish Republic slid into eclipse and the United States rose to the dignity of nationhood.

In area the two countries were at the time nearly equal. The population of Poland came to twelve and a half million, "not counting the population increment between the first two [partitions] and [the third and final partition in] the year 1795;"[1] the population of the United States amounted to not quite four million.[2] Poland at that time had behind her eight hundred years of recorded history — a colorful history woven out of labor and struggle, achievement and reversal, victory and disaster — a history of social evolution over a span of over thirty generations. Still more noteworthy, the Polish Republic comprised a voluntary union of Poland and Lithuania (the latter including what was then called Ruthenia and is now the Ukraine and Byelorussia) which over the centuries were gradually becoming transformed by a process of cultural integration into one people, and if only on that account constituted a phenomenon such as the United States were in their own turn to become.

An awareness of these truths facilitates an examination of partial parallels, and a still more probing study leads to the conclusion that kinships and mutual influences have long existed between the two peoples. Offhand one can spot evidence of these influences in the participation of Poles in the American Revolution of 1776-83 and in the American Civil War of 1861-65. Names of those who gave their services in the struggle for the independence and preservation of the United States include those of generals such as Kościuszko, Pułaski, Krzyżanowski, Karge and Shoepf. The search for still earlier affinities will conjure up the image of Dr. Curtius, who as early as the colonial period established the first college in North America.[3] In passing one must mention the first arrivals from Poland: craftsmen who are recorded in the early annals of America not only for having founded the production of glass and wood tar, but also for having organized the first strike in America: a strike which, employed successfully in the struggle over equality of rights, earned them recognition as the first heroes in American history.[4]

History also recalls the American physician Dr. Paul Fitzsimmons Eve, who participated in the Polish Uprising of 1830-31 (and whose home at 619 Green Street in Augusta, Georgia, is today a historical monument);[5] as well as the American novelist James Fenimore Cooper's organizing, during that Uprising, of an American-Polish committee of assistance for the Poles who were fighting for their independence.[6] Nor can we pass over the fact that the "Blue Division" — so called by the Poles after the color of the soldiers' uniforms and formed of Polish-Americans with the official approval of the United States government — fought during 1919-20 to secure the rights of the Polish nation to the historical soil of the Republic; or that American pilots headed by General Merian C. Cooper — a relative of James Fenimore Cooper's and at that time a young lieutenant colonel in the Polish Air Force — blasted out renascent Poland's eastern borders even as, toward the end of World War I, she made her return debut to the map.[7]

But in fact the roots of mutual Polish-American influence go back deeper still.

PART I
Kinships

CHAPTER 1

AMERICA TO THE END OF THE EIGHTEENTH CENTURY

I. The discovery of the continent to the Constitution of 1789

The American hemisphere has been discovered no less than three, and possibly as many as five or more, times. There being no evidence of *Homo sapiens* in America at an earlier time, the first discoverers and denizens — arrived between twenty-five and twelve thousand years ago — are taken to be a group of people whose physical characteristics indicate their origin in Asia.[1] How they traversed the distance — whether by foot across an ice-covered Bering Strait, or by some sort of primitive raft — will in all likelihood forever remain their own secret. It is possible that they crossed over on dry land during a period of greatly lowered waters[2] whose occurence is pointed to by recent scientific findings.[3]

These men from Asia fanned out over the North and South American continents. Those who settled in the areas about the Isthmus of Panama and along the shores of the warm-water oceans, developed interesting cultures. However, those who scattered out over the mountain, plateau and plains areas of the North American continent never strayed far out of the Stone Age.

This tremendous range of cultures among the same race inhabiting both the American continents, and the lack of any intermediate cultural forms, struck the early scholars and prompted the Frenchman de Guines to theorize, backed up by Chinese literary classics, that the Chinese were in contact with America about 2,250 B.C. and revisited it about 500 A.D.[4]

De Guines' theory of 1761 seemed in 1831 to collapse beneath the critical blows of the Prussian scholar Klaproth, but our own time continues to supply a growing knowledge of the Indians and with it de Guines' revitalized arguments are taking on a compelling force.

Next to discover the hemisphere framing the western Atlantic were the Norsemen. The names of two are known: those of Bjarne Heriolfsson and Leif Eriksson, who — independently of each other — reached the northern coast of North America at the turn of the eleventh century.[5] The attempts at settlement made at that time were unsuccesful, though for over five hundred years Norse settlements did flourish in Greenland. Subsequently the Scandinavian-descended population died out in utter misery, forgotten by their mother country,[6] and the Norsemen appeared to suddenly lose interest in the northern rim of the Atlantic and turned their attentions instead to the European continent.

The Polish contribution to the discovery of America was recorded in 1597 by the Dutch geographer Wytfliet, who stated that the honor of a "second discovery" of America "fell to *Johannes Scolvus Polonus,* who in the year 1476 ... sailed beyond Norway, Greenland, Frisland, penetrated the Northern Strait under the very Arctic Circle, and arrived at the country of Labrador and Estotiland.'"[7] Scolvus has since become known to Poles as Jan of Kolno.[8] Morison is skeptical about this Jan of Kolno, but — as he himself recounts — another American historian, George Bancroft, once dismissed the Norse sagas that were first adduced as evidence for the now well established Norse expeditions to America as "mythological in form and obscure in meaning."[9]

On the twelfth of October, 1492, a Genoan in the service of Spain, Christopher Columbus, landed on an island known today as Watling Island or San Salvador, which he mistook for the Indies.[10] There ensued further expeditions of discovery by Columbus and by his imitators, and their result was the gradual colonization by Europeans of the entire New World.

England, in the period from the beginning of the seventeenth to the middle of the eighteenth centuries, took possession of 325,000 square miles in the northern part of North America.[11]

The English colonies were organized by companies — corporate bodies to which the Crown granted royal charters — and by individuals or groups of individuals who received a territory together with the power of exercising authority on behalf of the Crown. Within the framework of either type of colony, the free settlers enjoyed certain fundamental rights: their freedoms, and participation in a limited local autonomy.[12]

Stretching as they did down the coastline over a distance of hundreds of miles, and taking in lands of diverse qualities and isobars and isotherms, all presenting diverse potentials for utilization, the colonies from their very inception displayed a heterogeneous character. Initially there were attempts at agricultural communes in which groups of settlers received tracts of soil which they divided up among them into homesteads, while preserving common ownership of pasturage and forest, as well as of tilled soil — which, however, was divided up for cultivation among the members of the community. This system did not persist for long; the communes were broken up, and after 1700 only completely private farms existed. Their sizes varied from that of bare self-sufficiency to that of large landed estates.[13]

During their early period, the Colonies were dependent for supplies on the mother country, and lacking as they did their own facilities for producing many objects of everyday use, they long accepted their state of dependence. England was then in the grip of mercantilism, in accordance with which the Colonies fulfilled certain well defined roles: they produced the raw materials needed by English industry and bought the finished products of that industry, while the shipping of both raw materials and finished goods brought profit to the English merchantmen.[14] Aside from that, the Colonies served to drain off England's excess population as well as elements for a variety of reasons considered undesirable by England.[15]

In order to ensure the full attainment of these goals, Parliament issued the "Navigation Acts,"[16] a set of regulations governing the commercial intercourse of the Colonies with other countries. The series of Acts of 1660, 1663, 1673 and 1696, together with the *Molasses Act* of 1733, put an increasingly tight rein on the independent economic operations of the Colonists. A thorn in the side of English industry was the developing native Colonial industry. In order to stifle competition, the English Parliament passed a number of laws: the *Woolens Act* (1699) forbidding the Colonies to produce woolen fabrics for export; the *Hat Act* (1732) forbidding the Colonies to produce hats; and the *Iron Act* (1750) enjoining the Colonies from producing certain articles of iron.[17]

The enforcement of these regulations required administrative vigilance on England's part; the tendency of the London government became to turn the Colonies — still at that time of diverse types — into homogeneous royal domains, and to consolidate small ones into larger ones. The royal governors — at times exceedingly despotic men — in implementing the policies of the London government antagonized the Colonists and in some places provoked conflicts.

The process of administrative homogenization led to the Colonies by 1754 being — save for Connecticut, Maryland, Pennsylvania and Rhode Island — all royal colonies. Their administration crystallized into a system under which:

1. the supreme authority in each colony was vested in a governor who enjoyed the power of vetoing acts of the colonial legislature, as well as the power of enforcing the Navigation Acts; an appointed council not only advised the governor but sat as the upper house of the colonial legislature and as the supreme court;

2. the members of the legislature, or more precisely of its lower house, were chosen by those citizens who could fulfill the property qualifications for voting; this body could make laws, subject to veto by the governor or by the royal Privy Council;

3. judicial powers were exercised in each colony by courts at three levels: local, county and superior; the judges were appointed by the king or, in his name, by the governor — which was not without its consequences for their rulings.[18]

The problems of the Colonies and their situation underwent drastic changes in 1763, when as a result of the annexation of Canada and the Floridas into the ethnically quite heterogeneous British domains, more new groups of entirely different cultural backgrounds entered into the picture. Moreover, while up till then the Colonies had had continually to reckon with the possibility of attack from French Canada, now the disappearance of France from North America freed the Colonists from that threat and consequently also from the necessity of hanging onto Britain's apron strings.

For England the eviction of the French from America meant a new situation, with its own attendant benefits and burdens. The English government attempted to transfer the financial burdens at least in part onto the Colonies by employing "requisitions" which nearly all of them refused to honor. Already during the Seven Years' War with France, the Colonies had exhibited their indifference toward Britain's interests by continuing to trade with French and Spanish possessions in the West Indies and by running the English blockades.

The Colonies had all the while been drifting away from the mother country, an effect augmented by the mass influx of Germans, Scotch-Irish and Negroes into the population. From all the groups there had gradually been developing a distinctly "American" type; a sense of separateness was ever more strongly manifesting itself, and a society intially founded with the idea of replicating English society was being transformed into something entirely new. Additionally, the existence of a virtually unlimited western frontier encouraged the development of strong personalities disinclined to acknowledge the traditional English social scheme.[19]

The old order was continued the longest by the Southern planters, tied to England by their lucrative tobacco transactions. Elsewhere the Colonists carried on — and had no intention of curtailing — a trade conducted with other countries without any regard for the English economy. They likewise demonstrated their independence of the Crown when, without waiting for the conclusion of the war with the French, they proceeded to move onto the lands being lost by France in the west, thereby rousing the displeasure and hostility of the local Indians.

English attempts at curbing these wildcat colonizations by individuals contemptuous of all authority and by self-proclaimed "companies" met with complete disobedience, thereby leading to an increasingly real menace of organized attack by the Indian tribes. The government in London felt obliged to station ten thousand troops along the frontier. Their expense was to amount to three hundred fifty thousand pounds a year; of this sum one third, by London's decision, was to be defrayed by the Colonies. The attempt to make the Colonies pay the special tax provided the first impetus for the organization of armed resistance against British authorities. Henceforth the Colonies and the Crown persisted unalterably on a collision course, as Parliament — dominated by adherents of George II, equally as ignorant as he of the state of affairs — enacted one law after another designed to discipline the Colonists.

The government instituted strict customs controls in the Colonies; the navy pursued smugglers, and the vice-admiralty courts operated without juries. The year 1764 brought the *Sugar Act* designed to put a stop to the Colonies' trade with the island possessions of France and Spain. The *Currency Reform Act* of the same year forbade the Colonies to issue paper money, thus aggravating the already short supply caused by the rigorously enforced customs duties. The year 1765 added the *Stamp Act;* henceforth legal and business documents, newspapers and other printed matter were required to bear revenue stamps. The purpose of the latter act was to raise funds needed for at least partial coverage of the costs associated with maintaining British troops on the American continent.

All these laws were greeted in the Colonies with vociferous discontent, which took the legal form of a resolution by the colonial legislature of Virginia — imitated by other colonies — denying Parliament's right to levy taxes and fees on the Colonies without their consent. The resolutions of the individual colonies were crowned by a resolution of the Stamp Act Congress of 1765 — the first joint action taken by the colonists. The well-to-do and educated segments of society acted through more or less legal channels; the organized merchants boycotted British goods (the "Nonimportation Agreements"); the lower orders simply exercised violence against the fiscal agents of the Crown.

Probably as a result of the troubles experienced from the commercial boycott, the English Parliament in its *Declaratory Act* of March, 1766, lowered the import duties on molasses, while at the same time affirming its inalienable right to legislate in all matters whatsoever for the Colonies. Practically at the same time, at the instance of Chancellor of the Exchequer Townshend,

Parliament lowered the English land tax, planning to offset the diminished government revenues through increased revenues from the Colonies. When the New York legislature refused to make appropriations for the English troops, Townshend secured the dissolution of the refractory legislature and strengthened the instruments of royal authority in the Colonies in order that they might execute a strict application of the Navigation Acts and thereby assure the collection of funds for the royal administration without His Majesty's Government having to seek the cooperation of the colonial legislatures.

In 1767 Townshend took a further step by obtaining from Parliament the power to impose customs duties on articles imported by the Colonies: on paper, painters' materials, glass and tea. Here it should be mentioned that during the previous period of crisis between England and the Colonies, the Americans themselves had acknowledged the British government's right to regulate trade between England and her colonies through so-called "external taxes." However, they did not recognize Britain's right to impose on the Colonies "internal taxes," or taxes designed to balance the English budget. Townshend, in introducing the customs law, described the customs duties as "external taxes," to which the Colonists objected that even such taxes were illegal if their chief purpose was not the regulation of trade.

The polemics concerning the Crown's rights in regard to the Colonies were the first essay at questioning the constitutional basis of English rule over the inhabitants of the Colonies. The conflict once again manifested itself on several levels: led by Samuel Adams, the radical intellectuals expressed their objections in written form in a "Circular Letter" calling upon all the Colonies to apply the Nonimportation Agreements; and the mob harrassed the customs agents, here and there tarring and feathering them. Troops sent to protect them were attacked by a street crowd on March 5, 1770, and the resulting "Boston Massacre" at long last demonstrated to England the gravity of the situation. A short time later there occurred a change of prime ministers, and with it — upon the urging of the new prime minister — repeal of customs duties in the Colonies, with the exception of that on tea.

If the Colonists did not carry off a complete victory, at any rate they acquired the conviction that through concerted and persistent action they could break down London's opposition. Nor did they forget the wrongs that they had suffered at the hands of the English authorities. Feelings ran particularly high among the lower classes, which were unable to reconcile themselves to a system in which the antiquated guild law hampered free employment, the requirement of property ownership deprived them of voting rights, and the church was legally a state institution. Although during the period from 1770 to 1773 there was a certain relaxation of tensions, it proved to be merely the proverbial calm before the storm; the repeal of duties brought about by the Boston demonstration failed to discharge tensions which had been building for years. In 1772 the Colonists organized "committees of correspondence" whose purpose was to register and publicize actions by the English authorities detrimental to the Colonies.

The year 1773 brought the *Tea Act,* releasing the British East India Company from customs duties on tea exported to America: a measure which, in conjunction with its provisions effectively eliminating American merchants from the tea trade, granted that company a monopoly on tea. The resentment of the well-to-do and of the masses was expressed in the so-called "Boston Tea Party," in which a consignment of East Indian tea was heaved overboard into Boston harbor.

Parliament next issued a series of measures known as the *Coercive Acts* (1774) which the Colonists christened the "Intolerable Acts." These acts struck at the vital interests and rights of the Colonies: the *Boston Port Act* closed down that port until Massachusetts made good the losses resulting from the Tea Party; the *Administration of Justice Act* deprived the New England courts of jurisdiction over cases involving royal officials; the *Massachusetts Governing Act* suppressed town meetings and made the upper chamber of the legislature appointive by the governor; and the *Quartering Act* gave the colonial governors the power to requisition buildings to house troops.

The Colonists called a Continental Congress. In September of 1774, fifty-five delegates from twelve colonies arrived in

Philadelphia. The Congress resolved to urge the Colonies to resist the English "Coercive Acts," adoped a *Declaration of Rights and Grievances* recognizing royal authority but denying Parliament's right to impose taxes on the Colonies, and established the "Continental Association," which subsequently engineered a suspension of trade with England.

In February, 1775, the British Prime Minister, Lord North, announced a *Resolution on Conciliation,* promising to lift the taxes from any colony that covered the expenses of its own government. The Continental Association rejected this declaration, and the English military command sent detachments to the town of Concord to seize the military supplies stored there by the Continental leaders. The colonial militia gathered to oppose the army, and on April 19, 1775, a skirmish took place in which eight militiamen were killed.

Bold and decisive steps were needed; on May 10, the Second Continental Congress resolved to organize an army and placed it under the command of General Washington. The skirmishes rose in frequency and intensity, eventually turning into full-scale revolutionary warfare that was to last for the next seven years. An attempt at conciliatory settlement via a petition of July, 1775, was hardly facilitated by the Crown's response: the King in August declared the Colonists rebels, dispatched mercenary Hessian troops to the Colonies, and declared a blockade of American ports.

On July 2, 1776, the Continental Congress directed a committee headed by Jefferson to prepare a document which on the fourth of July was adopted as the "Declaration of Independence." For the first time the word "independence" fell openly, expressing the desire of the colonial population for a joint existence as a separate nation; but seven years of bloody struggle were required to turn the word into the deed.[20]

At the behest of Congress, all the former British colonies, with the exception of Connecticut and Rhode Island, drew up their own constitutions based on the principle of a tripartite government:

1. The executive power was vested in a governor with a one-year term of office.

2. The legislative power was reposed in a legislature comprising members with a short duration of office.

3. Justice was to be dispensed by life-term judges appointed — depending on the state — either by the governor or by the legislature.

Each of the constitutions incorporated a section — a "bill of rights" — guaranteeing civil liberties: freedom of speech, of press and of religion; immunity from arbitrary arrest; and the right to trial by jury.

Here and there the constitutions did contain provisions that stood in conflict with democratic principles. Thus the rights to vote and to seek office remained contingent on property ownership, and so most of the citizens were barred from either voting or holding office. Some of the constitutions expressly restricted the rights of certain categories of the populace, such as Jews, Catholics and atheists.

The considerable similarities among the constitutions notwithstanding, the differences among them — derived largely from their somewhat divergent sociopolitical patterns developed during the colonial period — bespoke the necessity of codification. Standing in the way of this were deep-seated feelings of separateness and an all but fanatical resistance, on the part of colonies just transformed into *states,* against any concessions to the other states. This situation indicated to the more politically mature leaders the necessity of laying foundations for a formal union of states.

The Declaration of Independence of 1776 was followed in 1777 by the Articles of Confederation, the first attempt at a constitution binding together all the states. But the result was merely a very loose union. Each state retained complete independence and sovereignty, and the United States were little more than a league of nations for the resolution of common problems. The Congress — a unicameral legislature which also functioned as an executive and judicial authority — was composed of delegates from the various states. A vote by two-thirds of all the states decided any measure, and the powers delegated by the states to Congress were restricted to:

1. the declaration of war and the conclusion of peace;
2. the drawing up of treaties and alliances;

3. relations with the Indians; and
4. the conduct of the mails.

Congress' functions as a joint government boiled down to the role of a common administrative agency for the states. Congress had no power to levy taxes or to regulate commerce, those powers being reserved to the individual states. This first attempt at a constitution created no single dispositional center, provided no coherent system for the administration of justice, furnished the joint government with no sanctions. The only true step toward genuine unification was the establishment of a common citizenship.[21]

The consequences arising from the impotence of such a Confederation were not long in coming. The once booming commerce with foreign countries stagnated; England refused to participate in any economic exchange, and worse still denied American ships access to the West Indies; Spain refused to engage in any trade.

In economic self-defense, the individual states proceeded to levy tariffs against each other. The result was an economic standstill which turned the dissatisfied populace against Congress — a helpless, powerless body burdened with responsibility for forty million dollars in war debts, lacking in power to tax, and dependent for its funds on the sale of land belonging in common to all the states and on so-called "requisitions," i.e. requests to the various states that they cover parts of the common expenses. This last means of covering the Confederation's expenses Washington termed "A timid kind of recommendation from Congress to the States."[22]

This situation was complicated to the point of chaos by the individual states releasing massive printings of paper money. Inflation grew, together with all the inescapable consequences. According to whether the debtors or the creditors held the majority, the legislatures favored either one group or the other. In Massachusetts, events culminated in a debtors' rebellion led by Daniel Shays, a former captain in Washington's army, which was put down only by troops, and in all the states there were demands for the abolition of all private debts and for an equal distribution of property.

There must have been some signs of positive change,

inasmuch as Washington noted during this period that the country was making good the destructions of the revolutionary period and was laying the "foundations of a great empire." At the same time he made no secret of his fears: "I am mortified beyond expression when I view the clouds that have spread over the brightest morn that ever dawned upon any country."[23]

A somewhat more sanguine view was given by Thomas Jefferson in a letter to Madison: "I hold that a little rebellion, now and then, is a good thing, and as necessary in the political world as storms in the physical."[24]

However, that the situation appeared grave is indicated in another piece of correspondence from the times. A former subordinate of his during the Revolution, General Knox, wrote Washington: "[The mob's] creed is, that the property of the United States has been protected from the confiscation of Britain by the joint exertions of all and therefore ought to be the common property of all."[25]

Confirmation of the alarming state of affairs is found in another letter from Washington: "There are combustibles in every State which a spark might set a fire in;" and in a letter from Stephen Higginson:

> we cannot long exist under our present system; and unless we soon acquire more force to the Union by some means or other, Insurgents will arise and eventually take the reins from us. We shall inevitably be thrown into ... convulsions which will result in one or more Governments, established with the loss of much blood.[26]

The difficult situation was complicated by strong pressures on Washington that, in order to save the country, he take power into his own hands and declare himself dictator — pressure which, however, the former commander in chief would not yield to.[27]

The discontent among the lower classes alarmed the well-to-do. The latter perceived the necessity of furnishing the government of the Union with force capable of checking the mob. After delegates from Maryland and Virginia had convened in

1785 for the purpose of discussing their common problems and in particular their disagreement about their rights on the Potomac River and Chesapeake Bay, it was resolved to call a conference of delegates from all the states to discuss commercial questions.

The following year, the conference took place as planned, but representatives of only five states showed up. Chiefly through the efforts of Hamilton, the gathering took a resolution not on the matters comprising the original purpose of the conference, but bidding all the states to send their delegates to Philadelphia for a convention to discuss necessary changes in the Articles of Confederation.

At Philadelphia, just as the Convention was to gather, former officers of Washington's assembled.

> Disgruntled at the refusal of Congress to grant them half pay for life, some of the military men through their exclusive and hereditary Society of the Cincinnati hoped to control and to invigorate the government, some of them even aspiring to a kind of army dictatorship.[28]

> These gentlemen, "panting for nobility and with the eagle dangling at their breast," could well become the nucleus of an American aristocracy or of a Cromwellian military government. And Washington was president of the Cincinnati![29]

The General regarded this circumstance as highly embarrassing. He saw it as

> serious and sufficient reason for his staying away. It had required the combined efforts of Madison, Hamilton, Edmund Randolph and Washington's especial friend General Henry Knox to get the General to Philadelphia at all; he feared that as president of the Cincinnati his presence would inconvenience the Convention.[30]

At the Convention all the states were represented save for Rhode Island. Fifty-five delegates assembled. They were mostly young; their average age — despite the attendance of several venerable members whose senior, Benjamin Franklin, numbered eighty-one years — was thirty-two.

From the beginning several men stood out: Washington (the president of the Convention), Madison, Franklin and Hamilton. Additionally influential — if not physically present — were John Adams (then the American minister to London) and Jefferson (away negotiating agreements and loans in Paris). Adams had just published the first volume of his three-volume work, *A Defence of the Constitutions of Government of the United States of America*, and Jefferson sent members of the Convention several hundred volumes from Paris: the new *Encyclopedie Methodique*, works on history, political science and the law of nations, and writings by Voltaire, Diderot, Mably, Necker and d'Albon.[31]

The members of the Convention represented an enlightened element well acclimated to public life. The majority had already served in Congress or in the state legislatures, and nearly all came from the wealthy classes. They did not include the leaders of the late Revolution; the signatures of Samuel Adams, Patrick Henry and Thomas Paine were not later to appear at the bottom of the Constitution. True, there was still Franklin, together with a group exhibiting democratic leanings, but no trace of the revolutionary fervor of several years earlier. Other men were putting their efforts to working out the new social foundations, but even those whose names reached Jefferson in Paris seemed to him "an assembly of demi-gods."[32]

These men proved equal to the undertaking, and although undeniably having a personal interest in the economic consequences of their work, they did not lose sight of their true goal: the preservation and strengthening of the Union. Realism and the clear recognition that the new law of the land would have to win acceptance outside the Convention to acquire the force of law, made the members realize the necessity of coming to agreement with their opponents, and distrust of aristocracy on the one hand and an aversion toward the system of democracy as experienced under the Confederation on the other, inclined them toward a path of moderation.

There were many problems. Virginia — one of the large states — submitted a plan envisioning a bicameral legislature in which measures would be passed by a majority vote, and which would likewise choose the President of the United States and the federal judges. The plan proposed by New Jersey — a small state — disagreed with Virginia's: it provided for a unicameral legislature, with each state enjoying a single vote, and empowered to set duties and tariffs, to regulate commerce in general, and to exercise sanctions in order to obtain from the states the so called "requisitions" needed to cover the essential expenses of the federal government.

The numerical advantage was with the large states, and had they wanted to, they certainly would have been able to force through their plan. It bespeaks their considerable political maturity that, instead, they sought to avoid further crises and to reach a compromise.[33]

II. The Constitution of 1789

The United States Constitution as it was finally worked out was founded on six cardinal principles:

1. The people were recognized as the source of the Constitution's force — as the superior of a government of limited powers;

2. a federation (tight union) supplanted the Confederation (loose union) of the states;

3. the federal executive authority was granted strictly delimited powers; the powers not granted by the Constitution to the federal government were *eo ipso* reserved to the state governments or to the inhabitants of the states;

4. the decision of the federal Supreme Court closed, without further recourse, any dispute between a state and the federal government or between one state and another. In subsequent decisions, the Supreme Court ruled that the states could neither tax federal agencies nor hinder their functioning on state territory;

5. the powers of the government were divided into legislative (the Congress of the United States), executive (the President of the United States), and judicial (a system of federal courts with

Bill of Rights

Bill of Rights

the Supreme Court at the top and with the judges installed for life terms); and

6. the Supreme Court was empowered to pass upon the compatibility of legislative acts with the Constitution (this doctrine actually being inferred subsequently from the doctrines of limited government and divided powers).

III. Ratification

The presentation of the draft constitution, in September of 1787, to the states for ratification signaled a violent campaign of opposition, led chiefly by liberals and by pre-Revolutionary radicals. The prospect of a strong government delighted neither those of limited means, who feared the suppression of the unrestricted printing of money by the states, nor the populace of the western frontier, who suspected that the federal government might trade away their access to the Mississippi. On the other hand, Jefferson was dismayed that the new constitution might produce a President who was "a bad edition of a Polish king."[34]

More than eager to endorse the Constitution were the people of means, concentrated chiefly in New England — the merchants and planters. They found themselves privileged by the constitutional allocation to them of senators equal in number with those of the large states; accordingly the Constitution was eagerly snapped up by Delaware and Connecticut.

Difficulties were caused by the state of Massachusetts, where the interests of the small property owners and of the unpropertied necessitated political promises and the pledging of an additional section guaranteeing civil rights. The same happened again with Virginia, and only the appending of the first ten amendments — known collectively as the "Bill of Rights" — made ratification possible. The ten amendments guaranteed:

1. separation of church and state and freedom of religion;

2. freedom of speech, press, assembly and petition for redress of grievances;

3. the right to keep and bear arms;

4. prohibition against peacetime quartering of troops in private domiciles without the consent of the owner, such quartering being permissible in wartime only in accordance with the law; and the nonseizure of private property for public use without just compensation;

5. personal security in one's lodgings, papers and belongings, and immunity against unreasonable search and seizure;

6. the rights of persons accused of crimes;

7. the right to trial by jury;

8. no excessive bail or fines, nor infliction of cruel or unusual punishments;

9. the preservation by the people of other rights not expressly mentioned in the Constitution;

10. the retention by the states or by their people of rights not specifically delegated by the Constitution to the United States.

IV. Amendments

The amendments to the Constitution did not stop with the Bill of Rights, and an analysis shows three periods to have produced them:

1. the period of 1789-1804, during which the first twelve amendments modified the original Constitution, making it more attuned to the realities and dominant concepts of the time;

2. the period of 1865-70, which brought three amendments resulting directly from the Civil War and from the freeing of the slaves; and

3. the final period, which has given the balance, in the main directed toward the democratization of American life.

The amending procedures, regulated by the Constitution itself, from the very beginning roused sharp criticisms. One of the most frequently advanced complaints has been that the mechanism is too slow and cumbersome. But the framers of the Constitution hardly wanted it otherwise. Hamilton argued that making changes easier would have deprived the Constitution of its intended stability.

A second prominent charge has been that the procedures for amendment are undemocratic. Demands have been voiced to permit initiatives by the people at large, or to submit proposed amendments to a popular vote. Strong objections have been raised against a procedure which makes it possible for thirty-eight states — regardless of their populations — to put through an amendment, with not much over a third of the citizens being theoretically able to exert a decisive voice against the will of nearly two-thirds. Similarly, thirteen states can block an amendment, even though their combined populations may represent not fully a twentieth of the total population of the states.

Nevertheless, the prevailing view is that an easing of the amending procedures would not be salutary to the mechanism of political change, and that the flaws in the existing procedures are compensated for in other ways: by legislation, by acts of the executive branch, by judicial interpretation and by custom.[35]

V. "Checks and balances"

One of the most striking comments on the United States Constitution is that it contains a built-in self-correcting mechanism,

> a realization in political form of the legendary perpetual motion machine. According to this view, our division of authority between states and nation under a federal system and our separation of powers and functions among three branches of the national government provided a series of institutional rivalries and internal checks which prevented any part of the system from breaking down or running too fast.[36]

The framers of the Constitution constructed a system to govern a federated country, with sufficient powers to counter centrifugal forces, while at the same time avoiding the danger of its becoming monopolized by one of its own branches. This last effect was achieved through a system of checks and balances.[37]

Legislative responsibility was vested basically in the Congress of the United States, but a bill passed by the latter becomes law upon signature by the President of the United States. However, a bill vetoed by the President can still become law, provided Congress upholds it by passing it once again.

The Supreme Court of the United States has the power to deprive any law of its force by formally, as part of a judicial

21

decision, asserting its incompatibility with the Federal Constitution. But the composition of the Supreme Court is dependent on nominations by the President and on the consent of the United States Senate, which by voting in the negative can prevent the installation of a presidential nominee as a Supreme Court justice. The latter was illustrated by the Senate in 1969 and 1970, when it rejected President Nixon's nominations of Judges Haynsworth and Carswell to the Supreme Court.

By the same token, the Senate can reject the President's nominees for the highest federal posts and refuse to ratify treaties concluded by him.[38]

VI. The general nature of the United States Constitution

The Constitution of 1789 was a work of compromise, and its essential purpose was to federate the United States and to assure them a republican form of government. Just after the announcement that a constitution had been drawn up, a lady passer-by in a Philadelphia street inquired of the senior member of the Convention, "Doctor Franklin, what kind of government have you given us?" The latter replied, "A republic, madam," then added, "if you can keep it."[39]

The framers of the Constitution drew up a brief and simple document; together with the amendments, it does not exceed six thousand words. It is lucid and logical; its language is uncomplicated, and it does not contain a superfluous or ambiguous word. Nonetheless, the Constitution is purposely "loose," permitting of free interpretation. This is illustrated in the clause pertaining to citizenship and in the clause enjoining the Federal Government "to provide for ... the general welfare of the United States."

The United States Constitution is characterized more by an avoidance of (often unpredictable) detail than by misleading provisions. It is precisely in this that American political scientists see "the work of plain honest men."[40] It is their approach that assured the Constitution its durability: the Constitution was created during the Enlightenment and has persisted essentially unaltered into this day of nuclear reactors and of voyages to earth's natural satellite.

VII. The sources of its success

It has been observed that this same Constitution, when transplanted to other soils — particularly to the South American countries — does not secure their stability but as a rule is eventually supplanted by dictatorships.

Two factors contributed to the success of the Constitution of 1789: favorable physical and social conditions, and the particular qualities of a people largely shaped by Anglo-Saxon culture. Clearly, too, its success was favored by the period of several decades separating the Revolution from the Civil War during which the United States were free of major upheavals, and which made possible the achievement of a large degree of national homogeneity as well as the development and accumulation of considerable resources.

The Americans showed a talent for developing their institutions which has been described as an

> "instinct for practical, workable government." While we began by viewing the Constitution as fundamental law, embodying a higher claim to obedience and moral respect than the day-to-day rules made by legislators and executives, we have also tended to approach the problem of adapting the Constitution to new conditions and crisis developments with a highly pragmatic perspective.[41]

It is proper now to examine certain institutions and procedures which play an enormous role in American political life today, even though they were quite unknown to the framers of the Constitution.

VIII. The government

The American's pragmatic approach to political problems is illustrated in the genesis and evolution of the government.

The cabinet ... grew up outside the Constitution and unknown to the law. President Washington looked first to the Senate to share some of his burdens and to offer him timely advice, and then to the Supreme Court. He was rebuffed by each of them in turn. And, finally, when the House of Representatives discouraged the appearance of his departmental heads in the midst of their deliberations, he was forced to turn in upon the resources of the executive branch. Washington came to rely entirely on his own subordinates, the heads of the four executive departments, for advice and assistance and thus the cabinet was born.[42]

IX. "Executive agreements"

The broadening of presidential powers came about through the granting to him of *carte blanche* authority to conclude international — "executive" — agreements without their having to receive the "advice and consent" of two-thirds of the Senate.

In the period from 1789 through 1941 the presidents of the United States made over 1,250 such international agreements — a third more than were concluded by the process spelled out by the founding fathers.

The power of "executive agreements," during the period of World War II, brought about Lend-Lease,[43] just as in 1933 it had the Roosevelt-Litvinov Agreement arranging American recognition of the U.S.S.R. and later would the Yalta Agreement of 1945.[44]

X. "Executive orders"

Another example of presidential powers which have arisen outside the original framework of the Constitution are the so-called "executive orders," which "are in plain fact laws made by the executive."[45] Whether they were anticipated by the founding fathers is unknown; the Constitution neither clearly authorizes nor forbids them. Their nature is illuminated by a remark of President Johnson's: "I don't care what the law says! I'm going to . . . if I have to issue a special executive order to do it."[46]

XI. The bi-structurality of the United States Constitution

The previously mentioned aids to constitutional evolution (legislation, acts of the executive, judicial interpretation, and custom) have been jointly described as "the living word and deed of living men."[47] They have produced a structure which the original Constitution did not provide for — a progressive layering on the British pattern, with an increasingly evident duality of construction:

1. a relatively strict construction — the original Constitution of 1789, together with the amendments; and

2. a loose construction, evolved either unofficially or semi-officially.

CONSTITUTION OF THE UNITED STATES — 1787

Preamble. Objects of the Constitution (cf. A. of C., Art. III).

WE THE PEOPLE of the United States, in Order to form a more perfect Union, establish Justice, insure domestic Tranquility, provide for the common defence, promote the general Welfare, and secure the Blessings of Liberty to ourselves and our Posterity, do ordain and establish this CONSTITUTION for the United States of America.

ARTICLE. I.

CONGRESS. Two houses.

Section 1. All legislative Powers herein granted shall be vested in a Congress of the United States, which shall consist of a Senate and House of Representatives.

HOUSE OF REPRESENTATIVES. Term and election.

Section 2. [1] The House of Representatives shall be composed of Members chosen every second Year by the People of the several States, and the Electors in each State shall have the Qualifications requisite for Electors of the most numerous Branch of the State Legislature.

Qualifications -- age, citizenship, residence.

[2] No Person shall be a Representative who shall not have attained to the age of twenty-five Years, and been seven Years a Citizen of the United States, and who shall not, when elected, be an Inhabitant of that State in which he shall be chosen.

Method of apportioning representatives. (Part in brackets superseded by Sec. 2 of Amendment XIV.)

[3] [Representatives and direct Taxes shall be apportioned among the several States which may be included within this Union, according to their respective Numbers, which shall be determined by adding to the whole Number of free Persons, including those bound to Service for a Term of Years, and excluding Indians not taxed, three fifths of all other Persons.] The actual Enumeration shall be made within three Years after the first Meeting of the Congress of the United States,

A. of C. = Articles of Confederation.

CHAPTER 2

POLAND TO THE END OF THE EIGHTEENTH CENTURY

I. The dawn of Polish history to the Constitution of 1791

The elements of Poland's genesis — and hence of her earliest political system — are lost to view in the proverbial mists of time. It is known that at the time of the references to Poland in the chronicles of Ibrahim Ibn Jacob in the tenth century, she was regarded as an organized country. Eastern merchants visited Poland without any apprehensions.[1] Her historical beginning must be regarded as coeval with her first certainly known political decision: the adoption of western Christianity

Poland's baptism promoted her to the status of a civilized nation, assuring her recognition as a state by the West and thus by all the world with which it was a political necessity for her to reckon, endowing her with an alphabet, and—by virtue of Europe's geopolitical situation—making Poland the eastern-most bastion of western civilization.

If we are to accept Gumplowicz's dictum that "the state is the product of force and exists by force,"[2] then consistency enjoins us from imagining that Poland's statehood sprang from some inspiration of sages or from the innate altruism or peculiarly peace-loving disposition of certain Slavic tribes. Probably a more accurate supposition would be that Poland arose through some one ruler subjugating a number of other tribes. Whether he acquired his position of preeminence by vanquishing first one neighboring tribe and then another, or whether the earliest settled tribes — having switched from pillage to agriculture — were then overpowered by a nomadic tribe still dwelling in the hunting and gathering stage, and whether its victorious leader thus imposed his rule upon the settled populace[3] — in all likelihood will never be determined. The fact remains that Poland's earliest historically demonstrable statehood is associated with the existence by 963 A.D. of a common ruler and that she is already by then embarked on the path of political progress, thus apparently confirming the theory that "without autocratic rule, the evolution of society could not have commenced."[4]

The rise of a common prince initiates a period of centralized rule which encompassed the totality of the national life. But the scope of the prince's — or later the king's — authority underwent changes, and the society proceeded to differentiate until in the period more or less beginning with the death of Kazimierz the Great in 1370 there came into existence a number of social classes with disparate rights and obligations. This period lasted until the second half of the sixteenth century, when Poland became a republic of the nobility, governed by that one social class, which dominated the king as well as the other social classes. Poland also became an elective monarchy, and this system of electing the king was regarded as a vital safeguard of "golden liberty," much as each election was viewed as the act of entrusting supreme power to the individual regarded as fittest by the electors. (In actuality elections were not a sixteenth-century invention; election of ruling princes had been known in Poland during the regional divisions of the twelfth century, and during the thirteenth had occurred when the prince's throne was required to pass not to his son but to another member of the family — to a close relation or to a member of a collateral branch.[5])

One of the milestones in Poland's political development was the privilege conferred by King Władysław Jagiełło in 1425, known as *Neminem captivabimus,* which by two and a half centuries antedated the similar English *Habeas corpus Act* of 1679. *Neminem captivabimus* was followed by the *Nieszawa Statutes* of 1454, granting legislative powers to the provincial *seyms* or parliaments. Half a century later, in 1505, *Nihil novi* was added, by which King Alexander obligated himself not to issue any new laws without the consent of the Seym and Senate, thereby giving the beginning to Polish parliamentarism.[6]

The year 1573 brought *Pacta conventa,* binding every newly elected king to affirm the rights and privileges conferred by his royal predecessors. The clause on "de non praestanda obedientia" gave the nation the right to resist the king if he should act contrary to the constitution and the law. It is not unreasonable to compare the position of the Polish elective king with that of a modern president; the difference resided merely in the fact that the king as a rule held power for life. Even the very name of the Polish "Republic," as Wagner observes, demonstrated the fact of power being wielded in common by the people. The full-fledged citizens (the "szlachta" — the gentry or nobility) participated in the government of the country, and this noble class approached ten per cent of the population.[7]

While in other European countries absolute monarchy was on the rise, in Poland over the centuries royal power was being progressively curtailed in favor of the sizable noble class. It deserves emphasis that, in contrast to the feudalism prevalent then in other European countries — and certainly in contrast to the extreme autocracy of Russia — in Poland the ordinary nobleman was the equal of the king. Poland had no native aristocratic titles, and when he was acclaimed king, the nobleman Sobieski clambered up onto the throne without the slightest hint of an inferiority complex. This unparalleled position of the Polish nobility was noted by von Moltke:

> No Polish noble was the vassal of a superior lord — the meanest of them appeared at the diet in the full enjoyment of a power which belonged to all without a distinction. It is here that we find the fundamental

difference between the Polish [political system] and the feudal states of the West and the despotism of the East.[8]

But Poland, exposed as she was to hurricanes of invasion from the southeast and north by the Mongols, Turks, Swedes and Russians, in the eighteenth century in response to the growing militarism of Austria, Prussia and Russia, failed to draw the proper conclusions concerning the changes going on about her. Economically and militarily weak, stunted in her intellectual development, demoralized, her class of fully enfranchised citizens committed to the single aim of enjoying themselves — she rolled with gathering momentum down the incline of progressive disintegration.

In this condition she entered the eighteenth century, from the middle of which the nation — or more precisely, the enlightened individuals within the nation — began to rouse themselves out of their lethargy. The year 1740 saw the founding of the Collegium Nobilum, and 1765 the creation of the Szkoła Rycerska (Military Academy); in that same year the National Theater arose. Literature, architecture and the fine arts flourished anew; thought concerning sociopolitical progress appeared.

Poland underwent a cultural revival, but unfortunately too late to forestall, in 1772, the first of the three progressive partitions of her lands, by Austria, Prussia and Russia. Nevertheless, this blow to Poland's sovereignty was sufficiently powerful to aid the enlightened element in their efforts: as early as 1775 there was a reorganization of the central authorities, creating Ministries (styled "Government Commissions") of National Education, of the Treasury and of the Army; municipal reform was initiated. In 1788 the Great Seym was convoked, but by the end of 1790 it had failed to accomplish much; only toward the end of that year did its effectiveness increase, and by March of 1791 it had passed an act on the reorganization of the regional Seyms, in April an act on the reorganization of the cities, and in May an act on the national government which established the Constitution of May 3, 1791.

The idea of introducing a constitution had advanced only with difficulty until finally the Seym's fragmentation into parties and factions and their fruitless, endless debates over trivia had convinced the more enlightened that in the existing atmosphere the redesigning of the social structure did not stand much of a chance. But politically mature minds were also aware of the discord that existed between two of the late partners in the criminal First Partition — Prussia and Russia — which offered a chance, not likely to be soon repeated, of introducing social reforms. The idea of drafting a constitution outside of the plenary Seym and then submitting it ready-made for a vote forced itself upon them.

As early as the end of 1790 and the beginning of 1791 there had begun secret caucuses bringing together the most mature members of the Seym: Stanisław Małachowski, Ignacy Potocki, Adam Czartoryski, Hugo Kołłątaj, Aleksander Linowski, and Lanckoroński. After Potocki's unavailing initial efforts, Father Piattoli, the private secretary to the King and a resident of the royal castle in Warsaw, was successfully recruited to win the King over to the idea of social reforms. There are conflicting versions as to who were in fact the authors of the draft constitution. The document was reputed to have been drawn up personnally by King Stanisław August, though he and, following him, others as well indicated Kołłątaj and Potocki to be the authors.[9] Pragier ascribes it to the afore-mentioned Father Piattoli.[10]

The minister of Saxony to Warsaw, Essen, was let in on the secret, inasmuch as it was important to gain the agreement of the Elector of Saxony to the provision restoring the Saxon dynasty to the Polish throne. The plan was realized slowly and prudently, and in the meantime the maximum attainable was secured from the plenary Seym: a *Regional Seyms Act (Prawo o sejmikach)* and a *Free Royal Cities Act (Miasta nasze królewskie wolne)*, both subsequently declared in the May 3d (1791) Constitution parts of the latter. The passage of these two acts must have been hailed as breakthrough events, as the foreign press devoted considerable attention to them, and the surviving notices are of a sensational nature and anticipate still more sensational events to come. "Political events are expected here," writes a contemporary correspondent, "which will excite universal astonishment." The article, written in Warsaw on the sixteenth of April, 1791, and reprinted from the London Press, continues:

Julian Ursyn Niemcewicz, 1757-1841

> The 14th of April, the day before yesterday, will hereafter be a memorable day in the annals of Poland. In the session of that day a law was passed by the Diet relative to cities and their inhabitants, which restores them to their primitive rights, associates them with the Legislative Power, and will serve as a basis for still more extensive regulations, to reduce the different orders of citizens, to that relative equality which constitutes the very soul of a solid and just constitution. Upon this occasion the plan of M. Suchorzewski, member for Kalish, was adopted. The substance of the principles which have been decreed agreeable to this project, is, "to destroy the difference of orders and classes, to grant liberty to all citizens, without distinction; to restore Nobility to its true origin, that is, to the prerogative of merit and virtue . . ." Poland may therefore date her restoration from that day; for, with such principles as these, uniformly followed up, she will become powerful from her external strength, and will be truly independent.[11]

The import of the sociopolitical restructuring underway in Poland prompts the author of the article to compare it with the French Revolution, and there follows a quotation from a speech by Deputy Niemcewicz castigating the privileged nobility and pointing to the example of democracy in America. (Hardly could Niemcewicz have foreseen that seven years later he would be entertained cordially by Washington at his residence at Mount Vernon.[12])

> None of us [Niemcewicz is quoted as saying] knows who were the ancestors or what was the religion of Washington and Franklin; but all of us know what important services these Illustrious Characters [have] rendered to their country. Let not, therefore, the modesty of citizens prescribe limits to our generosity. Let us not ask, nor look into old papers to ascertain what they have a right to demand; but let us grant them, out of our own free accord, all that the welfare of our own country requires that they should possess.[13]

Royal Castle in Warsaw

As the prospect of a possible detente between Russia and Prussia gained urgency, the tempo was stepped up and a somewhat broader group was admitted into the secret in order to assure the bill the greatest possible support within the Seym. The Easter recess appeared to complicate the undertaking: the recess lasted until May 2, and under the established order of business the first two weeks of the month were to have been devoted to fiscal matters. The fear of an improvement in Russian-Prussian relations capable of bringing the Constitutional project to nought dictated the earliest possible introduction of the act, even if it meant violence to the Seym's calendar. May 5 was set as the day.

About a week earlier the circles of bitterest opposition to social reform, tipped off about the progress on the draft constitution, had called for a meeting of their own to be held on May 4. It looked as though there would be strong organized opposition; accordingly, with the approval of the King, the reformers decided to steal a march on the conservative block by introducing their bill on May 3. But the circumstances which obliged haste necessitated that even this date be set forward by a day; already on the evening of May 2, at an informal gathering in the palace of the Radziwiłłs, the draft was read out, and that same night a meeting took place at the residence of the Marshal of the Seym, Stanisław Małachowski; there an "assurance" was written out, by which the participants, eighty-three in number, obliged themselves to "the bravest possible support of the act, pledging . . . the undertaking with the watchword of love of Country and with their own individual honors."[14]

The next day's session of the Seym opened with a report on the state of foreign affairs, after which the King directed the secretary to read the draft constitution. The resultant discussion lasted until late in the evening, a veritable tourney of oratory. The Constitution had the support of the majority, but far from the still legally required unanimity. Nevertheless, ignoring the formal niceties, the King arose and swore an oath which rendered the Constitution law. In their turn, at the cathedral the oath was taken by the deputies who had come out in favor of the Constitution. However, it was not officially registered — a fact which its opponents the following day attempted to take advantage of by moving that it be invalidated on the grounds

Warsaw, Radziwill Palace

King Stanisław August Poniatowski, 1732 - 1798

King Stanisław August leading the throng to the St. John Cathedral, May 3d, 1791

Front page of the Polish Constitution of May 3, 1791.

that it had not been passed by even a simple majority of the votes. The forceful arguments of the social reformers overcame their resistance: the *Government Act* was signed at the Seym's meeting of May 5 and registered the same day.

One must consider as an integral part of the May 3d Constitution the *Mutual Declaration of the Two Peoples* (i.e. of Poland and the Grand Duchy of Lithuania, the latter including Ruthenia) of October 22, 1791, which closes with an affirmation of the unity and indivisibility of the Republic and with a resolution incorporating that Declaration "inter pacta conventa."[15]

The American press recorded these events of May 3, 1791. In a lengthy resume it presents not only the facts, but also King Stanisław August's speech and a twelve-point summary of the new Constitution.

> He [the King] said in substance that notwithstanding all assurances to the contrary, there was an alarming rumour, confirmed by the advices daily received, that the three neighbouring powers (Russia, Prussia and Austria) would make up and terminate all their jealousies and divisions, at the expense of the possessions of the republic; that the only method of assuring to Poland the integrity of its possessions, and of preserving it from the ruin which foreign politics were preparing for it was to establish a Constitution, which should secure its internal independence. That in this view there had been prepared a plan of a Constitution founded principally on those of England and the United States of America, but avoiding the faults and errors of both, and adapting it as much as possible to the local and particular circumstances of the country.[16]

The American journalist's comment appears quite apropos. The principle contained in the May 3d Constitution, that "the King, doing nothing of and by himself, is answerable for nothing to the people," is a transplant of the principle in English constitutional law which holds that "the king can do no wrong."

Both in Poland, under the Constitution of May 3, and in England the respective minister is responsible for the king's acts. Perhaps the very fact that Europe found in the Polish Constitution something already familiar to her, caused her to greet it with applause, and even Edmund Burke himself deigned to admire it.[17] In this connection, it is said that when he described it as "the noblest benefit received by any nation at any time" and averred that "Stanislas II [August] had earned a place among the greatest kings and statesmen in history," he was actually giving vent to his pleasure at the discomfiture experienced by Catherine the Great.[18]

But a more probing scrutiny of the first written Polish — and European — constitution shows it to bear a greater kinship to the United States Constitution than to the British, although there is no doubt that the latter had already been made use of in some measure as a model by the Americans.

II. Kinships between the Polish Constitution of May 3 (1791) and the United States Constitution

Both the United States Constitution of 1789 and the Polish Constitution of 1791 bear out von Mohl's dictum that it is circumstances that compel changes in social systems.[19] In both cases the constitutions were forced by the necessity of remolding a malformed system with strikingly inadequate governmental powers. Both constitutions — deliberated and drawn up in secret and only later submitted for approval — set out to strengthen the cohesiveness of the body politic: in America a federation (tight union) displaced the Confederation (loose union); in Poland, integration into a single henceforth indivisible state supplanted the erstwhile union of Poland and the Grand Duchy of Lithuania, and the springs of the Republic's impotence — the free election of the king and the *liberum veto* — were swept away.

(Actually, royal elections were not *per se* destructive of the state; they were not the cause but the consequence of sectional divisiveness. The elections *became* perilous when they led to vote-buying by the candidates for the Polish crown. And the *liberum veto* — conceived as a guarantee to the several lands that they would not in consequence of the union be drawn into situations contrary to their own interests, e.g. into wars in the eastern territories — was rendered destructive by ignorance, private interests and venality. Apart from its sad existence in the United Nations, it is also found in the United States: the verdict of a trial jury is required by law to be unanimous. Certain religious organizations in the United States respect the veto, holding that if an individual withholds his support, then he must have good and weighty reasons for doing so; discussion continues until the matter has been clarified, and finally either unanimity is secured or the proposal goes down to defeat. This procedure is based on the principle that each honestly cast vote must carry weight, and that if the group cannot convince the individual, then this indicates a lack of strong arguments on the group's side.[20])

The distribution of powers in the state, under both the American and Polish constitutions, shows their authors to have accepted Montesquieu's concept of the division of powers, based on the idea that, "in order to prevent abuses by any of the branches of authority which could turn it into a tyrannical power, one [branch] ought to check another through a proper system of balances."[21]

Furthermore, Montesquieu saw utility in a bicameral legislature, in that, "The legislative body being composed of two parts, they check one another by the privilege of rejecting."[22]

This recommendation of the French thinker's too registered approval with the fathers of the respective constitutions: both established a bicameral legislature. Even the very order in which each constitution deals with the three branches of governmental power — the legislative, executive and judicial — lends confirmation for the common origin of the concept.

The legislative branches

These, under both constitutions, comprise bicameral bodies.

United States	Poland
Congress in composed of a House of Representatives and Senate.[23]	The Seym was composed of a Chamber of Deputies and a Chamber of Senators.[24]

The lower chambers
1. Members are elected from among, and by, the enfranchised citizenry and represent all the people.

Voting rights *were* conditional — in accordance with the laws of the respective states — on property ownership.	Voting rights were conditional on ownership of land; the landless nobility were barred from the regional seyms.
The House of Representatives chooses its own presiding officer (the Speaker).[25]	The Chamber of Deputies selected its own presiding officer (the Marshal).[26]

2. The lower chambers enjoyed legislative initiative.

All bills for raising revenue shall be introduced only in this chamber. All other bills may be initiated from either chamber.[27]	All bills were to be considered first in the Chamber of Deputies.[28]

The upper chambers
1. The Senators were not popularly elected.

The Senators *were* selected by the legislatures of the respective states.[29]	The Senators were appointed by the King.[30]

2. An executive functionary presided over the Senate.

The Senate is presided over by the Vice President of the United States. He votes only in the event of a tie.[31]	The Senate was presided over by the King, who was entitled to his own vote as well as — if the need arose — to a tie-breaking vote.[32]

3. The Senators do not represent all the people.

The Senators — two from each state — represent their own respective states.[33]	The Senators represented the highest spheres in the country.[34]

4. The peculiar role of the Senate.

In contradistinction to the Chamber of Deputies — the "temple of legislation" — the Senators were assigned by the May 3d Constitution the role of seniors privileged to express reservations. In the case of civil, criminal and political laws, these reservations led to the suspension of the law in question as passed by the Chamber of Deputies "until the next regular Seym, at which, if it be passed a second time, the law suspended by the Senate must take effect." At a session of an extraordinary Seym, the Chamber of Senators could express disagreement, but this could not result in the suspension of a law.[35]

The Senators, men of well stabilized views and of great political experience — as was to be expected of them by virtue of the positions which they occupied — were to constitute a balancing element which with a sober cautionary word exerted a check upon over-hasty decisions. But they themselves were not to take part in decision-making.

It was a similar case with the United States Senate. A compelling picture is provided by Kennedy.

> [The] very concept of the Senate, in contrast to the House, was of a body which would not be subject to constituent pressures. Each state, regardless of size and population, was to have the same number of Senators, as though they were ambassadors from inidividual sovereign state governments to the Federal Government, not representatives of the voting public ... the Senate was to be less of a legislative body ... and more of an executive council, passing on appointments and treaties and generally advising the President, without public galleries or even a journal of its own proceedings.[36]

The powers of the legislative chambers

In the most important matters of state, both the United States Congress and the Polish Seym were furnished with enormous powers of decision. They levied taxes and fiscal duties; they had responsibility for debts and government loans; they decided about war and peace as well as about the making of treaties; finally, they were empowered to influence the personnel make-up of the executive branch[37, 38] and to impeach those who exercised the highest executive powers.[39, 40]

"The House of Representatives . . . shall have the sole power of impeachment."[41]

"The Senate shall have the sole power to try all impeachments."[42] "no person shall be convicted without the concurrence of two thirds of the members present. Judgment in cases of impeachment shall not extend further than to removal from office, and disqualification to hold and enjoy any office of honor, trust, or profit under the United States; but the party convicted shall, nevertheless, be liable and subject to indictment, trial, judgment, and punishment, according to law."[43]

"Desiring that the Guardians of the National Laws [i.e. the royal cabinet: the King cannot be held to account!] shall be bound by a strict accountability to the nation for any misconduct whatsoever by them, we do determine that if ministers shall have been indicted of a breach of law by a deputation appointed to examine their deeds, then they are to be held responsible in their own persons and out of their own property. In any such indictments the gathered estates shall by a simple majority vote of the conjoint chambers convey the accused to parliamentary courts for just punishment commensurate with the crime or, their innocence having been established, for their release from further proceedings and punishment."[44]

The executive authorities

"The executive power shall be vested in a President of the United States of America." The President shall be chosen by electors; the electors shall be selected by each state in

"We repose the supreme authority in the execution of the laws in a King within his council." The Constitution puts an end to royal elections, but establishes "elections

45

accordance with its own laws.[45] Thus the President is chosen through indirect elections.

through families": in the event of the Saxon dynasty expiring, the nation (the Seym) will choose a new dynasty.[46] Thus the King is in a sense indirectly elected at the election of a new dynasty.

1. The President and the King enjoy decision-making powers.

The President has the power, with the consent of the Senate, to make treaties and to appoint government functionaries.[47]

"The King's decision, after all the opinions [of the Guardians of the Laws] have been heard, shall prevail, in order that there may be a single will in the execution of the law." (But the minister is accountable for the King's acts.)[48]

2. The American President and the Polish King both are assured a legislative initiative by their respective constitutions.[49,50] Both also call their legislatures into session.

The President may convene the legislature on exatraordinary occasions.[51]

The Seym is convened by the King, and only in the event of his refusal to do so or of his death or grave illness is this done by the Marshal of the Seym.[52]

3. The executives both in Poland and in the United States are constitutionally responsible for informing the legislature on the state of the union.

The President "shall from time to time give to the Congress information of the state of the Union..."[53]

The executive "shall conduct only interim negotiations with foreign states and shall take temporary and current measures in matters involving the safety and peace of the country, about which it shall apprise the next gathering of the Seym."[54]

4. The defense of the country is regarded of such import that both the constitutions place the command of the armed forces in the hands of the head of state.

"The President shall be commander-in-chief of the army and navy of the United States, and of the militia of the several States when called into the actual service of the United States . . ."[55]

"To the King shall belong the supreme dispositions of the armed forces of the country in time of peace and the appointment of the commanders of the army."[56] The army "shall remain always in obediance to the executive."[57]

5. The head of state makes appointments to the highest offices in the government.

The President appoints ambassadors, diplomatic representatives and consuls, judges of the the Supreme Court, and other functionaries. The appointments go into force "by and with the advice and consent of the Senate." When the Senate is in recess, the President fills vacancies, but such appointments expire at the end of the next session of the Senate.[58]

The King names the members of the government, senators, bishops, senior government officials, judges of the Supreme Court and diplomatic representatives. (Upon the demand of two thirds of the conjoint chambers, the King is required to relieve a minister from the Guardianship of the Laws or from his office and to name another.[59] Here the powers of the Seym exceed those of Congress; this was a parliamentary government.)

6. The respective constitutions emphasize the executive nature of the President's and the King's authority.

The President "shall take care that the laws be faithfully executed."[60] He will "preserve, protect, and defend the Constitution of the United States."[61]	The King, together with the Guardianship of the Laws, shall "take care that the laws are executed."[62]

7. The executive has power to initiate international treaties, but they acquire force only after legislative ratification.

The President is empowered to make treaties "by and with the advice and consent of the Senate."[63]	The King together with the Guardianship of the Laws is empowered "to conduct provisional negotiations with foreign [representatives]" but these acquire force of law only following ratification by the Seym.[64]

8. Both constitutions furnish the executive with the power to act by force if need be.

The President has at his disposal the state militias, which — though called out by Congress — have the assignment of enforcing the laws of the Union, as well as of suppressing insurrections. "Governing such part of them as may be employed in the service of the United States" is reserved to Congress, and they are trained uniformly "according to the discipline prescribed by Congress."[65]	The executive "shall act of itself, the laws permitting, where the laws require supervision of their execution or even the application of force."[66] "Thus the national army may be used . . . in aid of the law, if any person shall be disobedient to its execution."[67]

9. The constitutions assure the material independence of the head of state.

The President receives compensation whose amount may not be changed during his term in office.⁶⁸

Neither the royal incomes nor "the prerogatives proper to the throne" may be changed.⁶⁹

10. The chief executive enjoys powers of clemency.

The President has "power to grant reprieves and pardons for offenses against the United States, except in cases of impeachment."⁷⁰

"The King, who shall preserve every power of beneficence, shall have power to apply the *ius agratiandi* in behalf of persons sentenced to death, except *in criminibus status.*"⁷¹

The judicial authority

In stating the powers of this branch, both constitutions are remarkably brief. Only the purpose of this branch, the provision of justice, is actually spelled out.

Automatic system of checks and balances

Like the year-and-a-half older American Constitution, the Polish May 3d Constitution had a system of checks and balances designed to safeguard society against a disproportionate growth in the powers of any one branch of government.

The Seym's Chamber of Deputies is made the basic source of laws. After passage by the Chamber of Deputies, bills go to the Chamber of Senators. But failure of passage by the Senators does not necessarily kill them, as repassage by the Deputies will make them law anyway.⁷²

The King chooses the Guardians of the Laws, but the Seym by a secret two-thirds vote may force the King to dismiss a minister and to appoint another.

The King conducts the government in the Guardianship of the Laws. But the Marshal of the Seym has a seat in the Guardianship, *sans* the right to participate in discussions. The King makes decisions, but they require a minister's signature. The ministers, aware that a decision may meet with disapproval by the Seym and that they may then pay for their endorsements with their own dismissal — forced upon the King by the Seym — are in no great hurry to furnish their signatures.

In the event of a general refusal to sign, the King is to abandon his decision, and in the event of his refusal to do so the Marshal asks him to call the Seym. In the event of delay, he calls the Seym into session himself. The Marshal may exercise this prerogative whenever he deems it proper, but the Constitution also enumerates circumstances when such a calling of the Seym is mandatory.[73]

Thus the Seym probably had the leading role: it ordained the law, decided about government expenditures, made international treaties, and maintained a check upon the executive. Much like the Congress in the light of the United States Constitution, the Seym appeared (even in spite of the system of checks and balances) the strongest branch of government, consigning the chief executive to a chronic state of impotence.

Additional kinships

1. The intellectual currents of the Enlightenment run through both constitutions. Both reflect the heritage of Locke, with his concept of limited government, and the legacy of Rousseau, who demanded power to the people.

"We, the people of the United States . . ." goes the preamble to the United States Constitution, "do ordain and establish this constitution for the United States of America."[74]

"All authority in human society," declares the Government Act of 1791, "takes its beginning in the will of the people."[75]

The source of authority is also indicated in the preamble to the Constitution: "by the will of the people the King of Poland . . . Together with the confederated estates . . . representing the Polish people."[76]

2. The stated aims of the two constitutions are virtually identical.

"to form a more perfect union, establish justice, insure domestic tranquility, provide for the common defense, promote the general welfare, and secure the blessings of liberty to ourselves and our posterity ..."[77]

To perfect the national constitution "for the general welfare," to "preserve the country and its borders;" to secure "external independence and internal liberty" to themselves and their posterity.[78]

3. Both constitutions reflect a concern for social equality. Nevertheless, one must bear in mind the early period and certain attitudes prevalent among the authors of the constitutions.

"No title of nobility shall be granted by the United States . . ."[79] This provision was dictated by the desire of the class framing the new system to secure for itself a position equivalent to that of the old titled magnates, and by a felt need to get back at the remaining ex-loyalists. There is no sense yet of the propriety of abolishing slavery: emancipation of the Negroes would have clashed with the interests of the wealthy and administered a jolt to an economy based on slave labor.

"We recognize the dignity of the noble estate in Poland as equal to any degree of nobility wherever it may be used."[80] This provision was a veiled slap at the magnates who sported aristocratic titles courtesy of foreign courts. The Constitution also opens up the possibility of ennoblement and attainment of officer's commission to the burgher class, and thus of membership in the class of fully enfranchised citizenry.[81] But there is not a word about freeing the peasants; that would have antagonized the still preponderantly backward nobility.

4. An indisputable goal of the two constitutions was to create a sense of the stability of the enfranchised citizen's rights, as stemming from his membership in society.

"No bill of attainder . . . shall be passed."[82]

"we shall permit no alteration or exception in the law directed against any person's property

51

> ... we affirm ... the personal safety of, and the security of any property rightfully belonging to, a person, this being the true bond of society ..."[83]

5. Both the American and Polish constitutions welcome able-bodied persons who are willing to work.

"The migration or importation of such persons as any of the States now existing shall think proper to admit shall not be prohibited by the Congress prior to the year one thousand eight hundred and eight ..."[84]

"Desiring as effectively as possible to encourage the multiplication of the people, we announce complete freedom to all persons either newly arriving or who, having removed themselves from the country, now wish to return to their native land, insofar as each person newly arrived from any part to the Republic or returning thereunto, as soon as he shall set foot upon Polish soil is completely free to apply his industry as and where he shall please, is free to engage in agreements for settlement, labor or rents as he shall agree and until termination of the agreement, is at liberty to settle in city or in village and is free to reside in Poland or to return thereunto, having previously acquitted such obligations as he may have freely ... entered into."[85]

The brevity of the American clause and the lengthiness of the Polish call for comment. The Polish Constitution addressed itself to free men, in part to fugitives from Poland; it detailed their rights from the moment when they would have settled upon or returned to Polish soil. The American Constitution guaranteed to the various states the unrestricted right to import slaves until the year 1808; the extension of the legal importation of slaves was one of the prices of compromise.

How powerful must have been the currents for and against the "peculiar institution" in the United States is eloquently attested by the fact that as early as 1783 Chief Justice Cushing of the Massachusetts Supreme Court declared slavery illegal in that state, but that his ruling was not published until 1874 — that is, after slavery had legally ceased to exist in all of the United States on July 1, 1865.[86] (Coincidentally, at just about the same time serfdom disappeared from Poland.)

The clause extending the legality of importing Negro slaves did not cloak some kind of pseudo-scientific racism of a Nazi stripe. The Negroes were in fact often admitted to a considerable degree of intimacy with the planters' families, as is evidenced by today's substantially bleached-out blacks. Toynbee indicates that there has never been any fundamentally black-white antipathy:

> The planters had illegitimate children by Negroes. George Washington caught a cold while visiting Negro quarters on his estate for this purpose. It is never put into the official biographies, but this was the cause of his death. After all, it was the normal thing for a gentleman to do.[87]

One of the great landowners was Jefferson, who took great personal satisfaction from his authorship of the Declaration of Independence declaring the "self-evident" equality of all men. Thanks to Jefferson, B. Banneker, a black mathematician and surveyor, was named to a three-man commission that worked out plans for the expansion of Washington, D.C.[88] Jefferson was a slave-owner. The paradox is explained by one of his biographers, who states that Jefferson

> was well aware of the contradiction, and over a period of 60 years sought some way to bring about a gradual

and voluntary emancipation. Meantime, to accomplish the other reforms he had at heart, he had to accept the institution of slavery, and make it as beneficient as possible for his own slaves. His position may be roughly compared to that of persons who today see grave moral evils of the existing capitalistic order, but who must live in, and by, that order, because there is no escape from it — unless they go to Russia, where they will find other and perhaps greater evils.[89]

Undoubtedly the same necessity of compromise forced progressive men such as Kołłątaj to give up the thought of making all the classes equal under the May 3d Constitution. In both cases the framers of the constitutions contented themselves with what appeared to be the maximum attainable.

6. It was not the intent of the constitutions' framers to destroy the achievements of earlier times; both preserve the old laws guaranteeing the personal security of citizens.

"The privilege of the writ of *habeas corpus* shall not be suspended, unless when in cases of rebellion or invasion the public safety may require it."[90]

Neminem captivabimus was preserved and extended to cover the burgher class.[91,92] (But its protection was conditional on property ownership in the city.)

7. A humanitarian concern is evinced in clauses referring to bail.

Article VIII of the Bill of Rights states that "Excessive bail shall not be required . . ."[93]

The Cities Act of April 18, 1791 — incorporated as an integral part of the Constitution — contains a clause excluding from the law of *Neminem captivabimus,* among others, "persons not posting sufficient bail with the court of law."[94] The use of the adjective "sufficient" instead of — say — "established" or "required" suggests that the intent was a reasonable bail.

8. The guarantee of free religious belief was a major advance of both constitutions, though not to an equal degree.

"Congress shall make no law respecting an establishment of religion, or prohibiting the free exercise thereof . . ."[95]

"All persons, of whatever persuasion, are entitled to peace in their faith and to the protection of the government, and therefore we ordain freedom for all rites and religions in the Polish Lands, in accordance with the laws of the lands."[96] The name of the article in question, "The prevailing religion," and the Cities Act incorporated into the Constitution, denying non-Christians citizenship in the cities,[97] shed doubt on the substantiality of the guarantee of religious freedom. These provisions reflected the traditionally privileged position of the Roman Catholic Church. Not without significance, too, was the economic competition from non-Christian — i.e., Jewish — merchants.

9. Finally, both constitutions took cognizance of the mutability of things and hence of the possible need for changes.

In the United States, constitutional amendments may be introduced at any time, in accordance with certain precisely spelled out requirements.[98]

The May 3d (1791) Constitution provided for changes every twenty-five years."[99]

CHAPTER 3

POLAND: 1791-94

I. The May 3d Constitution to the Kościuszko Constitution

The blow of the First Partition had made it possible for more modern political views to come to the fore and to exert an influence on Poland's social development. The possibility of detente between two of the partitioning powers — Russia and Prussia — and of their renewed intrusions into Poland's internal affairs had made dispatch of the essence. In part that is why the May 3d Constitution had not gone very far in the way of reforms; it had not gone into the details of the country's government but had created only the basic skeleton of the system, which was to have been fleshed out later through appropriate legislation. This, however, never came about; instead, there followed regressive laws nullifying the May 3d Constitution and substituting a different law of the land.

Professor Kutrzeba notes acts of the Targowica Confederation of 1792, repudiating the May 3d Constitution, and of the Grodno Seym of 1793, at a single fell blow sanctioning a Second Partition and introducing the *Cardinal Laws*.[1] Writing before Kutrzeba, Franciszek Kasparek breaks off the history of Poland's constitutional evolution at the May 3d Constitution, indicating unveiledly that forces inimical to Poland had brought that Constitution to nought: "The external causes that prevented the implementation of these redemptive laws and brought about the fall of Poland's political existence are generally known."[2]

Kutrzeba states that "these circles connected with the Confederacy [which regarded the Constitution as going too far in the way of reforms] resorted to foreign assistance."[3]

It is known that "At the Seym in Grodno on the sixth of September, 1793, a committee was delegated to work out a different form of government and was presented the ideas approved by Sievers [the Russian ambassador] or developed at his initiative."[4] The statute established under the dictation of, or in collaboration with, the ambassador of the partitioning power is striking in that, while it does away with the May 3d Constitution, it was itself modeled in a certain degree upon it. Kutrzeba points out that "often in the arrangement of the various parts of the system use was in fact made of it, and certain dispositions established under it or in elaboration of it were even copied almost verbatim from it."[5]

The framers or instigators of the Cardinal Laws proceeded to neutralize all that was not to their own liking. In retaining certain of the mechanisms introduced by the May 3d Constitution, they did so partly to assuage those who had greeted the May 3d Constitution with enthusiasm. The Cardinal Laws are marked by sheer cynicism. There can be no other description when, for example, they in advance deny the force of law to the cessions of Polish territory subsequently carried out by the government and legislature. The purpose of the Grodno Seym was quite obviously to ratify the treaties with Prussia and Russia by which Poland ceded sizable territories to them. Its second goal was to formally rescind the May 3d Constitution and to supplant it with something more in line with the purposes of the partitioning powers and of their adherents.

In carrying out these missions, the Grodno Seym did not advance Polish political thought but set it back. The Cardinal Laws, though in places aping the Constitution of 1791, are not derivative of it. This prompts us to exclude them from consideration as a *Polish* constitution and rather to undertake a closer inspection of the *National Uprising Act* of 1794 and of the latter's derivatives.

The Uprising was preceded by Kościuszko's mission to Paris in January of 1793. Kościuszko attempted to secure the assistance of revolutionary France for Poland's struggle for independence; he pledged — in the event of France's engagement — an uprising by the peasants and townspeople. He made assurances of the King's readiness to abdicate in favor of a republic, as well as of the Polish army's participation in France's war with Prussia. The French were prepared to go along with the proposal, but the eruption of war with England in July, 1793, and the invasion of France put an end to plans for joint Polish-French action.

Kościuszko's mission hung fire while the leaders of the independence movement organized a new Polish army which was placed under Kościuszko's command.[6] The National Uprising Act made Kościuszko "the one supreme leader and governor of the entire uprising." The Act also authorized the Leader to appoint a body, the Supreme Council, to carry out the government of the country, as well as provincial commissions, a supreme criminal court and provincial criminal courts. The Supreme Council was to function through departments administered by appointees of the One Supreme Leader.

The Uprising Act equipped the Leader with dictatorial powers: he could make changes — of organization as well as of personnel — in the Supreme Council; military matters were reserved to him exclusively, and the Supreme Council was charged with immediately executing all his orders.

The Decree of May 10, 1794, embraced the country progressively within its jurisdiction as the Uprising grew, and the expansion of jurisdiction was marked by the setting into motion of provincial commissions of public order. A new scheme of territorial organization developed, harking back to the memorable laws of the Four-Year (or Great) Seym.

Kościuszko — a liberal who had fought for the independence of the United States, where he had made himself known as a champion of men's equality unqualified by the color of their skins — no doubt sincerely desired to make all citizens equal before the law, but taking a realistic appraisal of the situation he only went so far as to assure the peasants, by the Połaniec Manifesto of May 7, 1794, certain rights which had not been granted them by the Constitution of 1791:

1. the protection of the national government;

2. freedom to change their place of residence, conditional on previous acquittal of debts and taxes and on informing the provincial commission of public order of the new place of residence;

3. a general, proportional reduction in the number of days worked on the property of the landlord (an interim measure, but to be made permanent by the legislative authority after the Uprising);

4. the irremovability of the peasant from the land, provided that he carried out his obligations; and

5. freeing of the peasant from his normal duties during his military service, the estate of his landlord in the meantime being guaranteed care.

The commissions of public order established supervisors in the proportion of one for every 1,200 households; these settled disputes. Appeal could be made to the parent commission of public order.

The provisions of the Manifesto were expanded by the Supreme Council's Act of July, 1794. Henceforth the landowners, municipal offices and hamlets would submit their nominations for supervisors, and the commissions would make their selections by secret ballot. The required qualifications pointed to the growing democratic spirit: a supervisor could be "of any estate or condition whatever, provided only that he be virtuous, judicious, not under suspicion of avarice or of harmful associations nor under a base obligation to any, be able to read, write and reckon, and enjoy a good reputation in his region."[7]

The duties of the supervisors included not only overseeing the peasants in their rights and obligations, but also resolving disputes between the peasants and their masters and maintaining public safety, keeping up the roads and bridges, and conducting a register of population.

A curiosity was the establishment of "supervision teachers." Anybody could become one, regardless of class, religious persuasion or condition, provided he could demonstrate a knowledge of the laws and displayed an unblemished patriotism. The supervision teacher was to assist the supervisors, chiefly by acquainting the people with the intent and substance of the measures issued by the authorities and by fostering in them a sense of the duties stemming from acts of private law and from the relationship of a citizen to the state.

The series comprising the Uprising Act (March 24, 1794), The Połaniec Manifesto (May 7), Kościuszko's Decree (May 10) and the July Act of the Supreme Council are expressions of Polish political thought desperately at work; the same thought that three years earlier had made itself manifest in the May 3d Constitution. In the altered circumstances a step forward was taken. Where the purpose of the May Constitution had — according to Kołłątaj — been a "mild revolution,"[8] the acts issued during the 1794 Uprising engineered a bloodless social restructuring. The monarch — the wielder of power — disappeared; the necessity of equalizing the classes found a clearer expression: anyone could become a supervisor, and the only qualifications were those of mind and character. Serfdom was not abolished, but it was curbed, and preparatory steps for its abolition were taken through the inculcation of a social awareness in the peasants. The latter were shown a way toward the attainment of complete freedom — through active struggle for the freedom of their nation.

The series of acts introduced during the 1794 Uprising, even as the Polish state was being liquidated, fulfill the criteria for a constitution in that they set down the fundamental principles of the social system, the manner of selecting the supreme agents of power and the limits of their competence, and the rights and duties of the citizens; more than that, they aimed at the education and enlightenment — indeed ultimately at the enfranchisement — of the largest social classes.

These acts of political reform are passed over in silence by Kasparek in 1877 and by Handelsman in 1922. They are

Tadeusz Kościuszko sworn as the Supreme Leader and Governor of the Insurrection — Kraków, March 24, 1794.

The Royal Crypt under the Wawel Cathedral

considered by Kutrzeba in 1905 and emphasized by Kukiel in 1961. Their consideration by Professors Kutrzeba and Kukiel is most definitely justified, since the social acts of the Kościuszko Uprising, taken together, form *sui generis* the first republican constitution of Poland.

It is true that it was conceived primarily as an instrument for the duration of the Uprising and that it bore no clear relationship to the 1791 Constitution; but it is likewise true that it advanced the latter's Article IV by providing government protection to the peasant and his land. This is hardly surprising when one considers that the authors of the measures introduced during the Uprising included a number of people whom the events of 1791 had forced to accept modest achievements. If the Uprising had proved successful, the new social norms would have become irreversible steps leading toward the healing of the Republic — which after all was the paramount aim of the Uprising, "the men whom Kościuszko led," as one historian writes, having been "pledged to the modernization of their country."[9]

Much as the May Constitution probably hastened the Second Partition in 1793, the Kościuszko Constitution — upon the collapse of the Uprising — speeded the final liquidation of Polish statehood in the Third Partition of 1795. But both constitutions, despite their tragic direct consequences, left the Poles a legacy of immense value: they documented the Polish people's resolute efforts to rebuild their government and their strength, the real guarantor of independence. Both were a source of moral support to the nation, as they produced an awareness that their country had succumbed not because it had begun to go rotten inside but because it had begun to regain its strength — a process which its militaristic neighbors had had no intention of permitting. It is to these two constitutions that one must ascribe the fact that generations "born in bondage [and] fettered in their very swaddlings" time and again rose up in armed rebellion. It was the heirs not of a Poland foundering in decay, discord and venality, but of the Poland preserved in the visions of 1791 and 1794, who with their superhuman efforts and sacrifice in 1918 restored Poland to the map of Europe.

II. Kinships between the Kościuszko Constitution and the United States Constitution

The framers of the Kościuszko Constitution can hardly be charged with imitating the American pattern. There are no analogies or even close resemblances either in form or in content. And yet there is something that connects them and makes them kindred: they are both the handiwork of enlightened men of the same period, informed by a genuine longing for individual as well as national freedom.

The strongest influence on the social legislation of 1794 was exerted by Kościuszko himself. The scion of eastern Polish-Lithuanian nobility, he acquired his sociopolitical beliefs early in life. This he revealed by not joining the Bar Confederation [1768-72]. His own ideological posture differed too much from that of the backward, even though patriotic, gentry of his times.[10] While away studying in Paris, he had "diligently read Rousseau and the Encyclopedists."[11] He left Paris intellectually formed and proceeded to America, where he spent seven years fighting for American independence. This period in his life exerted substantial influence on the Polish Uprising of 1794. It is considered evident, first of all, in his enthusiastic endeavor to introduce the peasant masses and plebs to his army.[12]

> Kościuszko was much closer in spirit [than his compatriot Pułaski] to the American farmers, with whose struggle against the tyranny of the British he deeply identified. Thus, in Kościuszko's scanty writings the American motif, the American mode of guerilla warfare waged by free farmers and puritan townsmen frequently recurs; he also often expresses his atttachment to the democratic traditions of America . . . this man, who imbibed the radical ideology of America and France and was to a large extent formed by it, did not dogmatically apply the ideas he was wedded to. He tried to adapt them to the existing structure, to the existing pattern of social and political forces . . . Through Kościuszko and what he stood for, words . . . acquired a new meaning. In the

18th century the words "my country" and "nation" had a different meaning than today. "Country" meant a man's patrimony, his farmstead or landed estate and "nation" was identified with the gentry. It was through the Insurrection that a transformation of ideas took place, ideas which to us seem simple and obvious in the sense they then acquired in the West thanks to America's War of Independence and the French Revolution. Such re-definition would not have occurred in Poland but for the events of 1794 . . .[14]

Kościuszko adopted more from the American than from the French Revolution. As the Uprising was embracing Warsaw, he took a position against military courts and resisting the pressures of the Polish Jacobins, and thus precipitated a major disagreement with Kołłątaj.[14] His position is very clearly set forth in a brochure printed in 1800, entitled *Can the Poles Break Free?* It did not issue from Kościuszko's own pen, but no doubt it did spring from his ideas — from "the idea of an uprising by the entire nation under its own power, with the entire mass of the people being drawn into the struggle by their emancipation and enfranchisement through a revolution similar to the French Revolution — but without the latter's fratricidal terror."[15] This approach laid him open to criticism by those who felt that "Kościuszko had raised his sword on behalf of insurrection, when he should have been fighting for social revolution as Kołłątaj urged."[16]

In summary, the set of social laws which were issued during the 1794 Uprising — considered here jointly as the Kościuszko Constitution — were of his own fashioning, and since he was, if not molded, then at least confirmed in his views by his observations and experiences while in America, his Constitution is likewise to an indeterminate extent a product of America. The Kościuszko Constitution sprang from ideas common to both the Polish and American peoples and is essentially more affined to the American Constitution of 1789 than to the Polish Constitution of May 3, 1791 — in its republican spirit, in its urgent sense of progress toward the freedom of man. But the Constitution of Poland in the future was — according to his own proclamation — to resemble the Constitution of the United States even more closely, when the National Uprising was victorious.[17]

The absence of superficial kinships between the two is a consequence of those "particular circumstances of the country" to which King Stanisław August had alluded when he introduced the May 3d Constitution. But the Kościuszko Constitution is related to the American Constitution in a profounder degree than to all the other Polish constitutions, since both were *par excellence* political and not legislative acts. Much like the American Constitution, the Kościuszko Constitution was "grounded on popular approval," which, as the American political scientist continues, "under the theory of popular sovereignty, was the only theoretically sound basis for a supreme political act."[18]

Thaddeus Kościuszko, 1746 - 1817

CHAPTER 4

POLAND: 1794-1831

I. The Kościuszko Constitution to the Constitution of the Kingdom of Poland at the time of the November (1830-31) Uprising

France — although her convention of 1792 had pledged her assistance to any country fighting for its freedom — was none too keen on coming to the aid of the Polish people. In the name of political realism the successive Jacobin leaders winked at the tragedy of the expiring Republic. For Napoleon, Poland was no more than another little square on the political chessboard of Europe; his position in regard to the Polish question shifted as, and to the extent that, involvement in it coincided with his own grand schemes. Some of his pronouncements must have electrified Poles with a considerable charge of hope:

"Russia annihilated Poland. France's indifference in this great matter was and always will be reprehensible."[1]

"It is in the interests of Europe, it is in the interest of France that Poland should exist."[2]

Thus he spoke when it suited his purposes to do so. Similarly, when it agreed with his own aims, he magnanimously accepted the Poles' offer to serve him with their arms.

Typical of Napoleon was the manner in which he brought to life a surrogate Polish state — the Grand Duchy of Warsaw — and then gave it a constitution. He neither cared about nor felt bound by the nature of the late Polish state. He was not struck by the fact that the territory of the new pseudo-state did not quite include even the area taken from Poland by Prussia alone in the three partitions between 1772 and 1795. Nor did he regard it meet to simply restore to the Poles a perhaps modernized May 3d Constitution, or to call even a symbolic constituent assembly.

As he was wont to do with all his creatures, he threw together a constitution for the Polish ersatz state. He made no effort to keep up appearances; he could have presented his constitution to the Poles in Warsaw, their capital since 1596, but he did not consider that a material question. On his way from Tilsit to Paris he bypassed Warsaw and stopped by at Dresden, capital of the King of Saxony, whom he made head of the Grand Duchy of Warsaw. It was as though he had decided to recognize Dresden as the new and fitting capital of the Poles.

There he was overtaken by the members of the Governing Commission, and there in their presence on July 19, 1807, he dictated the constitution (or at least its basic principles). His minister Maret and the members of the Governing Commission participated in the actual drawing up of the constitution. Napoleon signed it on July 22 and immediately set out again for Paris: and that was that. On July 23, "to the [Governing] Commission's remarks and presentations respecting certain of [the constitution's] features, His Excellency Minister Maret answered that this constitution, composed and signed by H[is] M[ost] G[racious] M[ajesty] the Emperor, may not be altered in any respect.[3]

Accordingly, the aforesaid constitution, prepared in conformity with the draft bearing Napoleon's signature, was signed and delivered to the newly created Grand Duke of Warsaw, the Saxon King Frederick Augustus I. Consistently enough, the original was deposited not in the archives of Warsaw but in those of Dresden.

The Constitution of July 22, 1807, was not a *Polish* constitution. It was ordained by an agency completely alien to Polish culture — by an Emperor of the French oblivious to the sensibilities and desires of the Polish.

The Constitution of July 22, 1807, bears no relation to the May 3d Constitution except in its restoration — in reduced rank — of a ruler from the Saxon dynasty to a hereditary Polish throne. No wonder that it not only did not attempt to revive the social reforms of the Kościuszko Uprising, but did not even want to recall them to mind. They would have been too democratic for ex-Republican Napoleon Bonaparte.

Napoleon's collapse buried the Grand Duchy of Warsaw and gave birth — by fiat of the Congress of Vienna on May 3, 1815 — to the next Polish pseudo-state, this time christened the Kingdom of Poland. The Kingdom of Poland comprised the mutilated territory of the Grand Duchy of Warsaw and was attached by personal union to Russia. The event did not pass without the institution of a new basic law. Although the writing of the new constitution had occurred earlier — most probably already in Vienna in May of 1815 — the final version bestowed upon pseudo-Poland bears the signature of the "czar and king" Alexander dated November 27 of the same year.

This constitution too — the second in a row granted to Poland by an external power, this time one of her partitioners — is no *Polish* constitution. The fact of its foreignness is unaltered by the intention expressed in the Principles of the Constitution of the Kingdom of Poland "that the new constitution to be bestowed upon the Kingdom of Poland may become more completely a national constitution and approach the Statute of May 3, 1791." The obvious intention of the czar-king's constitutional decree was to ensure the inseparability of the Polish ersatz state from Russia and to impose on it political patterns congenial to the czar and his ministers. During the elaboration of the constitution

> Alexander had made . . . next to nearly every article extensive autograph pencilled remarks of a restrictive character, very premeditated and calculated to leave him loopholes for autocratic license in the

constitutional structure, and then had heard an oral report regarding certain important articles (e.g., concerning budgetary matters) presented to him by Novosiltsev, a Russian senator and member of the provisional government, formerly a supposed friend of Czartoryski and of Poland and henceforth revealing himself as the most implacable and harmful foe of the Kingdom of Poland and of the Poles . . .[4]

The November (1830-31) Uprising shook the spurious foundations of the symbiosis that had been imposed upon the Poles, and an early problem of the Uprising became the constitution. With passing time the prevailing opinion among the leaders underwent a decided shift from that verbalized by Roman Sołtyk — "our last law is the Constitution of the Third of May; I regard all the changes effected since as illegal" — to the much more practical view that "the constitution is binding insofar as it is not changed by enactments either already passed or to be passed by the chambers of the Seym, which latter is the proper and now the sole legislative authority of the Polish Nation."[5] And so after the initial period of the Uprising, when power was constituted not so much in reference to legal foundations as to actual exigencies, the 1815 constitution was retained in effect, modified by — at times, quite fundamental — amendments.

A key measure is the *Government Act* of January 29, 1831, passed after political relations with the Russian Czar had been severed, invalidating portions of the 1815 constitution respecting the union of the Kingdom of Poland with Russia. The rest of the constitution was retained in force, although actual practice compelled the Seym to apply it in loose fashion. The Act of January 29 cleared up the situation resulting from the disappearance of the Russian ruler from the Polish throne: "The execution of royal power under the Constitution is entrusted to the National Government of the Kingdom of Poland, insofar as the present law shall provide; the remainder of such power remains with the two chambers."[6] Under the remodeled Constitution — and this is spelled out still more explicitly in the *Oath Act* of February 8, 1831 — Poland was a constitutional monarchy; the oath of office was rendered to the Seym.[7] The powers of the Government included part of the royal powers and were set out definitively in the *Government Act* of August 17, 1831. From that day forth the Government comprised the President, elected by the joint Chambers, within his Council of Ministers. The President appointed the ministers, who had an advisory voice, and made decisions at sessions of the Council. His decision was confirmed by the signature of one of the ministers.[8]

In this constitution there is no more anathemizing of the old sources of the Republic's impotence; the Constitution simply introduces the principle of deciding acts by a majority vote of the Chambers in place of the *Liberum veto*, and outlines the succession to the throne in "a constitutional representative monarchy . . . with the right of succession secured to the family elected . . ."[9]

The need to symbolize the union of the old Republic's lands was not overlooked. The *National Colors Act* of February 7, 1831, "in consideration of the need to ordain a uniform symbol under which Poles are to rally," had already established the national colors "of the coat of arms of the Kingdom of Poland and Grand Duchy of Lithuania."[10] The *Powers of the Supreme Commander Act* of January 24, 1831, had also shown itself mindful of the union of the lands when it had established, as part of the supreme commander's insignia, "on the epaulets two hetman's batons crossed." — The symbolism of the two batons is obvious; they cannot designate the joint powers of the grand hetman and of the field hetman, since the field hetman was subordinate to the grand hetman, and so it would have made no sense to cross two emblems representing different levels of authority. But the Crown grand hetman and the Lithuanian hetman *were* on equal footing; the powers of *these*, the supreme commander could reasonably unite. (It is a curious thing that the symbol of the double batons has been retained on the marshal's uniform of contemporary Poland.) And again somewhat later, "desiring that all the parts of the late Kingdom of Poland formerly subjugated to the force of Russian autocrats . . . may have a part in the present councils concerning the weal of their common country,"[12] the *Representation for Lithuania and Volhynia Act* of May 11-19, 1831, had ordained the participation of Lithuania and Volhynia in the Senate and Chamber of Deputies.

Collateral to the efforts at adjusting the political framework to the needs of the Uprising was an effort to completely change the constitution. The memorials to these efforts are the preserved but never inaugurated draft constitutions from the years 1830-31.[13] The earlier draft — dating from the period when it was believed feasible to maintain the Polish-Russian personal union (hence certainly from before January 25, 1831) — predicated the coexistence of the two states on the separateness and independence of the Polish nation, and did this by means of a proposed amendment to the constitution of 1815. This draft drew the lessons of the previous fifteen years and was directed toward the elimination of everything that had shown itself harmful to the relationship between the two nations. The second project, drawn up after the formal dethronement of the Czar, broke completely with the 1815 constitution.

As has been noted, neither of these projects ever became law; nevertheless they are valuable to the study of the evolution of Polish political thought, of which they are indisputable expressions — something that cannot be said either of the document dictated by Napoleon for the Grand Duchy of Warsaw or of the one framed by Czar Alexander for the Kingdom of Poland. If the present study does not take these constitutional projects under closer scrutiny, it is only because its scope is limited to actual operating constitutions.

II. Kinships between the Constitution of the Kingdom of Poland at the time of the November (1830-31) Uprising and the United States Constitution

The Poles in 1830-31, waging open warfare to liberate themselves from St. Petersburg, were in a situation analogous to that of the American Colonists when they were struggling to free themselves from London. And much as the American revolutionaries set about creating a constitutional framework (the Articles of Confederation) in 1776 soon after declaring their independence, the Warsaw revolutionaries too altered their framework during the actual course of their struggle, through flexible application of a system of amendments.

The Americans preserved certain institutions from their colonial period, but they built anew whenever they either did not wish to preserve the old system or did not wish to copy the British pattern. The Polish revolutionaries similarly kept what suited them, changing what they felt required change.

A comparison of the Constitution of the Kingdom of Poland at the time of the Uprising with the United States Constitution ratified in 1789 reveals a whole series of kinships.

Three branches of power

These are the legislative, executive and judicial.

Bicameral legislature

In the Kingdom of Poland both chambers — the Senators and the Deputies — are empowered to initiate legislation, on a par with the Government.[14] (From August 17, 1831, on, the two chambers acted as joint chambers, "pending the liberation of the capital."[15]) A bill passed by one of the chambers goes immediately to the other, and on its passage by that chamber becomes law.[16] A bill passed by one of the chambers but rejected by the other "shall be discussed further in both chambers jointly, which . . . shall decide by a simple majority vote."[17]

The lower chamber

This chamber was elected by the full-fledged citizens.[18]

The upper chamber

This was chosen through indirect elections.[19]

Joint chambers

The two chambers jointly make the most momentous decisions: in "the selection and removal of the persons comprising the Government," in questions of war and peace, and in the ratification of treaties.[20]

The executive branch

Its structure and prerogatives show scarcely a faint kinship with the American executive. The manner in which the head of the Government is selected and the manner in which his authority is exercised are different.

Somewhat analogous to the corresponding function of the President of the United States is the appointment, by the President of the National Government, of the highest dignitaries in the Kingdom: of ministers and other functionaries, of the commander in chief, of the generals, of clerics below the rank of bishop, and of "diplomatic agents."[21] The President, in his Council of Ministers, disposed of the Government's revenues in accordance with the budget approved by the Seym, but by the *Government Act* of August 17, 1831, "Only the President himself or his substitute shall have the decisive voice, and the Ministers shall sit with an advisory voice."[22] The Government — by the afore-mentioned Act of August 17, 1831, the President — had power to remit or to reduce sentences.[23]

The judiciary
Still conspicuous by its absence from this Polish constitution is an element quite basic to American administration of justice, the jury system. The Kingdom possessed an analog of the American Supreme Court; this was the Supreme Tribunal, the highest court of appeal but not empowered to issue binding interpretations of the law. The Supreme Tribunal did include judges appointed for life, but it also included a number of senators appointed for a limited term.[24]

General principles and guarantees of the law
1. Guarantee of religious freedom. The Constitution of the Kingdom still features a provision making "religious persuasion ... an object of particular attention by the Government,"[25] but the modified Constitution does show some progress: whereas the Czar's version had set adherents of various Christian denominations equal in their civil and political rights, from May, 1831, on the right to vote was granted to citizens from both "of Christian or Mohammedan persuasions;"[26]

2. guarantee of personal liberty: similarly as *habeas corpus* in the United States,[27] *Neminem captivabimus* assured personal security to all citizens of the Kingdom of Poland;[28]

3. freedom of the press (though in the Kindgom,[29] as contrasted with the United States,[30] limited in extent)

4. the privilege of posting bail; [31,32]

5. the right to speedy trial in a competent court of law, and immediate release if investigation provides no grounds for trial;[33,34]

6. the obligation to inform the accused of the causes of his detainment;[35,36]

7. the right to hold property;[37,38]

8. proscription against punishment inflicted outside the law or the courts;[39,40]

9. the right of persons of foreign extraction to be naturalized and to seek public office[41,42,43] (except for the offices of President and Vice President of the United States[44])

10. the right to move about freely (the kinship being only with the first paragraph of Article I, section 9 of the United States Constitution)[45,46]

11. repudiation of confiscatory powers;[47,48]

12. guarantee of the validity of public debts;[49,50]

13. the source of governmental powers: the remodeled Constitution of the Kingdom of Poland does not have a separate clause concerning the source of the Government's powers, but the people and their will, as expressed through the Seym, are clearly indicated to be the source. This is made unequivocal in the prescribed oath of office: "I pledge my faith to the Polish nation and to the Polish people, as represented in the Seym. I swear that I shall recognize no authorities save those that the Seym has established or shall establish . . ."[51] The analogy with the American Constitution[52] is in this matter complete.

Checks and balances

The American Constitution worked out in Philadelphia shows internal consistency. The system of "checks and balances" prevents excessive growth in the powers of the several branches of government, and the amendments strive to secure individual and civil liberties. Those who in 1830-31 in Warsaw undertook to remake their constitution — probably at times to the sound of distant cannonade —were not as consistent. Their amendments do not form a well planned out series, and their checks and balances are only rudimentary.

The joint chambers selected the head of the Government (the President), who made decisions "in council," and "Every decision by the President in the Government's name shall issue from and — in order that it may have the force of law — shall be pronounced in council and shall be certified by the endorsement of one of the Ministers comprising the Council." But his entire Council consisted of his own appointees.[53]

The lack of certainty in the morrow characterizing the period of the November Uprising, and particularly the internal struggles over power and over the definition of its limits, inevitably had to leave an impress of instability on the remodeled Constitution.

CHAPTER 5

POLAND: 1831-1921

I. The collapse of the November (1830-31) Uprising to the Constitution of 1921

With the collapse of the 1830-31 uprising, the laws enacted during its duration expired irreversibly. Russia returned triumphant, and with her came the *Organic Statute for the Kingdom of Poland* of February 26, 1832. The Statute bestowed upon the people of vanquished Poland by the "czar and autocrat of all the Russias, king of Poland, etc., etc., etc." can hardly be treated as a *Polish* constitution: any more than can the series of successive constitutions granted to the Free City of Krakow in 1818, 1833, 1837 and 1842. Accordingly they will not be discussed in the present volume.

The Poles had long to wait for a constitution of their own devising. Their circumstances were unimproved by the Springtime of Nations (1848) or by the January (1863) Uprising, and the great war that in the view of the more enlightened offered the only hope for breaking up the partitioning empires and restoring Poland's independence did not materialize. The beginning of the twentieth century roused fresh hopes with the Russian revolution of 1905. The latter expired, and in turn the prospects for war in the Balkans fell through. Finally the long awaited and providential First World War arrived.

Token Polish volunteer units entered the war, at first only on the Austrian side but later recruited also by the Russians to counterbalance the effect of Austria's Polish Legions. These Polish units fought on the historic soil of the Republic, without any political status, and with no guarantees regarding any national future. The first mention of the necessity to restore Poland had occurred in Petersburg on August 20, 1914, in a conversation between the Russian Foreign Minister Sazonov and the French Ambassador Paléologue.[1] However, two years of bloody struggle were required before the political biddings began with the November 5, 1916 declaration of the German and Austrian emperors, vaguely promising the restoration of the Kingdom as a state. In his subsequent New Year's message, Czar Nicholas II listed as one of the aims of the war the "creation of a free Poland made up of all three parts up to now separated from each other."[2]

On January 22, 1917, President Wilson delivered his "Peace without Victory" address, in which he attempted to reason with the belligerents. The need of solving the problem of independence for Poland was touched. But there does not seem to have been a single uniform view of the Polish question among the Triple Entente, as is indicated by a report from the American Ambassador in Italy to his Secretary of State, dated one day before Wilson's message, in which he "reported . . . the Vatican's anticipation of British consent to Russian hegemony over Poland . . . England had dictated Russia shall have [the] whole of Poland . . . and Galizia."[3]

The Chancellor of the German Reich, disturbed by Wilson's official pronouncement, requested an authoritative commentary. Bethman-Holweg "was satisfied only when the American Ambassador in Germany, James Gerard, represented Wilson's speech as having 'undoubtedly' referred to 'Poland as constituted by Germany and Austria themselves.' "[4] And the Austro-Hungarian Minister of Foriegn Affairs, Count Czernin, "on

January 24, 1917, in reply to Wilson's '14 points' . . . declared that 'if, after the conclusion of peace, Poland wishes to come to us, we will welcome her willingly.' "[5]

To the German offer to form a Polish volunteer army, the Poles responded with a demand for a Polish government and seym. The Germans agreed to some concessions: General Beseler issued a decree setting up a Council of State and a Seym for the Polish Kingdom. The decree contained a provision requiring acts passed by the Seym to have the concurrence of the government — that is, of the governor, who was himself — which in itself sufficed to make it unacceptable to the Poles.

On the basis of a new proclamation issued on January 14 after consultation with the Poles, Beseler appointed an Interim Council of State. Its head was a monarchist, Wacław Niemojewski, and the director of its military commission was Józef Piłsudski. On January 17 the Council set up a special commission to draw up a constitution and regulations governing elections to the Seym.

The draft constitution envisioned a revived Polish constitutional monarchy with a bicameral legislature, where the Senate — representing the various social classes — would be half elective and half appointive. The Catholic Church was to enjoy special status as "the prevailing religion."

In face of the growing complexity of the situation, as Piłsudski defied the Interim Council of State to prevent the Polish army from swearing allegiance to the emperors of Austria and Germany and was imprisoned in the fortress at Magdeburg, Germany, the Council of State dissolved itself. A short time later, by the will of the two kaisers, a Council of Regency was appointed which was to constitute the supreme authority in the Kingdom until such time as power was taken by a king or regent. The legislative authority was the Council of State, and the executive the Government (led by Jan Kucharzewski) which decided that the adoption of a constitution would be the business of the first Seym. The draft worked out earlier by the Interim Council of State died somewhat later, a creature ill adapted to its period.

The Council of Regency, together with the Government and the Council of State under its aegis, were a stage in the evolution of Poland's political independence, but they were incapable of satisfying the needs and aspirations of a nation eager for independence: if nothing else, the newly created system of government was very conservative and suffered from the handicap of its origin in the blessing of Poland's Teutonic occupants.

On November 7 in Lublin, freshly liberated from the Austrians, a Provisional People's Government came into existence, with the leader of the Polish Socialist Party, Ignacy Daszyński, as Premier. The Government included Tomasz Arciszewski, Medard Downarowicz, Marian Malinowski, Jędrzej Moraczewski, Tomasz Nocznicki, Juliusz Poniatowski, Wacław Sieroszewski, Błażej Stolarski, Edward Śmigły-Rydz, Stanisław Thugutt and Bronisław Ziemięcki. The Government was composed of members of the Polish Socialist Party and the Polish People's Party and nonpartisans. Colonel Śmigły-Rydz headed the army, as deputy to Commandant Piłsudski.

In their pronouncements this Government proclaimed a radical sociopolitical restructuring,[6] and displayed overt animosity toward the Council of Regency and the government sponsored by the latter, demanding its resignation and even going so far as to threaten the use of force against it.

In addition to the two afore-mentioned bodies which regarded themselves as the legitimate governments of Poland, there existed at the time three others desirous to take power over the entire emergent country: the Polish National Committee in Paris, the Commission of Liquidation in Krakow, and the Polish People's Council in Poznan.

The situation became somewhat clearer when Gemany collapsed and declared herself a republic — an immediate consequence of which was Piłsudski's release from Magdeburg. On November 10, 1918, he was greeted at the railroad station in Warsaw by a representative of the Council of Regency; on November 11 the Council of Regency turned military matters over to him, at the same time offering him the formation of a national government. Piłsudski summoned representatives of the Lublin government for talks, which apparently turned out according to his lights, as by November 14 the Council of Regency had placed power in his hands — binding him to pass it on to the national government to be created on the instructions of the Seym — and then had dissolved itself.

Without waiting for the Seym to come into existence, Piłsudski the same day announced the formation of a Provisional Government, and at the same time disavowed the so-called Lublin Manifesto, indicating that he would leave any sweeping sociopolitical reforms to the future Seym: a position which, however, did not deter him from issuing a decree proclaiming an eight-hour work day, etc. The earlier formation of a government at Lublin, and its radical program, did not make Pilsudski distrustful of its members. Their readiness to step down from the political arena several years later elicited words of high praise from him.[7] Daszyński was given the assignment of forming a government, but he was unable to carry it out due to the reluctance of the conservative factions to work together with him. He was replaced by another old Socialist, Moraczewski, whose reputation was redeemed by his service as an officer in Piłsudski's Legions.

Professor Kukiel sees Moraczewski's government as a new version of the Lublin government; the difference between them consisted in the rejection of social changes without prior approval by the Seym.[8] That is apparently how Piłsudski himself saw the new government, as indeed is indicated in the very wording of his *Decree on the Supreme Representative Authority of the People's Republic* of November 22, 1918, which opens: "Pursuant to the decree of the 14th inst., the President of the Ministers has presented to me a project, approved by the Provisional People's Government of the Polish Republic, for the formation of a supreme representative authority . . ."[9]

Next was the decree of November 28 promulgating the voting regulations and setting elections to the Seym for January 26, 1919. On February 10 the Seym was opened, and on February 20 Piłsudski turned over to the Seym his power as interim head of state. That same day, the Seym resolved to entrust him once again with the office and set forth the principles by which the Government was to govern. The act by which this was accomplished, familiarly termed the Little Constitution, formed the basis of governmental activities for the period of the next two years, during which the political parties were to work out drafts of the final constitution.

The projects were all as one in striving to establish a

democratic system. The Constitutional Club desired a federal system; the other parties wanted a homogeneous state. There were projects for a unicameral Seym from the Polish Socialist Party and the Liberation Party ("Wyzwolenie"); there were also projects, from the "government group" and the National-Popular Union, which urged a unicameral Seym with an additional body — A Guardianship of the Laws — to review the Seym's acts from the standpoint of their formulation and constitutionality. Under the "government" project, the head of state would have appointed one third of the members of the Guardianship of the Laws. The project of the Constitutional Club insisted on a bicameral legislature composed of a Seym and Senate.

There was incomplete agreement among the parties as to the scope of powers to be vested in the head of state. While the Constitutional Club, Liberation, the Polish Socialist Party and the "government group" wanted to ensure supreme power, both military and civil, to the head of state, the National-Popular Union did not want to grant him the powers of commander in chief.

The various parties also took different views as to the election of the head of state. Some (the "government group" and Liberation) called for popular election; others (the Constitutional Club and the Polish Socialist Party) viewed election by the legislature as more appropriate.

The projects also contained provisions seeking to advance certain special party interests. The Polish Socialist Party insisted on a separate title in the constitution setting up a special chamber within the Seym to monitor the workers' interests. The project of the National-Popular Union sought to assure a privileged position for the Catholic Church, particularly through a clause making membership in that church a *sine qua non* for a candidate seeking to become head of state.

Already in July, 1919, the draft prepared by the Constitutional Commission was before the Seym, and the debate over it — suspended in connection with the Polish-Soviet War of 1920 — was renewed in October, 1920. The country buzzed with public meetings, debates and press campaigns. The draft was sent back to the commission, and debate was postponed, and then the draft was accepted after the second reading: in spite of which, at the third reading, the leftist factions attacked certain of its details, chiefly the state's relation to non-Catholic denominations. The readings were concluded with the compromise of March 16. On March 17, 1921, the constitution of the new Poland was officially proclaimed.

At the time of her disappearance from the international stage in 1795, Poland had been a monarchy. The Council of Regency had shown a failure to grasp the changes that had occurred in the minds and feelings of the people when in their constitutional project of 1917 they had envisioned a revived Poland with a king once again at the top. In the new Poland there was no room for a king. This conviction was given expression right from the start in all the successive decrees of the new Poland's supreme authorities, and was confirmed in the March (1921) Constitution when the latter restored to the Polish state its pre-partition name of the Republic.[10]

The people were declared sovereign; the government's powers were divided — after Montesquieu — into legislative, executive and judicial;[11] civil liberties were guaranteed.[12]

A Seym and Senate were established as the agencies of legislative power;[13] the Seym shared the legislative initiative with the Government.[14] The Seym was assured the leading role: "there will be no law without the concurrence of the Seym, as expressed in the manner established by regulations,"[15] a statement which takes on a clearer significance when it is realized that the Seym itself was the author of the regulations in question. In practice, the Senate constituted a council of elders designed to apply the brakes to any overhasty proposals.

Executive power was exercised by the President of the Republic "through Ministers responsible to the Seym and by officials subordinate to them."[16] Not himself subject to parliamentary accountability, the President could be impeached only for treason, unconstitutional acts or infringements of the criminal code.[17]

The President,[18] the Chairman of the Council of Ministers, and the individual ministers were subject to impeachment by the Tribunal of State; impeachment required a vote by two-fifths or at least half the statutory number of deputies.[19]

The Tribunal of State was a body elected, from outside their own number, by the Seym (which elected eight members) and the Senate (which elected four members) immediately upon their constituting themselves, for the duration of the legislature. The Tribunal of State was presided over by the Chief Justice of the Supreme Court.[20]

The judiciary comprised a system of courts whose precise organization was left to subsequent legislation.[21] The only courts expressly referred to in the Constitution were a "supreme court for civil and criminal matters"[22] and military courts whose attributes would be "defined in separate laws."[23]

The judges, appointed by the President, were assured an independent status.[24]

The Constitution provided for the division of the country into decentralized administrative units[25] and for future legislation establishing "administrative" courts to pass upon the legality of administrative acts of the central, provincial, county and local governments.[26]

II. Kinships between the March (1921) Constitution and the United States Constitution

From the outset, even in its statement of aims, the March Constitution matches its sister American Constitution. The passage bracketed by the words, "We, the people of Poland . . . do ordain and establish this constitution," is in perfect consonance with the preamble to the American Constitution. In both cases, the basis of the constitution was a profound desire to secure for the nation the conditions requisite for an undisturbed existence and for the fullest possible development. The Polish Constitution of 1921 may have taken an additional step forward in making its avowed aim "the good of renascent humanity." But, then, perhaps this addendum resulted more from the felt need of an ancient people to document the idea that, in returning to the political map of the world, they were resuming their unprescribed rights and role within the community of nations.

Supremacy of the Constitution

The supremacy of the constitution vis-a-vis other laws is indicated by clauses in both Constitutions. [27, 28]

Division of power

Like the United States Constitution,[29] the March (1921) Constitution[30] distributes governmental powers among three branches: legislative, executive and judicial, considered in that order.

Legislative branch

The United States Constitution and the Polish Constitution of 1921, in aiming to balance the powers of the three branches of government, in reality reposed the greatest power in the legislature — or, to be more precise, in its lower chamber.

The original role of the United States Senate in Kennedy's exposition[31] resembles that of the Senate of the Polish Republic under the March (1921) Constitution. Both Senates were to have constituted bodies of older and wiser men (no women, originally, in America!) if need be blocking the passage of untimely legislation. In the United States the Senate, so construed, underwent a fundamental metamorphosis when the Federalists split into two factions over foreign policy. "The Senate became a forum for criticism of the executive branch, and the role of executive council was assumed instead by a Cabinet of men upon whom the President could depend to share his views and responsible to him."[32] Gradually the United States Senate became a full-fledged partner of the House of Representatives, and this of course destroyed the strongest kinship between it and the Polish Senate set up by the March Constitution.

The introduction of direct popular elections for the United States Senate in 1913[33] created another affinity when the 1921 Constitution made the Polish Senate subject to direct popular elections,[34] but any further relationships are strictly of a superficial nature. Whereas the American Senate rose to become a tremendously influential body, the Polish Senate — as ordained in the March (1921) Constitution — could just as well have ceased to exist without loss to the government or the nation.

The role of the legislature proper — in Poland between 1921 and 1935, and in the United States immediately after 1789[35] — was carried out by the lower chamber, and it was this chamber which attracted those interested in active politics.

The two constitutions contain a number of similar provisions respecting the two chambers:

1. each of the chambers judges the validity of the elections in

which they were elected (though, in Poland, only in uncontested cases)[36, 37]

2. each of the chambers determines the procedures for its own hearings and voting, and imposes disciplinary measures upon its own members;[38, 39]

3. members of the chambers are privileged from arrest (although this immunity is somewhat differently established)[40, 41]

4. members of the chambers are compensated in accordance with law;[42, 43]

5. members of the chambers may not, during their terms, hold any other paid government offices: in the United States, this refers to all offices under the authority of the United States;[44] in Poland, the offices of ministers, under-secretaries of state and professors at institutions of higher learning are exempted from the restriction.[45]

Senate

Both in the United States[46] and in Poland under the March Constitution the Senate receives bills passed by the lower chamber. It may then introduce emendations or reject the bill, which action in the United States has a bearing on the subsequent career of the bill, while in Poland the Seym could either consider or reject the sense of the Senate by a majority vote of eleven-twentieths of those voting, and repassage by the Seym — either with or without the Senate's emendations — made the bill law, and the President of the Republic was obliged to order its formal promulgation.[47]

Lower chamber

1. Both in the United States[48] and in Poland under the March Constitution,[49] the lower chamber is elected in popular ballotting;

2. the minimum required age for candidacy is 25;[50, 51]

3. candidates must be citizens of their countries;[52, 53] sex is immaterial to eligibility;[54, 55]

4. the lower chamber has the power of legislative initiative, which it shares with other agencies: in the United States, with the President[56] and Senate, while itself having exclusivity only in regard to bills for raising revenue;[57] in Poland, only with the Government;[58]

5. The lower chamber has the power to impeach;[59, 60]

6. the chamber selects its own presiding officer and other officials.[61, 62]

Apart from the foregoing, rather minor similarities, there are no significant kinships between the lower chamber of the United States Congress and its opposite number in Poland under the March (1921) Constitution.

Executive

1. Executive authority is exercised by the President,[63] but in the Polish Republic "through Ministers responsible to the Seym and by officials subordinate to them,"[64] which provision straightway makes the relationship between the roles of the two presidents a remote one;

2. the Presidents both of the United States[65] and of Poland[66] are chosen through indirect elections (but by different methods).

3. "Before he enter on the execution of his office" (the respective provisions begin identically) the President takes an oath. In the United States the oath is fundamentally — though in practice not entirely — secular in character,[67] while in Poland the formula is strikingly religious;[68] but in essence the two oaths affirm the assumption of identical obligations.

4. The President appoints the highest functionaries of the state. In the United States, he enjoys complete freedom in his appointments, but they go into effect only with the "advice and consent" of the Senate;[69] in Poland, the President freely appointed and relieved the Premier, and at the latter's instance the ministers; and he filled the highest civil and military offices upon recommendation of the Council of Ministers; however, in the event of a vote of non-confidence by the Seym, either the entire Government or individual ministers had to resign.[70]

5. The President appoints judges: in the United States federal judges "by and with the advice and consent of the Senate,"[71] in Poland all judges upon recommendation of the Minister of Justice;[72]

6. the President has supreme charge of the armed forces: in the United States he is commander in chief;[73] in Poland he was relieved of that authority in time of war, but he appointed the

commander in chief upon recommendation of the Council of Ministers, submitted by the Minister of Military Affairs.[74]

7. The President receives foreign ambassadors, [75, 76] appoints his own diplomatic representatives[77, 78] and represents the nation abroad: in Poland by the express letter of the Constitution; in the United States by interpretation of the basic law, the President being "the official channel" in "the maintenance of day-to-day intercourse with foreign governments;"[79]

8. the President concludes agreements with other nations. In the United States all such agreements theoretically require ratification by the Senate,[80] but in practice the number of "executive agreements," regarded as binding even without legislative ratification, is constantly growing; in Poland, agreements of particular importance to the nation require the consent[81] or "notification of the Seym."[82]

9. The President convenes the chambers of the legislature: in the United States, on extraordinary occasions;[83] in Poland, routinely;[84]

10. the president adjourns the two chambers of the legislature: in the United States, "on extraordinary occasions," under certain specified circumstances;[85] in Poland, both routinely and under certain circumstances with the consent of the Seym;[86]

11. the President has power to issue orders: in regard to the United States, executive agreements and orders have already been discussed; in Poland, the President issued orders in pursuance of, and in reference to, specific laws, and his orders required the endorsements of the Premier and the competent minister;[87]

12. the President grants reprieves, commutations and pardons according to his own lights. In the United States he has "power to grant reprieves and pardons for offenses against the United States, except in cases of impeachment;"[88] in Poland, he has power to grant pardons and commute sentences, except "in regard to ministers impeached by the Seym."[89]

13. The President receives compensation for his services.[90, 91]

Judiciary

Under the March (1921) Constitution, the administration of

justice for the first time approached the American system, thanks to the introduction (on a limited basis) of the jury system. In contradistinction to the United States,[92] the juries in Poland were competent to pass judgments only in political crimes and in crimes entailing grave penalties.[93]

Judges held office for life[94, 95] and were appointed by the President (in the United States, only federal judges being appointed by the President).[96, 97]

Guarantees of civil rights

In the United States Constitution, the guarantees of civil rights appear in a "Bill of Rights" that was tacked on as a kind of postscript. Similarly, in the March Constitution they appear in almost the final chapter, just ahead of the brief sixth and seventh chapters, dealing respectively with amending procedure and transitional procedures.

Chapter V of the March Constitution, relating to civil rights, outweighs its American counterpart — or perhaps archetype — in sheer bulk, but there are some striking similarities between them:

1. Social equality. Where the United States Constitution declares that "No titles of nobility shall be granted by the United States,"[98] and amplifies this through the Thirteenth Amendment of 1865, the March (1921) Constitution asserts almost in the tone of the American Declaration of Independence that "All citizens are equal before the law," and directly after this disowns family and class privileges, coats of arms and hereditary titles.[99]

2. Freedoms. Under both Constitutions, citizens (in the United States Constitution, "the people") are guaranteed the freedoms of speech,[100, 101] of press and assembly,[102, 103] and of petition.[104, 105]

3. Further developing the idea of freedom are clauses granting liberty of residence, occupation and disposal of property.[106, 107]

4. Freedom of religion. Freedom of religious belief and practice is granted by both Constitutions. But, as previously in the the Constitution of May 3d (1791) and next in the Constitution of the Kingdom of Poland of 1830-31, in the March (1921) Constitution [108] the clarity of the clause assuring religious freedom is — in comparison with that of the United States

Constitution[109] — obscured by the traditional privileged status accorded the Catholic Church. This time the latter has received a kind of *primus inter pares* position: it "holds the chief place among the equally privileged confessions."[110]

The Polish Constitution additionally contains a clause pledging the government not to refuse its recognition to "new or hitherto not legally recognized confessions."[111] However, this should not be regarded as an attempt to subject the faiths to the government, but as an expression of the rejuvenated Polish state's concern lest excessive denominational proliferation impair the already uncertain homogeneity of the nation.

One must bear in mind the historic role of Polish Roman Catholicism, which during the country's political eclipse constituted the strongest factor unifying the nation, annihilating as it did the borders between the three separate sectors at least in terms of religious belief.

5. Guarantee of personal liberty. The March (1921) Constitution did not reactivate the senescent *Neminem captivabimus* but established new guarantees — in accordance with the principle of equality before the law, applying to all persons without regard to class origin — against restrictions on personal liberty, except as the law may prescribe. This analog of the Anglo-Saxon *habeas corpus*[112] makes arrest and body search in principle conditional on a court warrant spelling out the reason. In exceptional circumstances court warrants issued *ex post facto* will fulfill the legal requirements for an arrest already carried out, but the absence of such a warrant within forty-eight hours after the arrest obliges immediate release.[113]

6. Inviolability of domicile. The concept that "an Englishman's home is his castle" was perpetuated in the American Bill of Rights, which guarantees "the right of the people to be secure in their persons, houses, papers, and effects, against unreasonable searches and seizures."[114] Similarly, the March (1921) Constitution in principle guarantees the security of domicile; entry, search and seizure of papers or effects may legally occur only in circumstances defined by law.[115]

7. Property rights. This is a fundamental concept of both Constitutions. The United States Constitution declares that "private property [shall not] be taken for public use without just

compensation."[116] The March Constitution declares property rights to be "one of the most important pillars of society [and] of the legal system ... and guarantees ... security of property, permitting ... the abrogation or limitation of property rights [only] in exchange for compensation."[117]

8. Guarantee of criminal proceedings in a court of proper jurisdiction: granted by both Constitutions.[118, 119]

9. Trial by jury. As mentioned earlier, the difference lies in the scope of the juries' competence: in the United States the accused is entitled to jury trial in cases of capital and other infamous crimes,[120] and in Poland in political crimes and in crimes subject to grave penalties.[121] American court procedure also provides for jury trial of civil cases.

10. Prohibition against cruel punishments: a humanitarian concern inherited from common antecedents, found in the Bill of Rights' proscription of "cruel and unusual punishments,"[122] and in the March Constitution's clause that "punishments involving physical torment are forbidden, and no one may be subjected to such punishments."[123]

A consideration of the civil rights guaranteed in the two Constitutions cannot but take note of the prudence which both societies display in making these guarantees conditional upon a state of peace and national security: conditions which make the existence of the civil liberties possible at all. "The privilege of the writ of *habeas corpus* shall not be suspended unless when in cases of rebellion or invasion the public safety may require it," states the United States Constitution.[124] But this provision for suspension of *habeas corpus* has been expanded by interpretation to include also declared or *de facto* wars.[125]

The March Constitution likewise provides for the restriction of civil liberties in times of public danger.[126]

The authors of the two Constitutions likewise provided for the use of force in the event of internal disorders of a scale such as to threaten the safety of the state. One of the powers of the United States Congress is that of "calling forth the militia to execute the laws of the Union, suppress insurrections, and repel invasions."[127] In Poland, "Armed force may be used ... to put down disorders or to enforce the execution of the laws."[128]

System of checks and balances

The framers of the United States Constitution made an effort to construct as balanced a system of governmental authorities as possible. They were in a particularly favorable situation in that they were not as divided in their political views as were the framers of the March (1921) Constitution. Whereas in the United States toward the end of the eighteenth century two opposed concepts can be distinguished — that of a strong federal government versus that of strong state governments — the Seym of the new Poland sported a broad spectrum of parties and outworn prejudices and animosities inherited from the period of the partitions. An example of their effects is found in the definition of the President's authority over the armed forces — limiting his powers in the event of war — pushed through by the National-Popular Union (later known as the National Democratic Party) against Piłsudski: a move which the Marshal took very much to heart and which influenced his consequent attitude toward the Constitution.[129]

From the absence of a primary concern for a balance of powers, the system of checks and balances suffered. Where Montesquieu had sought a balance among the branches of government — and even a balance between two legislative chambers — the March Constitution introduced a division of authority but practically frustrated any possibility of a balance of powers.

The legislature comprised two chambers, of which the upper lacked any sanctions. The Senate could only, by a three-fifths vote of the statutory number of its members, give its consent to the President for dissolving the Seym. But in that event the Senate itself was automatically dissolved. Thus the Senate's dissolution of a refractory Seym could only amount to a suicidal exercise in power. Consequently the Seym remained practically safe from the Senate.

The two chambers — jointly known as the National Assembly — elected the President. The President, pursuant to his authority, appointed the Premier and ministers (in addition to filling the highest civil and military offices) but all his appointees — either together or individually — were obliged to tender their resignations upon the demand of a simple majority of the Seym. The Seym also monitored the expenditures of the executive authority through a Supreme Comptroller's Office responsible to the Seym.

The executive branch too had the right of legislative initiative, but the fate of its bills rested entirely in the hands of the Seym. The only unquestionable authority of the chief executive in the legislative field was in the promulgation of laws.

Judges were to be subordinate only to the law; they were all appointed by the President. The Chief Justice of the Supreme Court headed the Tribunal of State, which could arraign the President and the members of the Government on charges of unconstitutional actions, treason or criminal transgressions. But the other members of the Tribunal of State were elected, from outside their own number, by the Seym and Senate.

The 1921 Constitution was particularly sensitive to the mood of the Seym. Consequently every major change in the Seym disturbed the equilibrium of the Government, which underwent changes too frequently to be able to develop truly effective, long-range policies. The basic flaw in the March Constitution was that it did not so much balance the powers of the executive as it neutralized them. In point of fact, it did the same to the powers of the upper chamber of the legislature.

Józef Piłsudski, 1867-1935

CHAPTER 6

Poland: 1921-

I. The March (1921) Constitution to the April (1935) Constitution

The period following the First World War was a trying one for the entire civilized world. Poland shared fully in the trials. To attempt to pinpoint the source of the trials in some one social factor would be a vast oversimplification; still, the present study will concentrate on just one of them: the political aspect.

Modern Polish politics evolved during the Partitions and was directed toward combatting the partitioning powers. Poland's political life after 1918 bore the consequences of that fact. The political activists and leaders were unable to set aside their old habits of thought and switch over from fighting the government to working together with it for the common good of society. Men who had dedicated the best years of their lives to the struggle for Polish independence — who had done everything in their power to prepare the Polish people for that struggle, who had joined the

Marshal Pilsudski in a political caricature

international movement (Piłsudski had participated in the Second International in 1889[1]) and had set the plight of the Polish nation before the leaders of the world, who had accepted the sacrifice of lives in the Russian Revolution of 1905, in the wars from 1914 through 1920 and in the Silesian Uprisings of 1919, 1920 and 1921 — found themselves unable now to look aside as Poland wrestled with her problems, under parliamentary governments which appeared to be leading her toward anarchy.

Ensconced within the privacy of his estate at Sulejówek, the ostensible ex-Socialist and the first organizer and commander of Polish armed forces since 1863, the former civil and military head of Poland, and her legal dictator from 1918 to 1921, fumed at the political situation. Finally, in mid-May of 1926, backed by his sometime officers and with the help of the railroad workers whose confidence he enjoyed, he forcibly took power. When subsequently elected president, Piłsudski would not accept the office; he felt that he could not "live without direct power, while the existing constitution imposes just such a separation between the President and the real power." Thus he concluded: "I would not be suited to such a position."[2] He saw "legislative chaos" and insisted that the President be given full authority.[3] He also discerned dishonesty in those who exerted an influence on the national economy.

From this appraisal of the situation sprang the so-called "August novels" amending the Constitution of March 17, 1921. First and foremost, they sharpened discipline among the deputies to the Seym by inaugurating automatic forfeiture of their seats upon the Supreme Court's ascertaining — at the instance of the Marshal of the Seym or of the Supreme Comptroller's Office — a violation of the provisions in Article 22 of the Constitution forbidding deputies (as well as senators) from drawing material benefits from their office apart from their salaries.

The August novels also established the times and procedures for budgeting as well as for setting military draft calls.

The President of the Republic was authorized by the August novels to dissolve the legislative chambers before the expiration of their terms and to declare new elections, though only once for any given reason.[4] During such time as the legislature was dissolved, the President had power, at the instance of the Council of Ministers, to issue orders having the full force of law — with certain limitations, particularly forbidding changes in the Constitution or in the voting regulations for the legislative bodies. The President could likewise issue such orders "at such times and in such matters as are indicated in this law."[5]

The August novels required that the President's orders be issued with express reference to the applicable provision in the Constitution; they had to be endorsed by the President and by all the members of the Government and published in the Legislative Journal of the Polish Republic. The continuance in force of these decrees was voted on at the next sitting of the Seym. They expired in the event that they were not submitted to the next Seym within fourteen days.

The novels of 1926 were a constitutional patchwork which did not give the President the powers that Piłsudski demanded the head of state have in order to be able to act effectively. Over the next several years people close to the great altar were to make pronouncements suggesting work underway on the next constitution. These found confirmation in February, 1931, when a draft constitution was formally laid before the Seym by the Nonpartisan Bloc for Cooperation with the Government.[6]

The veil surrounding the secret was lifted by the president of the Nonpartisan Bloc, Walery Sławek, at a convention of ex-Legionnaires on August 6, 1933. "He predicts government by elite, he says that from now on the destiny of the nation is going to be guided by the best citizens, who elect the senators; he downgrades the Seym and creates a superior office that will resolve disagreements between the Seym and Senate."[7] "Voting rights to a Senate with broader powers than the Seym's belong to those who have been decorated with military orders."[8]

This did not seem to be how the Marshal wanted the future constitution; "the [political] opposition says . . . he declared that . . . he does not intend to make use of the military-elite idea . . ."[9] "Work began again,"[10] and the result was most unexpectedly crowned with success by the act of January 26, 1935.

While Piłsudski's statements — whose tenor is confirmed by Sosnkowski[11] — indicate his desire to base the Polish political system on the American model, the manner in which his Constitution was enacted departed from the American legislative style, if not from the manner in which the American Constitution was assembled. We shall use the accounts of two diametrically different witnesses: a parliamentary reporter for the Jewish press, and a National Democratic deputy.

On January 26 at ten o'clock in the morning, the "constitutional proposals" prepared by the Nonpartisan Bloc were read before the Seym. They were given recognition as a constitutional draft by a rather fortuitous majority and were passed following three readings on the same day. The whole proceeding had a blitzkrieg quality about it. The sharp protests raised by National Democratic Deputy Stroński, adverting to Seym regulations and to the Constitution, were ignored by the Marshal of the Seym, Świtalski. Vice Marshal Car pointed to the provision in the regulations (Article 18) allowing "the Seym [to] resolve to curtail formal proceedings by: a) waiving the printing of bills or minutes, b) permitting immediate debate on a bill without the bill's being referred to committee."

"In this manner the constitutional proposals introduced at ten a.m. were transformed into a constitutional bill and passed, following three readings, at a few minutes after eight [the same] evening."[12]

Deputy Stroński's account agrees with the foregoing picture, which he completes by stating that the bill passed by the Seym on January 26, 1935, was sent to the Senate, which returned it in March with recommendations for amendment. The Marshal of the Seym averred that a simple majority of the Seym would suffice either to carry or to reject the amendments proposed by the Senate; Deputy Stroński objected to this in the Seym on March 23, lodging a formal demurrer on grounds that the letter of the law concerning change of the constitution had been violated. The Seym, at its session on March 26, 1935, rejected Stroński's objection.

On April 23, the new constitution was passed in its final form, and its passage — according to Deputy Stroński[13] — in violation of the law and in the absence of any appellate authority rendered the Constitution the new law of the land.

The present study regards constitutions not as legal documents but as political instruments. The fact is that the April (1935) Constitution was recognized by the Polish nation as the law of the land. Indirectly it was recognized by all the governments — including that of the Soviet Union — which during World War II recognized the Polish government in London.

Even assuming — after certain of its critics — that the April (1935) Constitution was indeed railroaded through, it was still a product of certain political views of the period, if not held by the majority of the Polish people, then at least by a goodly portion of them. It was not imposed or granted from outside. It was the work of the people who had been instrumental in the restoration of Polish independence and who — whether right or wrong — persisted in the conviction that this entitled them, in the interests of preserving and furthering the well-being of the country, to shape the Polish political reality without necessarily consulting the rest of the Polish people.

The fundamental principles of the 1935 Constitution are set forth by its co-author, Stanislaw Car, in his preface to the official English-language edition. These principles, in order of appearance, may be summarized as follows:

1. Under the new Constitution, the President of the Republic ceases to be just the executive head of the government and becomes chief of state, reconciling the activities of the highest authorities;

2. the government remains the agency of the President, appointed by him, but still under the political and constitutional control of the legislature;

3. the legislature acts in the domain of legislation and in supervision of the Government; under certain circumstances, the legislature may demand the resignation of the Government;

4. the Constitution breaks away from parliamentary government and makes the legislature a mouthpiece of public opinion, providing liaison between the Government and the people.[14]

The Seym is elected in popular ballotting. Elections to the Senate — under the new voting regulations — are not popular (the new system thus marking its conscious departure from "the mechanical, universal and absolute equality propagated by the Declaration of the Rights of Man and the Citizen of 1789"[15]). A new principle is introduced: "The rights of a citizen to influence public affairs will be estimated according to the value of his efforts and services for the common good."[16]

The April (1935) Constitution is symptomatic of an "opposition to political parties — only too numerous and far from being the disseminators [sic] of sound principles amongst the electorate of the country."[17]

Car's preface also announces Poland's entry into a new political era: "The new order will likewise be found to operate against professional parliamentary politicians in accordance with the ideal, so forcefully expressed in 1898 by Poincaré: *'il faut arracher la politique aux politiciens...'* "[18]

What the introductory commentary by the Vice Marshal of the Seym neglects to say is that the new Constitution has made a radical departure from the Montesquieuan division of powers. The coequal legislative, executive and judicial authorities have been superseded by the Government, the Seym, the Senate, the armed forces, the courts and a Supreme Board of Control — all subordinate to the President of the Republic. It puts the new system into sharp relief to add a basic innovation that Vice Marshal Car does not mention: the President of the Polish Republic is now held "responsible before God and history."

II. Kinships between the April (1935) Constitution and the United States Constitution

The intents of the constitutions

The April (1935) Constitution lacks a preamble stating the intent of its authors. But the intent behind it is clear in the already quoted comment on the March (1921) Constitution by Józef Piłsudski, as well as in the statements of his close collaborator Sosnkowski. It is also confirmed by Car's preface to the English-language edition of the 1935 Constitution:

> Upon the conclusion of the Great War [World War I] Poland... maintained the system of parliamentary government by her Constitution of March 17, 1921. This system did not, however, pass the test of life. Its lacks and faults [held] up the normal development of

State life amidst the more complicated relations of the post-War period.

For this reason the Polish nation as a whole very early realized the need for a reform of the system . . .

Poland decided to revert to her old State and national traditions of liberty, adapting them of course to the needs of modern times and reconciling them with the spirit of the present age.

On the other hand, constantly bearing in mind what experiences she had in history, she cannot but guide herself with a political realism which obliges her not to forget that only a strong and authoritative State authority can assure the Nation a free untrammelled existence and the State an independent position amongst the other countries and peoples.

This is the basic thought from which the new structure of Poland issued as the synthesis between the individual liberty of man and the dignity of the authority of the State; it is fully in accordance with the principle of "a free citizen of a strong State."[19]

The authors of the American Constitution, too, desired nothing else.

The supremacy of the Constitution

Much as is the case under the United States Constitution,[20] the April (1935) Constitution clearly states: "No legislative act may be contrary to the Constitution."[21]

Division of powers

As has already been mentioned, the 1935 Constitution eschewed Montesquieu's classic tripartite division of powers, in its stead setting up a double-decker system consisting of the head of state, the President, to whom are subordinated, all on the same level: the Government; the Seym; the Senate; the armed forces; the courts; and the Supreme Board of Control (a comptroller agency). (Actually, the establishment on July 15, 1936, of a "first person in Poland after the President of the Republic, to whom all — with the chairman of the Council of Ministers [Premier] foremost — ought to display their respect and obedience": General Śmigły-Rydz, [22] introduced a kind of trinity once again.)

Despite the striking difference between the American system and the new Polish system, it is interesting and productive to seek out the kinships between the two systems. Such a search leads to the conclusion that the differences should not be overstated.

The legislative chambers

In both systems there are two legislative chambers:
1. a "lower" (the Seym; the House of Representatives); and
2. an "upper" (the Senate).

Provisions relating to the members of the legislative chambers

1. The members of the legislative chambers can be disciplined by their respective chambers;[23, 24]
2. the members of the chambers are sworn in:[25] in Poland a solemn vow is required, without any religious overtones;[26]
3. the members of the legislative chambers receive compensation for their services;[27, 28]
4. the members of the chambers, within certain limits, enjoy immunity from arrest and from questioning outside their chamber about their statements made in the chamber.[29, 30]

Provisions governing sessions of the legislative chambers

1. The sessions are, in principle, public;[31, 32]
2. publication of minutes of public sessions is authorized.[33, 34]

The lower chamber

1. It is elected through popular suffrage;[35, 36]
2. candidates must be citizens of their country;[37, 38] sex is immaterial to eligibility;[39, 40]
3. the lower chamber has the power of legislative initiative, sharing it with other bodies: in the United States with the President[41] and the Senate, and having exclusivity only in legislation pertaining to revenues;[42] in Poland the Seym shared legislative initiative only with the Government;[43]
4. the chamber elects its own presiding officer.[44, 45]

The upper chamber
1. On receiving a bill passed by the lower chamber, the upper chamber may reject it or propose amendments;[46, 47]

2. the upper chamber — like the lower — reconsiders bills which, after having been passed by both chambers, have been turned down by the President;[48, 49]

3. the chamber has an influence on the composition of the Government: in the United States, the Senate gives its "advice and consent" in respect to appointments made by the President;[50] in Poland, it participates — without the right of initiative — in considering motions by the Seym demanding the dismissal of the cabinet or of a minister;[51]

4. the upper chamber is elected: in the United States entirely so, except when, in the event of a vacancy occurring before the end of the term, the governor of the state appoints a senator for the remainder of the unexpired term;[52] in Poland, two-thirds of the Senate is elected, the other third being appointed by the President of the Republic.[53] An additional difference is that in the United States all the senators — apart from the exception mentioned — are popularly elected (after May 31, 1913) while in Poland they were elected only by voters meeting certain requirements: personal merit, educational attainments, or the confidence of their fellow citizens.[54] Here one must observe that during the early period of American independence the United States Senate, which was intended by the authors of the Constitution to comprise a social elite, matched the concept of the elite Polish Senate under the 1935 Constitution.

The President
1. The President is chosen by the people indirectly,[55] in Poland by an Electoral Assembly comprising certain government officials and seventy-five electors chosen by the Seym and Senate;[56]

2. before assuming office, the President takes an oath: in the United States, the oath may be replaced by an affirmation without religious overtones;[57] in Poland the President's oath had a quite religious character, invoking "God Almighty united in the Holy Trinity" and closing with an invocation of "God and His Son's Holy Passion."[58] The oaths state the duties of the

President: in the United States, the preservation, protection and defense of the Constitution;[59] in Poland, the defense of the sovereign rights and dignity of the state, the application of the Constitution, the administration of equal justice to all citizens, the averting of evil and danger from the state, and solicitous care for the welfare of the state.[60] (The expression "care for the welfare of the State" is reminiscent of Article I, section VIII of the United States Constitution, listing the powers of Congress: "The Congress shall have power to ... provide for the ... general welfare of the United States," a provision which American political scientists view as one of those generalizations that "lend themselves to more than one interpretation."[61])

3. The President appoints the highest officials of the state: in the United States, his appointments require "the advice and consent of the Senate," and only when the Senate is not in session does the President fill vacancies on his own, his appointments then expiring at the end of the next session of the Senate;[62] in Poland the President appoints the Premier, and upon recommendation of the latter the ministers and other high government officials[63] "as freely as he sees fit;"[64]

4. the President has the power to dismiss high functionaries: in the United States, this power was interpreted into the Constitution by the Supreme Court;[65] in Poland this power is explicitly spelled out by the Constitution;[66]

5. the President appoints judges. In the United States the President appoints federal judges "by and with the advice and consent of the Senate."[67] In Poland under the April (1935) Constitution, the President appoints all judges;[68] the Constitution is silent on nominations, but the route probably led through the office of the Minister of Justice.

6. The President is the supreme head of the armed forces. In the United States[69] he is even called the "commander-in-chief," and his superiority is emphasized by the subordination of all forces to the Federal government, constitutionally denying to military commanders the power of independent action. In this sense the two Constitutions are in complete accord.[70]

7. The President represents the country abroad:
    a) he receives representatives of foreign countries;[71, 72]
    b) he appoints his own representatives to foreign

countries — in the United States "by and with the advice and consent of the Senate,"[73] in Poland according to his own judgment;[74]

c) he makes international agreements: in the United States "by and with the advice and consent of the Senate,"[75] through "executive agreements,"[76] or through "joint resolutions" — Congressional resolutions passed by a simple majority and confirmed by the President;[77] in Poland the President concluded and ratified international agreements, and only commercial and customs agreements and agreements entailing a permanent burden on the national treasury, imposing new burdens on the citizens or causing change in the national boundaries required the consent of the legislative chambers in the form of a law;[78]

8. the President convenes and adjourns the legislature: in the United States, "he may, on extraordinary occasions, convene both houses, or either of them, and in the case of disagreement between them with respect to the time of adjournment, he may adjourn them to such time as he shall think proper;"[79] in Poland, the President "convenes and dissolves the Diet (Seym) and Senate [and] opens, adjourns and closes sessions of the Seym and Senate;"[80]

9. the President promulgates laws. In the United States, he signs bills passed by Congress, and they are proclaimed law; in the event of his refusal to sign, the bill may become law if it is repassed by a two-thirds vote of each of the chambers; a bill may also become law if within ten days the President has neither signed it nor registered his opposition to it, except in the event that in the meantime Congress has adjourned, which is assumed to be the cause of the bill's not being returned to the chambers.[81]

In Poland, the President of the Republic signs bills and orders their promulgation in the Legislative Journal;[82] however, if within thirteen days the President rejects the bill with the demand that it be reconsidered, and if the legislative chambers repass it unaltered in the manner prescribed by law, the President signs it and orders its promulgation in the Legislative Journal.[83]

10. The President is empowered to enact laws. In the United States, the President's power to do so developed, via broadening

interpretations and practice, into so-called "executive orders," already discussed. In Poland, the 1935 Constitution gave the President the power to issue decrees with the force of law, stating both the cirumstances under which they may be issued and the scope of their force;[84] the President's decree became exclusively decisive in organizational matters of the Government, the supreme military command, and the administration of the state;[85] in the event of a formally declared state of war, presidential decrees had the force of law in all matters, excepting changes in the Constitution;[86]

11. acts of the President do not require a minister's endorsement. In the United States this principle is strictly adhered to; in Poland only presidential acts based on his constitutional prerogatives do not require such endorsement, whereas all others require the signature of the respective minister;[87]

12. the President has powers of clemency: in the United States he may "grant reprieves and pardons for offenses against the United States, except in cases of impeachment;"[88] in Poland the Constitution sets no limits to the powers of clemency enjoyed by the President;[89]

13. there is a connection between the function of the President's successor and the presiding officer of the upper legislative chamber. In the United States, the President of the Senate and the Vice President of the United States are the same person; in circumstances described by law, he becomes President of the United States;[90] in Poland, this duty devolved upon the Marshal of the Senate.[91]

The Government

1. This body conducts the business of the country at the highest level. In the United States, as mentioned earlier, the Government is not provided for in the Constitution: "The Cabinet ... grew up outside the Constitution and unknown to the law."[92] Nevertheless, the government does exist, and the Cabinet members "direct great specialized operating departments"[93] and are the chief advisers of the President;[94] but the actual role of the Cabinet and of its members is entirely dependent on the role assigned to them by the President, ranging from that of advisors to "very close to being an agency of collective responsibility."[95]

In Poland the Government directs the national affairs not reserved to other authorities;[96] the ministers direct the work of their respective ministries,[97] and the powers of the Council of Ministers and of the individual ministers are defined by presidential decrees;[98]

2. the government plays a role in the legislative forum. In the United States, the President enjoys a "message power,"[99] submitting in person or in writing "information on the state of the Union," either at the opening of a congressional session or in the form of "special messages" in the course of the session.[100]

In Poland, direct contact and cooperation between the Government and legislature were assured by the participation of the Premier, ministers or delegated officials in sessions of the Seym, with the right to speak out of turn. The deputies had the right, in accordance with regulations, to interpellate the Government, and the Premier and ministers were bound to provide answers or to justify their refusal to do so.[101]

The judicial authority

Here again there is a lack of close kinship between the provisions in the American and Polish Constitutions. The similarities are limited to:

1. the existence of a Supreme Court functioning as a court of appeal; [102, 103] and

2. judges appointed by the President, in principle for life,[104, 105] though the 1935 Constitution did make provisions for deviations in this matter.[106]

Guarantees of civil liberties

1. Freedom of religion, of speech and of assembly. The United States Constitution's guarantee is stated as a prohibition against Congress making any law "respecting an establishment of religion, or prohibiting the free exercise thereof; or abridging the freedom of speech or of the press; or the right of the people peacefully to assemble, and to petition the government for a redress of grievances."[107] The corresponding article of the April (1935) Constitution has a somewhat different character, as it states that "The State assures its citizens . . . liberty of conscience, speech and assembly . . . The limit of these liberties is

the common good."[108] In the United States the legislature is enjoined from attempting to curb the basic or natural rights of the people; in Poland the state is empowered to assure the citizens' liberties. While Article I of the U.S. Bill of Rights limits the powers of Congress vis-a-vis the people, Article 5, paragraph 3 of the April (1935) Constitution hints vaguely at the limits of citizens' liberties.

2. Freedom from bills of attainder. The corresponding clauses in the two Constitutions are not quite equivalent, but they show a basic kinship of concept. "No bill of attainder . . . shall be passed."[109] "No law can bar a citizen from seeking redress in the courts of justice for his injury or damages."[110]

3. *Lex retro non agit.* Both Constitutions express an identical idea: "No . . . *ex post facto* law shall be passed."[111] "No one can be punished for a deed not prohibited by law before it was committed."[112]

4. Personal liberty. In the United States this is guaranteed by the privilege of *habeas corpus*, which "shall not be suspended, unless when in cases of rebellion or invasion the public safety may require it."[113] In Poland under the April Constitution, "No one can . . . be detained without a judicial warrant longer than for . . . forty-eight hours."[114]

5. Guarantee of trial by the proper courts. The United States Constitution declares that "The trial of all crimes, except in cases of impeachment, shall be . . . held in the State where the said crimes shall have been committed . . ."[115] The 1935 Constitution states that "No one can be deprived of the court of justice to which he is by law subject . . ."[116]

6. Inviolability of domicile. This civil liberty, though stated somewhat differently than in the March (1921) Constitution, is still basically comparable with the corresponding guarantees in the United States Constitution, and the comparison drawn in regard to the 1921 Constitution still holds for the 1935 Constitution.

7. Protection against unreasonable search. Both Constitutions forbid unjustified searches. In the United States, "no warrants shall issue but upon probable cause . . . and particularly describing the place to be searched, and the person or things to be seized."[117] In Poland, "A law shall define under what

conditions the search of a citizen's person or home may be executed or the secrecy of correspondence be infringed."[118]

8. Inviolability of documents and correspondence. In the United States the Constitution guarantees the safety of "papers,"[119] which would seem to include documents and correspondence. In Poland, the 1935 Constitution guarantees separately the secrecy of correspondence, [120] and having guaranteed "personal liberty" and "inviolability of domicile", makes "the search of a citizen's person or home" (and presumably therefore also the inspection of papers and documents) dependent on "a law" later to be enacted defining the circumstances under which such actions shall be permissible.[121]

9. The political equality of the sexes. This is assured by both Constitutions.

10. Freedom from discrimination due to origin. In the United States, this guarantee was introduced with the Negroes in mind and in the first instance bound only the states.[124] Nevertheless, "equal protection is now construed as contained within the broad concept of due process of law, and therefore is binding upon the national government as well."[125]

In Poland, the treatment of this freedom was influenced by abandonment of the concept of equality proclaimed in the American *Declaration of Independence* of 1776 and in the French *Declaration of the Rights of Man* of 1789. According to the April (1935) Constitution, "The rights of a citizen to influence public affairs will be estimated according to the value of his efforts and services for the common good."[126] These rights, so defined, were not to be restricted on account of the citizen's origin.[127]

11. Freedom of religion. The 1935 Constitution retained in force Articles 110-116 of the 1921 Constitution; accordingly, the parallel drawn earlier between the corresponding provisions in the latter and in the United States Constitution still holds for the 1935 Constitution. The April (1935) Constitution further emphasized religious tolerance when it stated that "The rights of a citizen to influence public affairs . . . cannot be restricted by . . . religion . . ."[128]

Legal sanctions

While guaranteeing civil liberties, the framers of the

Constitutions drew a clear distinction between liberty and license. The United States Congress has the right to use the state militias (today, the National Guard) "to execute the laws of the Union [and to] suppress insurrections..."[129] In Poland, "In case of resistance ["to the aims of the State"] the State applies means of compulsion."[130]

Amendments to the Constitution

The respective provisions differ in their procedures, in the United States making the legislature sovereign and in Poland stressing the role of the President.[131]

Checks and balances

Detailed analysis of the April Constitution will uncover no automatic system of checks and balances of the American type; it has been eliminated entirely and superseded by a new mechanism built into the office of the President: "His role as the supreme arbiter of the State is to reconcile the activities of the highest organs of the country, and especially those of the Government and the parliament; in the event of conflicts arising, his duty is to remove friction and to restore the proper balance within the State."[132]

III. The letter, the appearances and the reality

The April Constitution came about through the inability of the March (1921) Constitution to accommodate Marshal Piłsudski. From the very beginning he had desired a different kind of constitution, and in this connection had made reference to the United States Constitution: "I am not saying that we should have imitated the United States down to the last detail... but we must seek in this area of ideas something that could be applied to Poland."[133]

He did not say it in so many words, but he probably envied the United States her freedom from a plague of endlessly intriguing political parties and coteries; her having a legislative chamber with a large influence on the President's highest decisions through its "advice and consent," but without exercising power for him; and her head of government not being constantly called on the carpet and threatened with unseating by some tactical conglomerate of opposition parties.

Piłsudski, in his own words, was "a child of liberty and sought power for the sake of that liberty."[134] But what he observed in Poland convinced him that "in a powerless nation grown feral in bondage, liberty produces an abuse of liberty..."[135] He saw "too much injustice in respect to those who devote their efforts to others..."[136]

Piłsudski's people drew up a constitution with the idea of basing Poland on the American system as they saw it, i.e., with strong powers concentrated in the hands of the President; their aim was to preserve civil liberties — to the extent compatible with the general national good; the lower chamber remained fully democratic, as in the United States; the upper chamber — patterned on the early United States Senate — became an exclusive body which might perhaps in the future, after the citizens had learned to think in terms of the general welfare, lose its elite quality. (It is interesting to note that in recent years there has been broad discussion in the United States of limiting voting rights to those who have a college degree.)

The fundamental difference between the 1935 Constitution — actually, between all the Polish constitutions — and the United States Constitution is that the latter, as mentioned earlier, is bistructural, whereas the Polish Constitution is quite rigid. In the United States, constitutional changes occur evolutionarily and continuously; in Poland they are abrupt. As a result, while the President of the United States over a period of time acquired powers essentially very similar to those granted to the Polish President under the April Constitution, in the view of his own society as well as of probably the predominant part of the western world the President of the United States is the executive head of the leading western democracy: while the powers of the Polish President, because of the abrupt, nonevolutionary change of constitution carried out in 1935, became for many — in Poland as abroad — symptomatic of an undemocratic political system.

Whereas the Polish President, responsible only to God and

history, is a "Caesar,"[137] no one for a moment saw any caesarist tendency when President Kennedy commended himself to the judgment of God and history. Critics of the 1935 Constitution were disturbed at the Polish President's powers to make decisions concerning war and peace and to conclude and ratify treaties, but they were not struck by the fact that the President of the United States was on his own responsibility concluding international agreements of such import as Lend-Lease, or that in 1950 a President of the United States by executive order, without any congressional formalities, dispatched American troops to Korea.

(A notable comment on the "caesarism" of the United States President has appeared in the U.S. Senate. "The Roman Caesars did not spring full blown from the brow of Zeus. Subtly, and insidiously, they stole their powers from an unsuspecting 'Senate,' " said Senator Church of Idaho, adding that Congress must take back its powers "usurped by U.S. Presidents since Truman."[138])

Critics of the April (1935) Constitution were shocked that, in consideration of the common good, the Constitution set *a priori* limits to civil liberties;[139] that it permitted detention without a judicial warrant for up to forty-eight hours.[140] But the same critics failed to notice that in the United States the privilege of *habeas corpus* may be suspended whenever the public safety may require;[141] just as they were silent when, reacting to the Japanese attack on Pearl Harbor in December, 1941, President Roosevelt ordered West Coast residents of Japanese extraction interned in "relocation centers," forcing them to liquidate their property for a fraction of its value. In the view of many political scientists, this act violated the Constitution, but the liberal Justice of the Supreme Court, Hugo Black, said in connection with the incident, "Hardships are part of war, and war is an aggregation of hardships. All citizens alike, both in and out of uniform, feel the impact of war in greater or lesser measure."[142]

The 1935 Constitution is not a copy of the United States Constitution, but it does show many kinships with it, the most fundamental being the resolve to assure Poland "liberty through strength," which the authors of the 1935 Constitution saw in the United States. The April Constitution is kindred with the United

States Constitution, but this time again Poland suffered the consequences of the "particular circumstances of the country."

IV. The Paris Declaration of September 30, 1939

In the final days of September, 1939, pursuant to the provisions of the April (1935) Constitution,[143] President Ignacy Mościcki, interned in Rumania, designated the Polish ambassador in Italy, Dr. Bolesław Wieniawa-Długoszowski as his successor in office. The objections of political opponents and the — under normal circumstances inadmissible — pressure of the French government forced President Mościcki to withdraw the appointment and to name another successor. This was the former governor (*wojewoda*), Minister of Internal Affairs, and Marshal of the Senate, Władysław Raczkiewicz.[144]

On September 30, 1939, President Raczkiewicz entrusted the formation of a government to Professor Stanisław Stroński, — already mentioned as a National Democratic deputy in the Seym — who stated that he would accept the assignment only on condition that the President declare to the government and the nation that he would not exercise the powers reserved to the President under Article 13 of the April Constitution, granting the head of state authoritarian powers. He had in mind particularly the prerogative of freely appointing and dismissing the Government, which he wanted supplanted by the President's decision concurred in by the Government.

President Raczkiewicz agreed and then pledged himself to pass the same condition on to any successor that he might designate.

This agreement, reminiscent of the old *pacta conventa* constituted according to Stroński "*in fact . . . the abolition of the authoritative [sic] element in the Constitution.*"[145]

This change made the positions of the Presidents of the United States and Poland more alike. In the United States, the President appoints members of the Cabinet "by and with the advice and consent of the Senate;" in the case of a Polish government being formed abroad, such a possibility did not exist, and so the next closest procedure to it was applied. The result was not a complete, but certainly a partial, analog of the American system — a Polish summary version of checks and balances.

V. The Polish Constitution after World War II

The conclusion of the Second World War found the legal Polish authorities sanctioned by the Constitution of April, 1935, abroad, while in a Poland of altered boundaries and with a substantially different population make-up, a new government came to power with the blessing of Poland's allies.

The new Republic recognized "the basic principles" of the March, 1921, Constitution, and the so-called Little Constitution of 1947 restored certain provisions of the latter constitution. The Little Constitution was replaced by the Constitution of July 18, 1952, as amended subsequently in September, 1954, December, 1957, December, 1960, May, 1961, December, 1963, November, 1973, October, 1975, and February, 1976.

The basic Constitution of the Polish People's Republic was ratified by a Seym whose election — at the instance of the Allies — raised protests from the governments of Great Britain and the United States.[146] As Bolesław Bierut expressed it on presenting the draft constitution to the Seym on July 18, 1952, "the shaping of our national, popular Polish constitution, independently of bourgeois cosmopolitan models, was made possible by that turning point in human history which was marked by the Great October Socialist Revolution."[147]

It is precisely on the grounds stated by Bierut that the Constitution of the Polish People's Republic is excluded from consideration in the present volume.

Map of Poland

PART II
Genealogy

Benjamin Franklin

CHAPTER 7

THE UNITED STATES AS CULTURAL PRODUCT

Political systems are integral with their cultures, and cultures evolve out of contacts with other cultures. Cultures isolated from the rest of the world and left to themselves — be it in a secluded mountain valley, on a God-forsaken isle in the middle of the ocean, on a scrap of inhospitable polar ice, in a desert oasis, or in some large expanse tightly sealed off from the rest of the world — falter in their development and become fossil evidence of the human mind's need for contact with other human minds charged with differing experiences, customs, beliefs, ideas and even superstitions. Only such a difference of charges can produce the potentials necessary to spark development.

It is not just a matter of opportunities for observation and imitation, although assimilation and imitation are in fact central to the learning process: no borrowed motif remains unaltered in its pristine form; the human mind grasps a thought, transforms it, and impresses it with its own peculiar stamp. Thus have art, languages, religions, philosophical concepts, laws, the military, social systems and all else that is a product of human thought developed.

The American hemisphere found itself within the compass of European culture when in the eleventh century the discovery of a new land by the Vikings first penetrated into the European consciousness. The stories told by sailors in seaport taverns stirred men's imaginations, until finally one of the more venturesome, Christopher Columbus, decided to see for himself.

The fossilized cultures which the Europeans found in the area of the present-day United States could not compete with the culture that the Europeans had brought with them. The Indians' contribution to the white man's culture was for the most part limited to some place names, a few hunting and fishing terms, and a variety of foodstuffs such as potatoes, squash and the turkey. The culture of the present-day United States was from their earliest settlement by white men a European culture.

The political reaction of the Indians to the arrival of European man was more notable. As early as the 1570's "a saintly prophet named Deganawidah, the son of a virgin mother whose face was pure and spotless, put an end to warfare among the five tribes and established 'The Great Peace.' " The prophet and his close collaborator Hiawatha organized several of the warring tribes into the Iroquois League, which according to some historians served as a model for the United States Constitution.[1]

White Americans are generally reticent concerning this putative Indian model for their Constitution, the traditional concept being that

> the framers did not go out of their way to invent political forms. Nor did they borrow far afield. Some of them were students of Vattel, Montesquieu, and other continental writers; some had read history and could cite the failures of ancient confederacies or draw illustrations from the experiences of France and other continental states. But, as an earlier writer has remarked, this knowledge taught them rather what to avoid than what to adopt; and insofar as they drew upon European sources at all, such sources were the common law, the principles of Magna Carta and the

Bill of Rights, the writings of Locke and Blackstone, and other characteristic products of their English motherland. In the main, however, this monumental heritage had passed to America far back in colonial days, and at the time when the national Constitution took form, was already deeply embedded in the constitutions, laws and usages of the states. In a very true and literal sense, therefore, the new instrument grew out of the political life of Americans themselves in the colonial and Revolutionary periods.[2]

The thrust of such explanations as this — aimed at dispelling any doubt concerning the American political system's pure Anglo-Saxon bloodline — does not prevent non-Anglo-Saxon relations from claiming kinship.

The Jewish-American scholar Abraham I. Katsh points out that "Judaism and American democracy have much in common."[3] He cites examples of Old Testament influence upon the founders of the United States and argues that "Hebraic idealism spurred our fathers to challenge monarchy and persuaded them to offer their blood in the Revolutionary War." In support of his thesis Katsh states that "There was a sufficiently widespread interest and knowledge of Hebrew in the Colonies at the time of the Revolution to allow for the circulation of a story that certain members of Congress proposed that the use of English be formally prohibited in the United States, and Hebrew substituted for it."[4] (It is interesting to note that a similar claim is made by Germans, who maintain that during the early period of American independence it was a toss-up as to whether English or German would become the common language of the new nation.) As evidence of the enormous influence of Jewish culture on the United States, Katsh adduces the Biblical verse inscribed on the Liberty Bell, "Proclaim liberty throughout the land unto all the inhabitants thereof." (Lev. 25:10)[5]

A book by the Slovenian scholar Joseph Felicijan propounds that "the ancient ritual of the installation of the dukes of Carinthia . . . served Jefferson as a pattern for the Declaration of Independence."[6] Felicijan points out that the Carinthian ritual was known to the Italian humanist Aeneas Silvius Piccolomini (later Pope Pius II) who described it in his work, *Cosmographia Pii Papae de Europa*, published in Paris in 1509. The ritual was cited by the philosopher Jean Bodin in his *Les six livres de la Republique* (Paris, 1576); Jefferson was in possession of Bodin's book, and his autograph notations prove his use of it. Felicijan maintains that "There undoubtedly exists a link between Bodin on one side and Puffendort, Locke, Rousseau and Jefferson on the other."[7]

The Polish claim to paternity of the United States Constitution was registered by the Polish ambassador to the United States, Tytus Filipowicz, in a lecture before the American Society of International Law on April 30, 1932. The Ambassador asserted that "the American reader of [Wawrzyniec Goślicki's] *The Accomplished Senator* will recognize in the pages of the 16th century Polish thinker a distinct similarity with the pattern of the American democratic ideal."[8] We shall return to the Ambassador's thesis later.

The process of the British Colonies' emancipation and transformation into the United States, as already recounted, would suggest that the independence movement was little more than the inevitable consequence of the faulty economic policies of the English government. But in reality it was not economic conditions that precipitated the Colonists' rebellion. The American historian John C. Miller holds that

> it cannot be said that Americans were driven to rebellion by intolerable economic oppression . . . In general, after the . . . depression of 1763-1765, the revolutionary period was an era of growth and prosperity for the colonies . . . It was the invasion of Americans' political rights by Parliament after the Peace of Paris which precipitated the struggle between the mother country and colonies . . . Economic grievances played a secondary part in the patriots' propaganda; from 1765 to 1775 political issues were kept uppermost.[9]

Paul Tillich claims that "Religion is the substance of culture."[10] The colonization of North America came about to a great extent as a result of cultural changes in Europe, including the religious wars and ferments of the time. The Reformation had sundered the unity of a considerable part of western and central Europe and subjected a number of countries to established national denominations, compelling various religious minorities to emigrate to the New World in search of religious freedom. (Some authors, such as essayist Gore Vidal[11] and the American Indian writer Vine Deloria, Jr.,[12] assert that what these fugitives actually desired was to impose their own religious views upon others, and that Europe would not stand for it.)

On their arrival in America, these sects established colonies and long strove to keep spiritual and political control of them. Exceptions were Rhode Island, Maryland and Pennsylvania, which as early as the middle of the seventeenth century permitted religious freedom. This freedom gradually spread among the smaller colonies, especially those harboring communities of settlers from a variety of countries.

This live-and-let-live attitude favored the spread of European ideas whose collective corpus is termed the "Enlightenment." These included concepts of rationalism, liberalism, tolerance, equality and democracy which, permeating the Colonial mind in the second half of the eighteenth century, prepared it to take up the struggle for independence.[13]

Not quite a hundred years earlier, the Colonists had not felt up to the task of independently framing their own social systems and turned to Europe for help. Carolina, for example, had commissioned young John Locke to draw up a constitution for her. His stratified system had provided for a "nobility bearing such titles as 'landgrave' or 'cacique' and [a] serflike class of leetmen."[14] This, according to another historian, was "the longest, most fantastic and reactionary of all colonial frames of government."[15]

Transformed by the thinking of the Enlightenment, the Colonies no longer turned to Europe for counsel; they now had their own educated men capable of studying the political systems of past and present and of selecting from these the elements that they deemed worthy of emulation.

For centuries medieval man had believed that the earth was the center of the heavens; that each event in the universe was especially arranged by God for their benefit; that the will of the Creator could be learned only by watching the evidences of his handiwork and searching Scripture; that life on earth was brief and unimportant, and that men should spend their limited earthly spans preparing for eternity instead of attempting to improve their lots on earth.

The first breach in this wall of tradition was made in the sixteenth century, when a Polish scholar, Nicolaus Copernicus, publishing a slim little book *De revolutionibus orbium coelestium* [1543], advanced the startling thesis that the earth revolved around the sun. The implications of this simple theory were staggering, for if ever a belief was undisputed it was that the earth, as man's habitation, was the center of the universe. Such a revolutionary hypothesis could not be accepted at once, but over the next centuries other scientists gradually added proof — Tycho Brahe of Denmark, Johannes Kepler and Gottfried Leibnitz of Germany, Galileo Galilei of Italy, Issac Newton of England — until by the end of the seventeenth century doubt could no longer be entertained by educated men. A new universe, far different from the medieval world, emerged. The earth appeared as only a minor planet revolving about an obscure sun in a vast cosmic ocean of heavenly bodies. God, it was supposed, did not rule this vast creation by special decrees but through a body of natural laws. And most important of all, thinking men realized that these truths had been learned not by searching the Scriptures or by reasoning from accepted propositions, but by questioning, investigating and drawing conclusions. Doubt rather than faith held the key to knowledge; truth could be found in the laboratory as well as in monastic cells.[16]

Scientists and philosophers had questioned the unimpeach-authority of the church in order to prove that natural laws rather than specific divine dispensation governed the universe. A natural corollary of this was the Enlightenment view that man's character and hence his social relationships were the product of his natural environment rather than of a special creative effort by God. The result was a revolution in social thought as epoch-making as the scientific upheaval; the seventeenth and eighteenth centuries saw a slow recasting of archaic ideas on man's relation to society, government and the economic structure. The future leaders of the American Revolution were impressed by Locke's argument, in his *Essay Concerning Human Understanding* (1690), that man possessed no innate ideas — ideas either of good or evil specifically implanted in him by God. From this proposition Locke argued that faulty institutions and inhumane social order warp human nature toward injustice and evil; conversely, improvement of the environment would improve man. By sweeping away poverty and ignorance, human nature could be altered and society advanced toward perfection.[17]

The influence of the Enlightenment on political thought was reflected in Rousseau's *Social Contract* (1762), in which Rousseau argued that men, when emerging from an original state of nature, had entered into social contracts with a central authority in order to secure legal protection and had surrendered certain of their freedoms in return; that consequently they had a right to expect their government to protect certain of their natural rights which they had not given up; and hence if any ruler interfered with their rights to life, liberty or property, they could justifiably overthrow him by revolution.

The Enlightenment approach to economic matters found expression in Adam Smith's *The Wealth of Nations* (1776). Basic to his views was the natural right of all individuals to improve themselves economically as well as morally and politically. This could be accomplished only if they were allowed to operate in an unrestricted environment where the sole controls were natural laws such as the law of supply and demand. Smith favored a laissez-faire policy on the part of government: abolition of laws restricting interest rates, stoppage of government meddling in economic affairs, dissolution of monopolistic trading concerns that controled foreign commerce, removal of trade barriers hampering the free movement of goods.[18]

The target of Enlightenment spokesmen was not governmental power to protect the public interest but the perversion of that power by powerful privileged interests, whereby the economic and political masters of monarchies, exploiting consumers and workers, had prevented the nations from achieving a greater total wealth and their peoples from gaining higher standards of living. The impulse behind the efforts of the *Illuminati* was a democratic one: the demand for a more responsive government and for an economy dedicated to the common welfare.[19]

The Enlightenment prepared the Americans not only for political revolution, but also for original work in the natural sciences. "Its impact had transformed scientific thought, weakened the hold of the churches, stimulated educational progress, recast economic theory and institutions and inspired so deep a respect for liberty and equality that the struggle for independence was almost inevitable."[20]

The eighteenth century brought the first major scientific contributions by Americans: by John Bartram, Cadwallader Colden and James Logan in botany; by the physicist David Rittenhouse, whose hypothesis on the structure of matter anticipated by over a century the comparable work of European scientists; by John Winthrop, mathematician, astronomer and physicist who in 1759 repudiated the medieval theory of earthquakes as divine retribution and offered the first scientific theory of the phenomenon; and finally by Benjamin Franklin, statesman and scientific and technical titan.

These scientific advances brought about a reassessment of religious concepts. The Calvinist church was compelled to beat a retreat from no longer tenable positions. The clergy split into two groups: one revised the old image of a God arbitrarily predestining certain individuals to eternal perdition for the sins of their first parents; the other adopted the deistic doctrines that were reaching them from Europe and gradually abandoned those tenets of faith that would not stand up to logical scrutiny. By this process they came to discard the miracles and prophecies of the Bible and to revere a God who ruled the universe according to rational laws. This new creed had its most numerous adherents among the educated upper classes, the lower classes being "largely within the orthodox fold"[21] and indeed making life difficult for such men as Thomas Paine, author of both the

Revolutionary-period *Common Sense* and later the uncompromisingly deistic *Age of Reason.*

The changes in the Colonies' religious life triggered changes in their economic concepts;

> prophets of the new freedom could express themselves as openly on economic as on religious subjects. During the eighteenth century their pamphlets, widely published by the colonial press, all stressed the twin themes that man's will rather than God's shaped economic developments, and that improvement was both desirable and inevitable . . . There remained only the question: would [the Colonists] resort to political revolt if the mother country seriously attempted to enforce any of its unpopular economic legislation?
>
> For this possibility the Enlightenment was also a preparation. The forward-looking political doctrines advanced by European scholars during the eighteenth century were readily accepted by countless Americans who found that the natural rights of philosophy fitted well into their spiritual and physical environment. They knew, as did Locke and Rousseau, that the first duty of all rulers was to protect the life, liberty, and property of their subjects. They accepted unquestioningly the right of any people to overthrow a tyrant who failed in this prime duty. They believed implicitly in certain basic rights: government by consent of the governed, the justice of revolution, the control of the state by popular majorities.[22]

The colonial press, influenced by the Enlightenment, sought to educate the masses. The attempts of the authorities to prevent this through censorship were to no avail. In 1745 the editor of the New York *Weekly Journal,* John Peter Zenger, was hailed into court for criticizing the authorities, but freed by the jury, which found that criticisms of the government were no libels if factually true.[23] Nevertheless, even as late as 1763, much still stood in the way of freedom.

An established church still dominated many colonies, Jews and Catholics were mildly persecuted in all, Americans still purchased Africans snatched from their homeland and sold them, property qualifications barred fully half the people from the franchise, restriction on freedom of expression remained, a vast gulf separated the upper class from the lower classes. Yet thinking men were already convinced that these autocratic vestiges must be swept away and knew that the assault had begun. Disciples of the Enlightenment, thoroughly committed to the principles of freedom, equality, and rationalism, only waited a favorable opportunity to translate their theories into action. The spadework for revolution was completed.[24]

The revolution that followed was victorious. The next step was the organization of a political system. The first phase was a loose Confederation; the second a United States based on a Constitution worked out by the most enlightened of contemporary enlightened America.

Puritans might lord it over Anglicans in New England, Anglicans might display their pretensions before Catholics and Quakers in Maryland and Virginia, Catholics might long for an establishment of papal authority over all, and Presbyterians might rule with an iron hand their communities on the frontier, but under Providence none of them was strong enough to get a mastery over the federal government, even if the Deists who wielded high powers in the drafting of the Constitution had been willing to bow before the winds of sectarian passion . . . the national government was secular from top to bottom. Religious qualifications for voting and office-holding, which appeared in the contemporary state constitutions with such profusion, found no place whatever in the federal Constitution. Its preamble did not invoke the blessings of AlmightyGod or announce any interest in promoting the propaganda of religion. Instead, it declared purposes that were earthly and in keeping with the progressive trend of the age — "to form a more perfect union, establish justice, insure domestic tranquility, provide for the common defense, promote the general welfare, and secure the blessings of liberty to ourselves and our posterity." And the First Amendment, added by the radicals in 1789, declared that "Congress shall make no law respecting an establishment of religion, or prohibiting the free exercise thereof." In dealing with Tripoli, President Washington allowed it to be squarely stated that "the government of the United States is not in any sense founded upon the Christian religion."[25]

The American Revolution had been prepared by the popularization of Enlightenment thought. " 'The Revolution was effected before the war commenced,' one of the greatest of the Revolutionary leaders, John Adams, afterward remarked. 'The Revolution was in the minds and hearts of the people.' "[26] And having once transformed men's minds, the Enlightenment placed its impress upon the subsequent Constitution of the United States.

Tracing the genealogy in turn of the Enlightenment takes us back two centuries to Europe in the midst of the "Second Reformation."

After the profounder meaning of the Copernican concept of the infinite universe had foliated in the minds of students — especially after Newton crowned it with his mechanistic view of the stellar system — a powerful group of English thinkers entirely discarded from their thought the God of the Old Testament and the cosmogony described in the Book of Genesis and elaborated by John Milton.

Out of England Deism was borne to France by Voltaire, where it became the creed of nearly all the skeptics who labored at the Encyclopaedia and at the new philosophy of naturalism and humanity.

From various directions the doctrine came into

America, spreading widely among the intellectual leaders of the American Revolution and making them doubly dangerous characters in the eyes of Anglican Tories. When the crisis came, Jefferson, Paine, John Adams, Washington, Franklin, Madison, and many lesser lights were to be reckoned among either the Unitarians or the Deists.[27]

The path that Unitarianism and Deism had taken in fact leads inexorably back to Poland during the Second Reformation.

CHAPTER 8

POLAND AS CULTURAL PRODUCT

I. Formative influences

Placed as she was between the Baltic and Black Seas, in a plain periodically swept through by powerful Eurasian tempests, where — to appropriate the expression which Marshal Piłsudski was to use in connection with the city of Lwów (now Lvov) — "all the winds from all directions make their rendezvous,"[1] it was to these same circumstances that Poland owed her cultural features.

From the hands of western Slavs she received not one by two sacraments: baptism, and marriage to the West. The young state entered into the orbit of western culture, and together with the teachings of Christ she acquired a sense of belonging not to East but to West, and a path to knowledge leading through the Latin alphabet.

The devastation wreaked upon Southern Poland by plague and by the Mongol invasions of the twelfth and thirteenth centuries caused Poland to welcome German craftsmen and

The Baptism of Poland, 966.

Jewish merchants into her borders, and this produced a beneficial result: the development of her cities.

Even the unfriendly relations with another group of Christians, the Teutonic Knights, and the need to contest before the Pope their forged claims to Prussian and Polish lands, brought a gain to Polish culture: the founding of the Kraków Academy (the University of Kraków, or — as it is officially known in honor of the dynasty that founded it — the Jagiellonian University) in 1364, ever since when its device has been "Plus ratio quam vis" (More reason than force). Some of its alumni, after having obtained their educations in Poland, pursued advanced studies in foreign institutions of higher learning. Their names include those of such outstanding men as Mikołaj Kopernik (Nicolaus Copernicus), Wawrzyniec Goslicki (Laurentius Grimaldus Goslicius) and Jan Zamoyski: all notable offspring of the marriage between Polish culture and the old culture of the West.

A major injection of Western culture occurred in the first quarter of the sixteenth century with the arrival of King Zygmunt I's bride Bona Sforza.[2] Erasmus of Rotterdam had words of admiration for Poland's subsequent cultural attainments;[3] and even if Poland was later to pay for this cultural injection when Queen Bona, following the heirless death of her son King Zygmunt II August, returned to Italy, taking the crown jewels with her, Poland still got far the best of the bargain.

But it was not only from peaceful contacts that Poles gained, if not their most precious, at any rate some very colorful acquisitions. They adopted armor — and attached wings to it; they took as their own the curved scimitar and eastern dress of the paynim — and made them the national property of the nobility; here and there they borrowed a Turkish word, for example naturalizing "kirmizidish" as "karmazyn" (crimson) and "filjan" as "filiżanka" (cup).

They took the art of printing brought to them by the Germans and assimilated it with the addition of diacritical marks to the type case.

Even into Christian beliefs and rites Poland wove strands of her ancient Slavic heritage following her conversion, by royal fiat, in 966 at the hands of her Czech cousins. Thus the nocturnal

Kraków, Jagiellonian University

The globe in possession of the Jagiellonian University, made around 1510, showing "America terra noviter reperta"

Warsaw, St. Mary's Church

Mikołaj Kopernik, 1473-1543

festivities of Kupała, involving the burning of bonfires, were converted to "St. John's Eve"; and the Israelite Mother of God was adopted as the patron saint of Poland and as Queen of the Polish Crown. (It is interesting to note that in 1729 the British clergyman Conyers Middleton wrote a series of *Letters from Rome* "showing in scholarly detail the residue of pagan rites in Catholic ritual — incense, holy water, relics, miracles, votive offerings and lights set up before sacred shrines, and the Pontifex Maximus [Great Bridgebuilder] of antiquity become the Supreme Pontiff of Rome."[4])

Culture is not content to *adopt*, it *adapts*, melds and homogenizes. From the church spectacles Polish culture fashioned the minstrel theater; the towering Gothic style of architecture, it modified to suit its own native landscape, transforming it into a distinctive Vistula Gothic; exposed to the beauties of Latin poetry, it quickly began producing its own verse; forming a state after the fashion of the West, in contrast to the ever more prominent despotism of the Western rulers it divested its own king of all his powers, introduced *Neminem captivabimus* which by two and a half centuries antedated the similar English *Habeas Corpus Act of 1679*, laid the formal foundations of parliamentary government with the law of *Nihil novi*, and never created a native aristocracy (as distinct from a hereditary nobility).

Each of these events was a milestone on the evolutionary road of Polish culture. A quite fundamental role in its shaping was played by geography. Noting the threats from East and West, Poland found a viable defense in rapprochement with the Grand Duchy of Lithuania, a political organism which had itself for similar reasons been formed from the linguistically quite different peoples of Lithuania and Ruthenia. The rapprochement introduced into the borders of a common state very diverse cultural elements. The Republic became an agglomeration of cultures, the maintenance of its unity requiring tolerance and equal treatment for all languages, customs and sects.[5] In no other way could a union have persisted for centuries of lands sporting Catholic, Protestant and Greek Orthodox churches, as well as synagogues and mosques, as described in a sixteenth-century book: "we saw a mass of various worships the like of which could have been seen but in heathen times — Roman Catholics, Greeks or Armenians, Jewish, Tartar, Karaimian."[6] The description is confirmed by a modern writer: "the Pole before Reformation had not been a religious bigot. He had for generations been used to seeing Roman Catholic, Greek Orthodox, Jew and Mohammedan live side by side in Poland in comparative peace and friendship."[7]

The acceptance of people regardless of their speech, their somewhat different modes of dress, or their worship of the same God under a different name in a different sort of holy place broadened the people's mental horizons. Minds reared under such conditions were freer of chauvinistic fetters, of the tendency to ascribe to their own community — be it linguistic, religious or ethnic — some spurious kind of cultural superiority.

An impressive example of Poles already in the first half of the fifteenth century is provided by Paweł Włodkowic (Paulus Vladimirus), rector of the University of Kraków, at the Council of Constance (1414-18) appealing for tolerance for pagans. That his theses, couched in the form of questions, proved to be questions cast into a void of incomprehension, was not his own fault and hardly detracts from his own stature.[8]

The atmosphere of tolerance was conducive to the formation of minds open to new ideas, capable of drawing comparisons without prejudice, or questioning deeply rooted traditional concepts. The role of tolerance as a factor in liberating the mind from deeply worn ruts is exemplified in the life of Kopernik. Born in Toruń, Poland, at the interface of two cultures — the Polish and the German — he must have learned to accept both even as a child. For four years — between the eighteenth and twenty-second years of his life, a time of great intellectual absorptiveness — he studied at the Kraków Academy, then a major center of humanist thought.[9] His mind thus trained, when he came upon the aspects of the motions of the heavenly bodies that could not be accounted for by the authoritative explanations, he would not be deterred from making inquiries aimed at establishing the truth.

Mikołaj Kopernik — a product of Polish culture, yet on intimate terms with a second culture and hence open to all cultures — admitted the possibility of a variety of approaches to the same problem, thereby fulfilling a condition indispensable to scientific skepticism. Kopernik's fundamental tolerance is confirmed by the fact that in a period of divisions and struggles within the church, while himself standing by Rome, he did not break off his friendly ties with clergy who joined the Reformation. None other than a professor at the University of Wittenberg — a stronghold of Protestantism — Georg Joachim von Lauchen, better known to the world as Rheticus, persuaded Kopernik to publish his revolutionary work on the motions of the heavenly bodies.[10]

For the Reformation came to Poland too: not through the cottages of the peasants, but through the houses of the enlightened: seeking truth and justice not with fire and stake, but with educated thought, phrased oftentimes in the language of the Romans.

In Poland the Reformation created no sensation, if only because the people were familiar with the religious freedom guaranteed to the Ruthenians, and because the memory of the recent Hussite wars and awareness of the existence of the Anabaptists in neighboring Bohemia had already for some time weakened respect for the distant papacy.[11] On various occasions Kraków, the seat of an institution of higher learning, had expressed and demonstrated views not entirely in keeping with official church policy.[12]

The Reformation was propagated chiefly by sons of the magnates and nobility studying at foreign universities. Along with their diplomas they brought back a new, critical outlook upon the world, encompassing as well the church, its hierarchy and the lesser clergy. The townspeople showed some interest in this new outlook, but the peasant masses — benighted and tied blindly to traditional worship — were lost to the Reformation.[13] Accessible to the Reformation were the nobility and the magnates, an element conscious of their own strength and hence of their invulnerability.

Not without great significance to the course of the Reformation in Poland was the presence of a relatively large group of Italian intellectuals who had either arrived together with the suite of Bona Sforza or who were later to join her court. One of them was Lismanino, royal secretary and the Queen's confessor who is supposed to have favored the Reformation. Undoubtedly also a sympathizer of the Reformation was Giorgio Biandrata or Blandrata, physician to the Queen and to her daughter Izabela.[14]

The accession of King Zygmunt II August to the throne in 1544 was marked by heightened activity among the Calvinists and the Anabaptists affiliated with them, and among the Lutherans, as well as by the arrival in 1548 of Bohemian Brethren expelled from their own country.

Attempts by the Catholics to have dissenters tried ended in a rebellion by the nobility against the Church, and in 1555 the Seym passed a law establishing freedom of all religions based on "the pure word of God."[15] The religious freedom until then enjoyed by the nobility was extended to the townspeople and peasants. The nobility were allowed to determine the religious practices on their own estates.[12]

The year 1573 further reinforced the foundations of religious freedom when the Warsaw Confederacy (one of those ad hoc organizations that arise periodically in Poland's history in times of crisis) enjoined peace among the faiths and bound the king by an oath to preserve religious freedom.[17]

The earliest evidence of Anabaptist thought in Poland — propagated half a century later by the Polish Brethren — is a series of polemics at the turn of the sixteenth century between Jan of Pilzno and Biernat of Lublin. The polemics are in reference to a now lost work by Biernat in which he denies on religious grounds the propriety of capital punishment, urging as the only permissible procedure the condemnation of the guilty person, and at most his incarceration for a period not to exceed fifteen years.[18] But, as Wilbur writes,

> Even before the Reformation the Catholic Church in Poland gave some signs of criticism of traditional dogmas. Early in the sixteenth century there had been published the so-called Krakòw Missal, with a commentary by Cardinal Hugo, in which it was explained that any prayer should be directed to the Father, or the Son, but never to the Holy Spirit, which is only a gift. This is . . . strangely like a teaching of Servetus and several of his early followers.[19]

Secemin, The Arian House

Górnicki notes the story of a Cracovian, Katarzyna Weigel, burned at the stake on April 19, 1539, for refusing to acknowledge a faith in Christ as the Son of God.[20] Another early example of Antitrinitarian thought in Poland is recorded by Frycz-Modrzewski. He recounts a conversation said to have taken place in 1546 among a number of humanists inlcuding himself and Lismanino, one of whom, referred to as "Spiritus," on hearing grace pronounced before a meal invoking God the Father, the Son and the Holy Ghost, asked: "Do you have three Gods?"[21]

The "official" beginning of Polish Antitrinitarianism may be dated from January 22, 1556, when a former instructor of logic at the University of Padua, Piotr Giezek, at a synod of Polish Calvinists in Secemin avowed an Antitrinitarian credo. He became an object of indignation, even as he drew a number of the clergy into a splinter group of the Reformed (i.e., Calvinist) Church in Southern Poland which with time became the so-called Lesser Reformed Church.[22]

Giezek had undergone a thorough change of attitudes in 1555 in Padua, under the influence of Mateo Gribaldi, a professor at the University. The latter had offered him his writings, and more importantly had imparted to him his own boundless resentment against Calvin, who had caused Servetus to be sentenced to death and burned at the stake in Geneva in 1553 for his opposition to the doctrine of the Holy Trinity.[23] Giezek had been influenced additionally by contact with German Anabaptist refugees in Moravia (who accordingly were called the Moravian Brethren). They lived in communes and — determined pacifists — would not even touch weapons, giving expression to their conviction by wearing canes at their sides.

Imbued with the ideas of pacifism and of contest by word and deed (reminiscent of the much later Thoreau, Lev Tolstoy, Gandhi and Martin Luther King), Giezek returned home with a cane in place of a scimitar, and additionally reinforced by the Anabaptist conviction that people should not be baptised as infants but only on attaining a mature age when they are capable of conscious religious belief.[24] Giezek's religious convictions are characterized by Wilbur in the following terms: "he accepts Scripture as the perfect standard of faith, containing everything

The Arian House in Raków

Faust Socyn, 1539-1604

Stanisław Lubieniecki, 1623 - 1675

Jonasz Szlichtyng, 1592 - 1661

necessary for salvation. One of its chief teachings is that the Father of Christ is the only and Most Highly God; and whoever recognizes him as the true God is not far from the Kingdom of God, be he Jew or Turk."[25] (These views accord well with the thesis that had been expressed over a century earlier by Paweł Włodkowic, questioning the moral right of Christians to convert dissenters or pagans by force of arms.)

Poland — Mecca to fugitives from the West European Inquisition and from Calvin's tribunals — was at the time harboring many Reformation thinkers who had fled the West. Escaping Calvin's violence, the former physician to Queen Bona, Biandrata, had returned, now as a radical reformer of the faith. In Pińczów, then the most important Calvinist center in Southern Poland, he found an agreeable group of adherents of Giezek's doctrines. Here he also met the former royal secretary and Queen Bona's confessor, Lismanino, and within a short time had drawn him completely away from belief in the Trinity. The group was augmented by Alciata and Gentile, both likewise refugees from Geneva and the Calvinist inquisition. A brief visit was paid by Lelio Sozzini (Laelius Socinus) and a somewhat longer one by Ochino, twice vicar general of the Franciscan order and once of the Capuchin.

Not without the influence of these arrivals from the West, at ease in debate and having a firm grasp of theology, the views of the Pińczów Arians developed and gained a growing following, their churches marking the routes between Gdańsk and Kiev and between Lithuania and the Carpathian Mountains.[26] (The "Arians" were so called by their antagonists after Arius, a presbyter who around 318 A.D. had held the belief that Christ, although superior to other created beings, was not of the same substance as God. The Nicene Council in 325 had condemned Arianism and declared the divinity of Christ as the Second Person of God, and next the Council of Constantinople in 381 had passed an article concerning a Third Person, the Holy Ghost.)

At length, losing favor with King Zygmunt II August, Lismanino left for Prussia (which owed its allegiance to the Polish Crown), and when the church reformers had become objects of especially violent attacks by both Catholics and Calvinists, Alciata left Poland; feeling insecure on Polish soil,

Gentile went to Moravia. The passage of a law permitting the expulsion from the country of foreigners considered undesirable on religious grounds forced Ochino to depart Poland.[27]

By his great activity, Biandrata drew upon himself the wrath of the Calvinist clergy. Pressed to the wall, he eagerly accepted an invitation to go to Transylvania, a mountain area of very mixed population in modern Rumania, where he became personal physician to King John Sigismund Zapolya and his mother Izabela, sister of the Polish King Zygmunt II August. Years earlier, in Krakow, this same Biandrata had been physician to both Izabela and her mother, Queen Bona.

Zapolya — in a different period of wars with the Hapsburgs and Turks and of struggles among various religious fanatics — believed in resolving even the most difficult problems through discussion. Like his mother who had been reared in Poland, Zapolya believed that "if people could be free to believe as they wished, without compulsion, one great impediment to the union of mankind would be removed."[28] This attitude in matters of faith made his views and Biandrata's kindred, and before long they were talking the same language as regards religious matters.

Biandrata's sphere of influence likewise encompassed Francis David, successively a Catholic, Calvinist and Unitarian clergyman in Transylvania. (It was in Transylvania that the name "Unitarian" was coined.) It is to David's influence that must be ascribed King John Sigismund Zapolya's declaration of religious tolerance at the Council of Torda in 1568, opening up to Transylvanian Unitarians the possibility of a normal life within the law.[29]

The Polish Brethren, as the Polish Arians called themselves, took their origin from Anabaptism and Antitrinitarianism, but they never made dogmas of these attitudes. They disputed, combined and dissociated themselves, held councils, overthrew doctrines and rejected traditions, continually seeking clear guides in the Bible for the conduct of individual and social life. An important year for them was 1580, when Faustus Socinus, sent by Biandrata, arrived in Kraków from Transylvania. He was a nephew of Laelius Socinus, who had twice visited Poland: once in 1551, probably as guest of Lismanino's, and again in 1558 together with Biandrata.

His paternal uncle's name facilitated Faustus Socinus' entry into the Lesser Reformed Church. He found the Church growing and its theology almost as advanced as his own;[30] but the Church was clearly in need of leadership, and within a short time Socinus had become a leading figure in it.

Since he was instrumental in narrowing down the excessive range of theological views held by members of the Church, its theology began — particularly outside Poland's borders — to be considered his own private theological system, and the entire religious group began to be termed "Socinians," even though many thinkers and writers contributed to the formation of the Polish Brethren's doctrines: Budny, Czechowic, Paleolog, Niemojewski, Moskorzowski, Ruar and — most mature of them all — Samuel Przypkowski, whose massive treatises concentrated mainly on the problem of church-state relations. Of the valuable works that Przypkowski bequeathed to the western world, the most important were *Animadversiones in Libellum cui titulus De qualitate Regni Domini nostri Jesu Christi, ubi inquiritur, an Christiano sive Regni eius subdito terrenae dominationes conveniant;* his *Cogitationes sacrae ad initium evangelii Matthaei at omnes epistolas apostolicas nec nontractatus varii argumenti praecipue De jure Christiani magistratus;* and his *Apologia prolixior tractatus de jure Christiani magistratus.*

Starting with a strict and absolute interpretation of Scripture, oblivious to established concepts, traditions and even popular customs, and only reluctantly keeping up with historical exigencies such as wars which increased the need for military service and for stronger governmental powers, the Polish Brethren slowly abandoned their sectarian positions for the attitude of the good citizen who does not reach out for what does not rightfully belong to him but who will defend that which does: weapon in hand, if the national good should require; in a court of law, if any should violate his own rights.

From total renunciation of all worldly authority — which they had accepted, if at all, only as a necessary evil — they gradually shifted to a position that accepted the possiblity of a Christian holding office, even one of leadership in the state,[31] and treating him like brother so long as he committed no iniquity nor any act contrary to the Gospel.[32]

But the Polish Brethren's adjustment to the dominant concepts and sociopolitical realities of Poland came only slowly, and meanwhile the Jesuits who had been brought into Poland set to work energetically to neutralize the influence of the Reformed Churches. They made particular efforts in combatting the Polish Brethren, who for their part reacted with a vigorous polemical campaign parrying the charges being levelled against them. They also planned a united front with the Calvinists and Lutherans; an expression of this latter fruitless effort was a volume prepared by them, *De Concordia et unione inter coetus Evangelicos et Unitarios,* published in 1624 and reprinted in 1630.[33]

A gesture openly inimical to the Polish Brethren was a law passed by the Prussian regional seym at Grudziądz in 1636, excluding them from the guarantee of the Warsaw Confederacy of 1573, and at the same time barring them from the Prussian seym.[34] The pretext for this grievous blow was supplied by a prank of two students attending school at the principal center of the Polish Brethren, Raków in Southern Poland: using a roadside cross as a target for their rocks, the students had knocked it down, thereby rousing the ire of the local Catholic population. Two years later, in 1638, by a decision of the Polish Senate, the entire Raków community — church, academy, printing shop and all — was liquidated. This did not mean the end of the Brethren's operations, but it did render them more difficult. There were many other communities of Polish Brethren stretching in a chain deep into the Ukraine, and there the Brethren stepped up their work.

The wars with Sweden (1601-29) had interrupted the ideological evolution of the Brethren. Freed from their earlier anti-war bias, they had gone to war.

While part of the nation had taken the side of the Polish king, Jan Kazimierz, part of it had accepted Swedish King Carl Gustav. These latter had included some high commanders together with their armies. If we are to believe Boy-Zelenski, Jan Sobieski himself (later King of Poland, 1674-96) and his cousin Opaliński had at first sided with the Swedish king.[35] It was mainly Protestants who had supported Carl Gustav, including a fairly large number of Polish Brethren, although some of them had sided with Jan Kazimierz. Many of the Brethren had thrown

153

in their lot with the Protestant invaders because they saw the Catholics as the greater of the evils.

In 1657, when the scales had begun to tip in favor of Jan Kazimierz, Carl Gustav drew the Hungarian Prince Rakoczy of Transylvania into the war (with the assistance of an unidentified Polish Brother who went to Transylvania specifically for the purpose of recruiting Rakoczy).[36]

Carl Gustav's defeat spelled the doom of the Lesser Reformed Church. The year 1658 brought a law depriving that Church of the right to exist (the *liberum veto* cast in the Seym by the lone remaining Polish Brother member, Tobiasz Wiszowaty, being disregarded!). Members of the Church were given a choice, within three years, between repudiating their beliefs and leaving the country. The time allotted to them was then cut back to two years — until July 10, 1660. The decided majority of the Polish Brethren chose to follow their consciences into exile.

II. The ideas of the Second Reformation in Poland

The Polish Brethren accepted the Bible, and hence revelation, as the basis of their religion, and attached prime importance to reason, which was in their view essential to a grasp of revealed truth.

> It (i.e. reason) is, indeed, of great service, since without it we could neither perceive with certainty the authority of the sacred writings, understand their contents, discriminate one thing from the other, nor apply them to any practical purpose. When, therefore, I stated that the Holy Scriptures were sufficient for our salvation, so far from excluding right reason, I certainly assumed its presence.[37]

The rationalism of the Brethren led them even to attempts at explaining miracles.[38] They eschewed the doctrine of the Trinity, as in their understanding the doctrine had no significance for the quality of the individual's life. They adopted the more congenial doctrine of the unity of the Divine Being, together with its corollary, the human nature of Christ.

The Brethren denied the Christian soteriology, finding no justification for the assertion that Christ's death had redeemed mankind. According to them, Christ was a man ordained by God to lead mankind onto the path of everlasting life through his teachings and example; he was supposed to influence man, and not God, by redeeming the sins of man through the sacrifice of his own life.

The concepts of sin, forgiveness and redemption came in for searching analysis by the Brethren. Socinus in his work *De Jesu Christi servatore* ("a book in which," says Charles Beard, "is to be found every rational and moral argument since that time directed against the theory of satisfaction"[39]) deduced that "If Satisfaction, then no Forgiveness of Sins; if Forgiveness of Sins, then no legalistic doctrine of Satisfaction." (A similar logic was applied to religious matters a century and a half later by Voltaire: "The two most important qualities attributed to God — omnipotence and goodness — are hardly even compatible with each other: because either He can make life on earth happy and will not, in which case He is not good, or He wants to but cannot, in which case He is not omnipotent."[40])

Nor did the Polish Brethren accept the idea of original sin; in their view it would have meant assigning man responsibility for transgressions not personally committed by him. On the other hand, they expressed a profound belief in free will, therewith conceding to man the possibility of attaining perfection. To them, the supreme value of Christianity was that through Christ it allows man to know God, and that through a life in accordance with Christ's teachings it assures him everlasting life.

On holy communion, too, the Brethren took a different view than the other Christian denominations; they saw it not as a sacrament so much as a ritual commemorating the death of Christ. Similarly, they ascribed no real significance to baptism in the salvation of souls; to them, baptism was merely a symbolic ritual.

From Christ's moral teachings the Polish Brethren deduced precepts of social coexistence and thus became social reformers. They started out in a radicalism akin to that of the Moravian Brethren but abandoned it. They disliked living in communes and subjecting themselves to the government of "elders"; they preferred to cultivate their own individual plots of land and, if the need arose, to share their produce with those in need of help. They began by renouncing the use of sanctions and thus waived the right to seek redress in a court of law. They also denied the Christian's right to participate in war or even to bear arms; they condemned capital punishment and physical mutilation, just as Biernat of Lublin had done in the fifteenth century.

After a hundred years of ceaseless debate and discussion, they had (although not unanimously) accepted the existence of worldly authorities to which Christians too should give their obedience. Samuel Przypkowski devoted a chapter of one of his works to demonstrating the propriety of governmental functions, and hence of authority.[41] The Polish Brethren also developed the concept of church and state as two distinct bodies.

"Both when the state with compulsory authority encroaches on the government of the Church," wrote Samuel Przypkowski, "and when the Church takes the sword which God himself has entrusted to it out of the hands of the civil authorities, there is a violation of justice."[42]

In time the Polish Brethren learned to reconcile Church membership with membership in a state, holding that it would be equally as absurd to bar a man from a state on account of his religion as it would be to expel him from a religious congregation on account of his ties with the state. "It is inconsistent with the nature of spiritual jurisdiction," wrote Samuel Przypkowski, "that the secular authority should command anything that properly concerns observance of the laws of Christ; in this respect religion not only does not ask help from the State, but defends itself against the interference of an outsider in another's sphere.[43]

This was the Polish Brethren's principle of the *separation of church and state.*

The Brethren likewise preached complete religious tolerance:

> Whilst we compose a Catechism, we prescribe nothing to any man; whilst we declare our own opinions, we oppress no one. Let every person enjoy the freedom of his own judgment in religion; only let it be permitted to us also to exhibit our view of divine things, without injuring and calumniating others. For this is the

golden Liberty of Prophesying which the sacred books of the New Testament so earnestly recommended to us, and wherein we are instructed by the example of the primitive apostolic church . . . one alone is our master, even Christ; . . . we all are brethren, to no one of whom is given authority and dominion over the conscience of another. For although some of the brethren may excel others in spiritual gifts, yet in respect to freedom and right of sonship, all are equal.[44]

This was the Polish Brethren's principle of *freedom of conscience*.

They did not seek to monopolize the path to salvation; they declared: "we firmly believe that whoever shall have trusted in God and Christ, and shall show himself obedient, will certainly obtain eternal life."[45]

In the same vein was the statement: "I do not condemn other churches, nor by any means despise them, but acknowledge all as true churches of Christ . . . and whoever keeps the same precepts [of Christ's] I consider to be a true member of Christ."[46]

The Polish Brethren had condemned war and punishment by death or mutilation, but with the passage of time, when on the one hand the Republic was threatened by enemies (in the Muscovite wars of the sixteenth century) and on the other hand Hugo Grotius had so convincingly argued for the legality of defensive war, personal defense, and courts and penalties,[47] they had modified their point of view, and a goodly number of Polish Brethren had taken part in the Muscovite wars, which were memorialized in verse by the Polish Brother Wacław Potocki. Among the participants in these wars was Samuel Przypkowski, who in his writings had argued that Christ's command that we love our enemies had referred to personal relations and that Christ had not forbidden war but had reckoned even with the possiblity that there would be enemies among his own followers. Christ had only forbidden men to hate.

A plea for humane moderation in punishment is found in Socinus' teachings at the synod of 1602, when he expressed a view then taking on clarity among the Polish Brethren, that one may lodge complaints before a court of law for inflicted wounds, since this was not connected with vengeance or with excessive punishment. However, he objected to the temporal courts sanctioning banishment, imprisonment or death against heretics: even as he rejected capital punishment altogether.[48]

Through Socinus' lips, the Polish Brethren advocated the principle of applying *no excessive or cruel punishments*.

CHAPTER 9

THE IDEAS OF THE POLISH SECOND REFORMATION ABROAD

I. The Polish Brethren in exile

The Polish Brethren scattered abroad. Seven of their new centers outside their native country can be distinguished: Transylvania, Silesia, the Rhine Palatinate, Holstein, Brandenburg, Prussia and Holland.

Small groups braved the snowdrifts of the southern mountain passes, the cold and hunger and robber bands of the trackless Carpathian Mountains, in order to reach Transylvania. There the decimated refugees found a haven with the Unitarian Chruch that a century earlier had come into existence as a partial result of Polish influences. Undoubtedly a certain number of today's Transylvanian Unitarians are naturalized descendants of the seventeenth-century Polish exiles.

The Unitarian Church in Transylvania is the only Unitarian church in the world with a continuous history of existence going back to the sixteenth century. However, apart from its name, which the English-speaking Socinians subsequently adopted, it has given nothing to the Unitarian churches of Great Britain or the United States. Based on principles set down in the sixteenth and seventeenth centuries, it is regarded by American Unitarians today as a doctrinaire establishment church.

Of the nearest centers outside Poland, the one in Prussia — in Koenigsberg and its environs — survived the longest. Instrumental to the Brethren's settlement there was a historian of the movement who was on close terms with a number of European courts, a close relative of Jan Sobieski's: Stanisław Lubieniecki, who paid for his zeal with his life, being — in all probability — poisoned to death.[1]

When religious freedom was restored in Poland in 1767, a small group of Polish Brethren returned home; the chronicles record the death of their last minister in 1803, and eight years later their last church in Poland ceased to exist. The last Polish Brother is said to have been a soldier of Kościuszko's, General Karol Sierakowski, who passed away in 1824.[2]

The Prussian census of 1838 lists the names Schlichtyng and Morsztyn, once well known in the Brethren's leadership in Poland, but the last traces of the Unitarians in Prussia disappear with the death of Karol Henryk Morsztyn in 1852.

The judgment issued on the Unitarians of Prussia by a German historian reads like a eulogy: "the distinguishing mark of their life, the showing of love toward everyone, their demand for freedom of religious life from all civil compulsion, praised even by Luther but forgotten again in early Protestantism, has entered on its victorious march in the social and liberal thought of the whole civilized world."[3]

It is a curious thing that, while the German Wotschke applauded the Polish Unitarians, at just about the same time the Polish poet Adam Mickiewicz was condemning them *ex cathedra* as a college professor, charging that their

> reforms in reference to matters of complete indifference to Poland, were no more than a ludicrous imitation of foreign models ... The English Unitarians to this day use the books printed up in Poland; their dogmas were established in a wretched little Polish

town . . . having gone farther than the Arians themselves, they ended up denying the divinity of Christ and going back to the Old Testament . . . Prince Radziwiłł, having long hesitated about which religion to pick for himself — Lutheran, Jewish or Turkish — had finally been heard to say that he intended to think up an entirely new one for himself.[4]

The Polish bard's allusions in his lecture to "dogmas" (when the Socinians had rejected dogma, assigning a decisive role to reason) as well as to the English Unitarians in 1841 still "using" books printed in Poland two centuries earlier, must surely be set down to poetic license. The poet had but a very limited knowledge of Socinianism and of the role of the publications, printed chiefly in Raków, which in the nineteenth century already constituted bibliographic rarities while in Great Britain the Unitarian Church was openly existing and its writings were freely developing the thought passed on to them by the Polish Brethren in the sixteenth century.

Mickiewicz's attitude toward the Polish Brethren did not prevent him from admiring the American poet Ralph Waldo Emerson, a Unitarian minister described by the Polish philosopher Tatarkiewicz as "descended from a family of ministers of the Unitarian sect, that most enlightened of Protestant sects, proclaiming freedom of religious thought." Emerson was the ideological heir of the ideological heirs of the Polish Brethren. According to Tatarkiewicz, his "lecture at Harvard University was virtually a declaration of the individual's independence from God: he held that everyone may and ought to create his own religion . . ." Mickiewicz corresponded with Emerson and was one of the first to appreciate his greatness, terming him "the philosopher who best reveals the needs of our age."[5]

The centers of the exiled Polish Brethren gradually expired. With the sole exception of the one in Holland, they played no significant role and left no lasting legacy.

II. Socinianism abroad

The potential market, in western Europe, for the thought of the Polish Brethren — whom we shall henceforth call Socinians — was appreciated by the leaders of the movement as early as the sixteenth century, when the first contacts with the West were established. Two ministers of the Lesser Church, Krzysztof Ostorodt and Andrzej Wojdowski, while sojourning in Leyden in 1597-98, had acquainted students at the University with Raków publications and won sympathizers for their sect.[6] The same works reached interested individuals in Germany, France, Holland and England. The dissemination of these publications, and with them of the thought of the Polish Brethren, was facilitated by widened personal contacts particularly at the turn of the seventeenth century.[7] Especially effective was a publication entitled *The Rakovian Catechism* (1605), next translated into German, whose Latin edition was dedicated to England's James I. Other works and polemical writings by Polish Brethren, Socinus chief among them, printed at Raków, Zasław, Łosk, Vilnius, Luebeck and Amsterdam, in German and Dutch, made their doctrines available (under the name of Socinianism) to western Europe, passing on the basic principles of tolerance and of the application of reason to religion.[8]

The results of Socinian contacts with the liberal Protestant element in the West manifested themselves earliest in Holland, where as early as 1585 a college rector in Antwerp published a paper in the Socinian spirit.[9] In some places, governments saw fit to take repressive steps; on March 8, 1599, the Dutch Estates-General condemned to burning the writings that had been brought into Holland by Ostorodt and Wojdowski and enjoined the two men to depart the country within ten days.[10]

As it transpired, the intellectual liaisons that had been established would not be destroyed: today it is known that Hans de Ries, Mennonite leader and evangelist in Alkmaar, and the later professor in Altdorf, Ernst Soner, continued to receive Socinian publications and to spread the ideas contained in them. As a result, the next generation of theologians was imbued with concepts that had been absorbed two decades earlier, and two men were removed from church positions for voicing Socinian views: in 1617 Adolf Venator, accused of denying the divinity of Christ and of "opening the gates of heaven to Jews, Turks, and heathen;"[11] and in 1619 Jan Geisteran, pastor in Alkmaar. In the same period Dirk Rafaelsz Kamphuysen was teaching at the Raków Academy and translating Socinian writings into Dutch.[12]

Socinian influences suddenly began showing up in published writings by respected theologians and candidates for professorial chairs. They are discernible in a work by Konrad Vorst entitled *Tractatus theologicus de Deo*. Vorst was also author of the introduction to Socinus' *De auctoritate sanctae scripturae* published in Friesland. As Cloppenburg diclosed, Latin editions of Socinian works by Socinus, Crellius, Smalcius and Voelkel were secretly distributed in Holland by Vorst's pupils and *De officio hominis Christiana* was "cum pluribus excursis Fausti Socini Opusculis, abunde in Belgium illatus."[13]

Polish-Dutch theological contacts not only did not die out, they flourished. Leading Raków Socinians such as Martin Ruar and Jonasz Schlichtyng journeyed to Holland, where they offered the help of the Polish Brethren to the Remonstrants in 1619 threatened with banishment. Socinian ideas must have exerted an extraordinary influence, inasmuch as the Dutch statesman and jurist Hugo Grotius, after having read the Socinians' writings, in his own *De veritate religionis Christianae* (1627) used only rational arguments and did not even mention the Holy Trinity, but placed his main emphasis on a "Christian" life rather than on faith. Grotius, although not agreeing entirely with the Socinians, completely accepted their moral tenets.[14]

The French philosopher and "father of the Enlightenment," Pierre Bayle, in his *Dictionary*, referring to correspondence from Holland (1638) with which he was familiar, records that "Magnam in his terris Socinianorum messem esse."[15] This state of affairs must have been an open secret, as a second edict of the Dutch Estates-General in 1653 forbade under pain of grave penalties the importation or distribution of Socinian publications and banned Socinian meetings. However, this edict did not diminish Socinianism's attractiveness, especially among the Mennonites and Collegiants,[16] who without leaving their own religious groups took a very positive attitude toward the thought of the Polish Brethren. On close terms with the Collegiants at that time was a young Jew, a refugee from Spain, Benedict Spinoza. A black sheep to the Jewish community on account of his doubts concerning Biblical interpretation, he attached himself to the religiously tolerant Mennonites and Collegiants and came into close contact with Polish Socinians, especially numerous following their reinforcement with exiles from Poland after 1660. The American author Wilbur sees Socinian influence in Spinoza's work *Tactatus theologico-politicus:*

"Their culture, their tolerant spirit, and their method of interpreting Scripture appealed to him, and his view of the Bible: that Scripture never teaches what is in conflict with our reason; that it can easily be understood by everyone; and that it leaves reason free — might almost have been taken directly from Socinus."[17]

The early contacts with Dutch intellectuals proved invaluable to the Polish Brethren as conditions in Poland became increasingly difficult and sheer survival became a major concern of their leaders. Although for a while longer they continued to give Raków as the place of publication of their books, these were more and more being printed in Amsterdam, which was next given the code name "Irenopolis."

A crucial series of publications by the Polish Brethren in Holland was the *Bibliotheca Fratrorum Polonorum,* edited by Andrzej Wiszowaty, bringing together the writings of many authors. Published in 1665 and 1668 (and misleadingly dated "post annum Domini 1656") it passed on the thought of the Polish Brethren to their heirs in the West. Their books spread over civilized Europe and were grabbed up, read and discussed, here and there creating an unfounded belief concerning the growing and mysterious influence of the Socinians. People even spoke about the possibility of their taking over Europe, if only some powerful ruler declared himself for Socinianism. But no such possibility every really existed, since no ruler, as Bayle pointed out,[18] saw any purpose in giving support to a sect totally lacking in martial spirit or in aspirations for power. The world was never threatened with a Socinian deluge emanating from Holland . . . but Holland did turn out to be an excellent base for the invasion of the British Isles.

III. Socinianism in England

The first known contact of the Polish Brethren with England dates back to 1574. A certain Ralph Rutter, a London merchant representing the Muscovy Company, having met Szymon Budny, an Antitrinitarian cleric in Lithuania, had fallen under the spell of Budny's eloquence and, won over to the ideas of the Arians (as they were then called), had set about spreading their teachings. His activity among the students at the University of Koenigsberg provoked sharp denunciation from the Lutheran bishop of Pomerania in a book entitled *Nebulae Arianae*.[19] Presently a silence fell: apparently Rutter had abandoned his proselytizing efforts.

The next evidence of contact between the Polish Brethren and the British Isles is found in a reference by Zeltner[20] to the visit of a Scot named Thomas Segeth to Rakow in the summer of 1612. He had gone there intrigued by Rakovian publications that had come into his hands. After a week's stay, he had left Raków for Holland, where in Altdorf he had visited his friend Martin Ruar. Ruar in a letter to Vogler had recorded Segeth's impressions of Raków; clearly the Rakovians had made a deep impression on Segeth: "he felt [reports Ruar] as though he had been transported into another world; for whereas elsewhere all was full of wars and tumult, there all was quiet, men were calm and modest in behaviour, so that you might think them angels, although they were spirited in debate and expert in language."[21]

Ruar, whose professor in Altdorf had been Ernst Soner, in 1614 went personally to Raków, where he joined the Lesser Reformed Church and in 1621 became rector of the Academy. He traveled a great deal over Europe, frequenting Holland, where he figured as representative of the Polish Brethren. Ruar was familiar, and often corresponded, with a number of outstanding theologians and philosophers, including Grotius and Marin Mersenn, a friend of Pascal and Descartes.[22] He also visited England where, as he mentions in one of his letters,[23] he was offered a chair at Cambridge. In 1646 Ruar settled in Gdańsk, where finally at an advanced age he formally became a clergyman and minister of a congregation.

Next we should mention the brief visit to England of Andrzej

Wiszowaty (grandson of Socinus and of his wife, born Morsztyn) during his studies at Leyden and Amsterdam. Closer personal contacts with England were established by Krzysztof Crell the elder when he went there in 1662 to secure help for the exiles from Poland. After Crell and Ruar, many years were to pass before the books printed at Raków, Vilnius and Luebeck would invade the British Isles for good.

The sixteenth- and seventeenth-century Polish-Dutch contacts were of an intellectual rather than of a mass nature. Only rarely would a small group move from one country to the other, as happened when the Dutch Mennonites were forced to migrate to Poland at the beginning of the seventeenth century or when the Polish Brethren migrated to Holland after 1660.

It was another matter with the Dutch and English. The wars and persecutions of the period caused major mass migrations, as a result of which during Queen Elizabeth I's reign alone, some sixty thousand Dutch people settled in England. These refugees must have brought along with their modest emigres' baggage, a sizeable dose of democratic ideas and some pretty well reformed religious views; it was noted that the newly arrived Dutch Anabaptists showed signs of Socinianism.[24] The Dutch settled mainly in eastern England where — curiously enough — Antitrinitarianism, ascribed to Arian influences, subsequently showed itself the strongest. One of the last heretics to be burned at the stake, in 1612, is called by the historian Fuller "our English Vorstius" and "an Arian."[25]

In the seventeenth century Holland became a land of considerable freedom and learning, and the University of Leyden particularly combined high academic standards with religious tolerance, making itself especially attractive, along with Edinburgh and Glasgow in Scotland, to British dissenters desirous of knowledge. There they came in contact with every manner of sect, among which an English traveler in 1643 found the Socinians, who "have also their public meetings in houses turned into churches."[26] The Britishers took back with them from Holland the "modern" ideas of the Polish Brethren. However, the Brethren's works began to draw real attention only when the *Catechesis ecclesiarum in regno Poloniae et magno ducatu Lithuaniae,* published in Raków in 1609 and dedicated to King James I, reached England.

King James ordered the *Catechism* with its gratuitous dedication burned, and a certain number of copies were; but the book survived, and there followed many more printings between 1609 and 1684. In addition to eight in Latin, there were two in Polish, three in Dutch and two in German.

The visits of the British students did not pass without their absorbing Socinian principles; an extant student's notebook contains a Latin summary of seven chapters of a book by Ostorodt, *Unterrichtung von den vernehmsten hauptpunkten der Christlichen Religion.*[27]

Cases are known of Britishers returning from Holland with respectable collections of Socinian literature, and a goodly quantity of it has been preserved to this day in English scholarly libraries and archives. There are allusions in many English theological publications of the time, as well as on recorded Calvinist and Catholic sermons, to Socinian books, which "have Clancularly crept in endeavouring to infect and poyson our faith."[28] As early as 1639 the Crown and the Church of England secured censorship of imported printed matter. But British publications — in theology, law, physics, philosophy and poetry — too henceforth required the imprimatur of the highest officials of the Church of England.

When the decree failed to produce the anticipated results, Archbishop Laud included among his Canons of 1640 one directed against "the damnable and cursed Heresie of Socinianism." The canon forbade the possession or reading of Socinian publications, which were to be available only to theologians and doctors of canon law. The canon provided for investigation of those supporting or defending Socinianism.[29] However, the canon never became binding law due to sharp opposition in the House of Commons, where it was described as conflicting with "parliamentary power, in determining an heresie not determined by law." Introduction of the canon, in the opinion of one member, would have permitted condemnation of a person without prior definition of "Socinianism," leaving it to private individuals to decide "whom they will judge and call a Socinian."[30]

However, there were efforts made to prevent the popularization of Socinian ideas through preventing their increase in Holland. Bayle notes an English effort to bring the attention of the Dutch Estates-General to the threat posed by the immigration into Holland of a certain number of Socinians from Poland in connection with the liquidations of their center at Raków.[31] Still another diplomatic intervention was caused by statements of Dr. S. Johnson, chaplain to the Czech queen at the Hague, who in conversations and scholarly debates had described Socinian ideas as "vera et solida theologia" and had pronounced Anglican arguments "pro divinitate Christi — futile, frivola straminea [so much straw]."[32]

The stories about Socinian influences invading the British Isles by way of Holland seem to have been justified but exaggerated. Merely labelling someone a Socinian hardly made him in fact an exponent of the principles held by the Polish Brethren. The word "Socinian" appears to have often had much the same epithet value as was attached between the two World Wars to "Bolshevik," or after the Second World War in some countries to "Socialist." Undoubtedly the thought of the Polish Brethren was at the beginning of the seventeenth century slowly spreading, particularly among English theologians, but much more water was yet to flow under London Bridge before Socinianism would really begin to take root in England.

Even thorough analysis of English theological writings of the time gives no complete assurance that certain arguments or ideas used in them had come into existence under Socinian influence, so long as there is no proof that the writings of the Polish Brethren had reached their authors. Hence it is important to establish the spread of Socinianism on the British Isles by determining the English translators of Socinian works.

IV. English translations of the Polish Brethren

The first English translations of the Polish Brethren were prepared by John Weberly,[33] but none of Weberly's translations were ever published. It is known for a fact that one of his manuscripts, ready for press, fell into the hands of the authorities and was confiscated. But it is impossible to establish which books Weberly translated.[34]

The second translator — and the first whose work survives —

was Thomas Lushington. He translated at least two books; the first was *The Expiation of a Sinner. In a Commentary upon the Epistle to the Hebrews,* published anonymously in London in 1646 (the original having been written by Jonasz Schlichtyng and published in Rakow in 1634).[35]

In 1650 Lushington published *The Justification of a Sinner,* a translation from the Latin original of Jan Crell and Jonasz Schlichtyng published in Rakow in 1628. Both of Lushington's books were free rather than literal translations, but "at every point Lushington follows the lead of his Socinian authorities."[36]

The next translator was Paul Best. As a young man he had studied at Cambridge, but his studies had been interrupted by travel. He had spent some time in Germany and had also visited Poland and Transylvania; he had returned very much under the spell of Socinianism (or of Unitarianism, in Transylvania).[37] Back in Cambridge again, he wrote out his new views on the Holy Trinity and showed them in confidence to a fellow student. As a result, in February, 1645, Best was arrested and placed on trial before the House of Commons. A Commons commission drew up a report establishing the law governing blasphemy and in Best's particular case recommended death by hanging, although it duly noted that common law also permitted burning at the stake.

Best spent about two years without sentence at Gatehouse Prison, after which he was quietly released. It is theorized that he was set free at the personal intervention of Oliver Cromwell. Best had once served in the parliamentary army, and his case was probably treated in accordance with Cromwell's letter to the Speaker of the House of Commons in which Cromwell expressed his desire that the authorities not discourage "those who had ventured their life for them, and come out expressly with their much-desyred libertie of conscience."[38] It is also possible that John Milton, an Antitrinitarian who did much propaganda work for Cromwell, had interceded with the latter.

During his extended stay in prison, Best wrote a *Letter of Advice unto the Ministers,* in which he undertook to demonstrate that heretics should be kept alive.[39] When his petitions did not bring about his desired release, Best wrote a treatise entitled *Mysteries Discovered* and a new petition to the House of Commons. In the latter he recounted his lot as a prisoner unjustly deprived of his freedom, set forth his religious credo, and ended with a plea for religious tolerance, citing Holland and Poland as examples.

Best termed Socinianism "that third Reformation which succeeded the Calvinian,"[40] and in his statement of Socinian principles recapitulated the views of the Polish Brethren. Mysteriously he succeeded in getting this work into print, prompting the authorities to issue an order for the immediate burning of all copies of it. Nevertheless — or, indeed, perhaps thanks to this order, which gave the publication notoriety — the effort to impound all copies did not succeed, and the remaining copies enhanced the attractiveness of Socinianism.

That the poet Milton was aware of the Best case seems beyond dispute. A copy of *Mysteries Discovered* preserved in the Bodleian Library at Oxford contains an extensive Latin autograph on the nature of Christ, presenting an Arian view akin to Milton's in his *Treatise on Christian Doctrine,* and the title page bears a brief note which experts ascribe to Milton.[41]

It should be stated that Best did not so much translate the works of the Polish Brethren as he freely interpreted them and popularized their thought. Beyond that, Best played a key role in introducing John Bidle to Socinianism.

Bidle, the son of a poor tailor, with a special talent for classical languages and literatures, was eighteen when he published his translations of Virgil. After obtaining his master's degree from Oxford, he became director of a school in Gloucester, where his work gained general recognition.[42] But at the same time through his own private (as he asserted) studies of the New Testament he developed doubts as to the doctrine of the Holy Trinity. Someone close to Bidle reported his cogitations to the city authorities, thereby causing his arrest. By declaring his credo in a manner permitting of safe interpretation, Bidle managed to secure his release,[43] but in his private theological studies he departed increasingly from orthodoxy. He set his views down in writing, and someone again reported him.

This time Bidle was relieved of his job and called before a parliamentary commission, next to be arrested and placed at the exclusive disposition of Parliament. Thus began the unique career of the convict-heretic, religious publicist and evangelist.

Behind bars, from which influential liberals (including some in Parliament) would now and again spring him, and while transitorily free, he wrote and like Best published his works, which spread like wildfire, frustrating the efforts of authorities to gather up the printings and solemnly burn them.

Bidle's departure from prison in 1652 coincided suggestively with a Latin edition of the *Catechesis Ecclesiarum Poloniae;* the appendix contained a biographical note on Socinus and a list of his works. Published anonymously, with Raków given as the place of publication but without the printer's name, it caused an investigation by a parliamentary committee that included Cromwell. The committee interrogated William Dugard, printer to the Council of State, as well as — for some uncertain reason — John Milton who, although not a Socinian himself, sympathized with the Socinian postulates of religious tolerance, of the role of reason in religion, and of the basing of religion on Holy Scripture.[44] Masson attempts to elucidate the mystery of the *Catechism's* publication by maintaining the Dugard was a Socinian and had issued the *Catechism* from his press,[45] but McLachlan's more convincing theory that Bidle himself was the moving spirit behind the publication is lent credence by the appearance a short time later of an English translation of the same book, under the title *The Racovian Catechism* (1652), printed in "Amsterledam for Brooer Janz."[46] "Amsterledam" is taken to be a cryptonym for London, and "Brooer Janz" a pseudonym for John Bidle.[47]

In 1653 further translations of Socinian writings were published by Richard Moone. One was of Samuel Przypkowski's *Fausti Socini Senensis vita,* with and introduction "To the Reader" by "J.B.," apparently Bidle. Another was a new edition of *Twelve Arguments against the Deity of the Holy Ghost,* a translation by Bidle which had been burned in 1647, published together with *The Testimonies of Irenaeus* [et al.] *concerning* [the] *One God and the Persons of the Holy Trinity, together with Observations on the Same* (originally published in 1648), under the joint title of *The Apostolical and True Opinion concerning the Holy Trinity.*

The next translation was *Dissertatio de pace, or a Discourse Touching the Peace and Concord of the Church* (London, 1653, printed by Ja. Cottrell for Richard Moone.) This was a translation of Samuel Przypkowski's original published in Amsterdam in 1628.[48]

Next to be published, the same year, was *Brevis Disquisitio, or a Brief Enquiry Touching a Better Way than Is Commonly Made Use of, to Refute Papists and Reduce Protestants to Certainty and Unity in Religion*, printed again by Ja. Cottrell for Richard Moone: the original being by Joachim Stegmann, former rector of the Raków Academy.[49]

February, 1654, brought a *Twofold Catechism: the One Simply Called A Scripture-Catechism; the Other, A Brief Scripture-Catechism for Children*, "by John Bidle, Master of Arts of the University of Oxford, 1654." According to Sandius,[50] this was a translation to a work in Latin by the Gdańsk Socinian Jeremiasz Felbinger, entitled *Doctrina syllogistica* (1646). Whether the *Twofold Catechism* was Bidle's own original work or in fact a translation of Felbinger, cannot be determined today for lack of any extant copy of Felbinger's work. But some food for thought is provided by a letter from Felbinger to Bidle, expressing pleasure at Bidle's having joined the struggle against the concepts of the Trinity and of Christ's godhood: that while he himself and others were fighting the good fight "in oris Sarmaticis pro Dei et Christi gloria," God was calling the faithful to action in distant lands. Felbinger urges Bidle to spread the word not only in England but also in America.[51]

Bidle's writings, especially those recounting his own life, permit of the possibility that when he had first been entering upon the path of religious heterodoxy, he had not been a "Socinian," though in all likelihood he had come across works by Polish Brethren already in the library at Oxford University. It is impossible to refute McLachlan's hypothesis that Bidle had been converted to Socinianism thanks to Best, together with whom he had served time at Gatehouse Prison in August of 1647.[52] Be that as it may, Bidle had embarked upon the Socinian path only gradually, and even as late as 1648, in publishing his *Confession of Faith*,

> had given serious thought to the whole doctrine of the Trinity and had become conversant with the works of

Socinus and his school. In his attitude to the Trinity and the Nature and Satisfaction of Christ he is Socinian, though on the character of the Holy Spirit he maintains his own peculiar doctrine, criticizing Athanasius on the one hand and Socinus on the other.[53]

With time he had come into closer and closer agreement with the Socinians; this is marked by his publication of a new Latin edition of *Catechesis Ecclesiarum Poloniae* (according to the original *Katechizm Rakowski* published in 1651 at Rakòw), initiating a series of translations from the Polish Brethren. This does not mean that Bidle accepted the ideas of the Polish Brethren slavishly. But, then, their writings were not — nor were they intended to be — compilations of dogma; their various writers were not always in accord with each other. They were united only by what set them apart from religious writers of many other groups: "they were scripturalists who admitted the place and use of reason."[54]

John Bidle died in prison on September 22, 1662. Altogether the "father of English Unitarianism" had spent about ten years in various prisons, nearly three of them at St. Mary's Castle on the Scilly Isles. He had borne the consequences of fighting the established Church of England. It would be two decades after his death before his own society would be able to view him and write about him objectively. The first to do so was John Farrington, a barrister in the Inner Temple.[55] Based on Farrington's work was the anonymous *Short Account of the Life of John Bidle*.[56] Posthumous accounts of him stress

> his great zeal for promoting holiness of life and manners; for this was always his end and design in what he taught. He valued not his doctrines for speculation but practice. The pragmatic character of Bidle's religion was, again, in line with the genius of the earlier Socinianism in Poland. Both Polish and English Socinians endeavoured to take seriously the ethical teachings of Jesus in the parables and the Sermon on the Mount.[57]

V. The first congregations of English Socinians

It had not been Bidle's intention to create a new sect, just as earlier it had not been the Polish Brethren's intention to create a separate church. Bidle had preached to those who would listen, and they had congregated at the places they knew he would be speaking. And it was these groups that had become the first informal congregations of English Socinians.

It is interesting that little groups of Socinians sprang up along Bidle's life path: in Gloucester (and in nearby Cheltenham) and in London. The leaders of these centers were men who had met him and fallen under the spell of his arguments and of his dynamic personality. Living testimony to Bidle's presence in Gloucester and its vicinity were John Knowles, Thomas Marret and John Cooper. Bidle's London contacts produced such Socinian activists as Thomas Firmin and Henry Hedworth.

Particularly important both to Bidle's own efforts and to the existence of the Socinian community in London was the aforementioned Thomas Firmin, a wealthy textile merchant and master stay-maker. It is conceivable that it was precisely his mastery of stay-making and thus his exceptional intimacy with an exalted clientele that gave him an otherwise completely incomprehensible immunity in his Socinian activities. His biography records a conversation between Mary II and Archbishop of Canterbury Tillotson, in which the Queen had urged the Archbishop to convert Firmin, and the churchman had assured the Queen that he had already on many occasions attempted to do so.[58]

Firmin had gotten his Socinianism from Bidle, probably in 1655. Firmin represented a rare combination of religiosity with business acumen; he had made a fortune which enabled him to pursue philanthropic activities. Bidle had taught Firmin a humanitarian approach to the poor: "This was one of Mr. Bidle's Lessons, that 'tis a duty not only to relieve, but to visit the Sick and Poor; because they are thereby encouraged and comforted, and we come to know of what nature and degree their straits are . . ."[59]

Firmin did not restrict his philanthropy to just his own compatriots and coreligionists. Without ceasing to be a pillar of

English Socinianism, he did his utmost to alleviate the plight of the French Huguenots in 1680, of the Calvinist refugees from Poland in 1681, and of the Irish Protestants in 1688-89.[60]

Strongly wedded to Socinianism, Firmin was on close terms with Bidle's friends, including the already mentioned Hedworth, Knowles, Cooper and Marret. All their names are associated with the arrival to England of Krzysztof Crell the elder (son of Jan Crell, rector of the Raków Academy and minister of the Raków congregation, one of the chief thinkers of the Polish Brethren in the early years of the seventeenth century, and author of a number of works, including — in collaboration with Voelkel — *De vera religione libri quinque,* published at Raków in 1630).

Krzysztof, or Christopher, Crell's arrival in England in 1662 was preceded by Hedworth's trip to Holland, where he was in close touch with the Polish Brethren and with the Dutch Remonstrants who harbored the Brethren. It appears that Hedworth brought Crell to England to help him raise funds to aid the exiled Polish Brethren.[61] There he introduced his guest to his coreligionists, whom he called "friends of the Archi-catholic faith."[62] There can be no doubt as to whom he had in mind in using this extremely rare name for the Socinians. (As a young man, the author of the present study heard his mother speak of her ancestors, "Old-Catholics, otherwise called Archi-Catholics," who used to gather at night in local groves for prayers and sermons: these apparent clandestine survivors of the Polish Brethren after 1660 had eventually died out in Poland.) The name is preserved in the title of a work by Tomasz Pisecius, *Manuductio in viam pacis ecclesiasticae, per archi-catholicam fidem.*[63]

Crell's English coreligionists carried on their fund-raising campaign wherever they could. Their efforts are known to have spanned the counties of Worcester, Oxford, Cambridge and London.[64] Parenthetically, the campaign did not yield impressive results, but that is entirely understandable in the difficult circumstances of the persecuted and infamized English Socinians. An exception to this general misery was Firmin, who generously opened his purse and alone was mentioned by name as a contributor in Crell's letter to his friend, Jan Naeranus, a leader of the Rotterdam Remonstrants.[65]

John Knowles paid for his part in the fund-raising with some unpleasant consequences: during a search of his lodging (his sizable correspondence having aroused suspicion) the authorities came upon a list of contributors. The officer conducting the search would not accept Knowle's explanation about assistance to "Polanders," and suspecting some nefarious plot, had dispatched Knowles to London for investigation. He was freed several months later. The official report damningly demonstrated Knowles' Socinianism, pointing to "communication he had with Mr. Bidle and the use of his blasphemous writings with which his study is well furnished."[66]

As a preacher, Knowles had often been accused of Socinianism; he had answered the charges with polemics which had featured verbal evasions and assurances that he had never read or seen any Socinian works. But it is proven fact that his library had contained two works by Socinus, *Socini Praelectiones* and *Socini Disputationes,* as well as a six-volume *Bibliotheca Fratrorum Polonorum.*[67]

An "independent Presbiterian" as a youth,[68] Knowles had early as a young preacher roused suspicions with his treatment of the Holy Trinity. His statement: "I have learned . . . not to trust others to try for me, or to pin my faith on author's sleeve, nor believe as the Church believes" shows Bidle's influence.[69] His views had crystallized into an increasingly distinct Socinianism and were expressed in his polemic *A Friendly Debate on a Weighty Subject . . . Concerning the Divinity of Jesus Christ* (London, 1650).

In connection with his sermons, Knowles had after a protracted struggle been relieved of his congregation in Chester. He had settled in Pershor, Worcestershire, where he had gathered about him into an informal congregation a small group of secret Socinians. After a dozen years or so, his presence at Pershor had been interrupted by the earlier mentioned episode when he had been arrested and sent to London, where he had remained for good after his release. Firmin had often gotten Knowles out of scrapes of this kind; probably this time too Knowles owed his freedom to Firmin, especially as the latter had for years been urging him to move to London and take over the pastorate of the local Socinian group, offering him room in his own home.[70] It cannot be determined whether Knowles took him up on the offer; but it is known that at the beginning of 1676 he was delivering sermons in the Socinian meeting place on Coleman Street, one of three then existing in London.[71]

In London Knowles also continued his writing. It is considered quite certain that a product of his pen is an anonymous pamphlet entitled *The Freeness of God's Grace in the Forgiveness of Sins by Jesus Christ* (1668); and under his own name he published *An Answer to Mr. Ferguson's Book, Entitled Justification Only upon a Satisfaction, Wherein He Is Friendly Reprov'd, Fully Silenc'd, and Clearly Instructed. Whereunto Is Added, A Compendium, or Brief Discourse Concerning the Ends and Intents of Christ's Death and Passion, Consider'd as a Ransom. By John Knowles, a Servant of Jesus Christ. 1668.*

Without going into Knowles' theological arguments, it may be stated that he was an heir of the Polish Brethren, although like Bidle he professed a somewhat modified brand of Socinianism, Knowles himself confirmed his bonds with the Polish Brethren: "And this the Poland Churches (whom I think Mr. F. counts for Socinians) do also profess, as may be seen in their Catechism, Printed post Annum Domini 1659."[72]

Knowles' friendship for the Polish Brethren is evidenced in his will, which established a legacy for "Christopher Crellius the elder" and "his exiled friends and countrymen that are in want ..." Knowles' will bequeathed his library to his nephews, except for the books of the Polish Brethren, which — in order to make them available to the broad reading public — he bequeathed to the public library in Gloucester.[73]

Of other early English Socinians already mentioned, John Cooper headed a small group in Cheltenham. Under Cromwell he was headmaster of a school in Gloucester, the same one in which Bidle had worked two years earlier; next Cooper became vicar of Cheltenham. With the return of the Royalists, he was removed and became preacher to a Socinian group. During this period he was on close terms with Hedworth, Knowles and Marret; this is shown by correspondence in which he says of the Polish Brethren: "Got knoweth I am very glad (my Heart) to find that in endeavours to do something in their behalfe thou needest no Argument for encouragement.They are bone of our bone and flesh of our flesh; or rather (hoc ordine inverso) they are our precedents in some great points of Religion."[74]

The next English Socinian, Henry Hedworth, had met Bidle in London. In 1662 he was in the circle of Firmin's intimates and frequently exchanged correspondence with Knowles. The preserved letters indicate that Hedworth sent Knowles a work by Daniel Zwicker, a Gdańsk Socinian, entitled *Irenicum Irenicorum* (Amsterdam, 1658) and "ye Exiles Epistle of ye receipt whereof yu didst never advise me." McLachlan surmises that this is a reference to a copy of a letter of June 17, 1661, to the Dutch Remonstrants from six Polish Brethren clergy sojourning in Silesia.[75]

Hedworth, author of several theological polemics, and considered closer ideologically to Bidle than were Knowles or Firmin,[76] spent most of his life in London, where he was very active in Socinian circles. He died in 1705; his will contained a bequest for Christopher, Jr., and Samuel Crell (sons of Christopher Crell the elder) and for Hopton Haynes, a friend of Isaac Newton's.[77]

Thomas Firmin, John Knowles, Thomas Paul Best, John Bidle and John Cooper formed a generation that did not content itself with clandestine reading of the Polish Brethren and with favoring each other more or less in secret with their doubts concerning the Athanasian Creed. They assumed the heritage of the continental Socinians, published their works, and gave rise to groups which were regarded by their opponents as religious congregations. And they steadfastly gave expression to their sense of close ideological kinship with the Polish Brethren — both in words (as in the passages just quoted) and in deed, as in their fund-raising in aid of exiled Polish Socinians.

The London Socinians provided Christopher Crell the elder, who visited England several times as a representative of the Polish Brethren, with a family in more than metaphor. While there, he met a Socinian woman, Alice Stucky, who had recently lost her husband and an exceptionally talented sixteen-year old son who, when barely thirteen, had translated Bidle's *Twofold Catechism* into Latin. On learning that Crell's children were living in squalid conditions in Holland, Mrs. Stucky had extracted from him a promise to bring them to England and entrust them to her care.

Accordingly, in 1668 Crell's two oldest children arrived in London; these were Christopher, Jr., and a daughter whose name is not recorded, whom Mrs. Stucky adopted. Later two other sons, Samuel and Paweł (Paul), likewise arrived.

Christopher, Jr., completed medical studies at the University of Leyden and was later admitted to Britain's Royal College of Physicians.[78] In gratitude he dedicated his dissertation "to Mrs. Stucky, who brought him up," also naming "Mr. Henry Hedworth and Mr. Thomas Firmin," in clear acknowledgment of his sense of debt to them for their help to him personally as well as to the Polish Brethren who had remained on the continent.

Christopher Crell, Jr., became known in London not only as a physician but also as an intellectual. Among his closest friends were Thomas Sydenham, "the English Hippocrates," and the famous philosopher John Locke. All three were physicians by education. A verse by Christopher Crell was included in the foreword to a posthumously published medical treatise of Sydenham's.[79]

The second son of the elder Christopher Crell, Samuel, after arriving in England studied at Oxford. He was friends with John Locke, Isaac Newton, and the Anglican clergyman (later Archbishop of Canterbury) John Tillotson, and Lord Shaftesbury. After his studies Samuel left England for forty years to be Socinian minister in Koenigswald in East Prussia, later returning to England to a handful of his surviving friends (Locke, among others, being now dead). He renewed and established some contacts; among his closest friends in this period were Isaac Newton and Lord Shaftesbury. Samuel Crell's time in London passed in seeing through the press his two-volume work, *Initium Evangelii S. Joannis Apostoli ex antiquitate ecclesiastica restitutum,* and in discussions with selected Anglican clergy, including Archbishop of Canterbury Tillotson.[80] In one of his sermons the Archbishop expressed himself quite favorably on the Socinians and then had to explain himself profusely; his attitude to the Athanasian Creed is likewise known from a letter to Bishop Burnet: "I wish we were well rid of it."[81]

Having published his work, Samuel Crell departed for Holland, where he settled in Amsterdam. The Collegiants gave him a modest pension, of which he spent the greater part on books. He passed away in 1746: the last of the Polish Brethren known to the great world, valued and respected for his knowledge, scholarly integrity and character.[82]

The presence of the Crells on the British Isles among the most enlightened English Socinians did not escape the attention of the enemies of religious liberalism. The Crells are denounced in a book by Dr. John Edwards,[83] who observes: "We are not sure that some of those who go under the name of English Socinians are not foreigners. Is not Crellius' stock somewhere harbour'd among them?" This is an obvious allusion by Edwards, living and active in Oxford, to Paul Crell, studying at that University, the charge of Lord Shaftesbury (a member of Charles II's council of ministers, and a founder of Carolina colony), who treated young Crell as a member of his own family. After completing his studies, Paul Crell left England to become a Socinian minister in Kąsinowo, where his father Christopher the elder had been minister before him.

Christopher Crell the elder had himself not settled in England permanently, but between 1662 and 1670 he had been there three times.[84] McLachlan, making reference to a letter of Hedworth's mentioning the departure for Holland of one "Mr. Spinoste," deduces that Crell, Sr., had used the name "Spinowski" in England; he adds that apparently his son Paul had abandoned use of that name, since in extant documents he always figures as Crell. Apparently associated with the presence of Christopher Crell the elder in England was the publication in London of an English translation of Jan Crell's *De uno deo patre*, as *The Two Books of John Crellius Francus, Touching One God the Father*. This translation was reputed to be Bidle's work, but a more likely guess is that Bidle, having met Christopher Crell the elder, who had probably brought more Socinian publications with him, had begun the translation, but that it had been completed by Knowles or Hedworth, and its publication had most likely been financed by Firmin.[85]

To round out the story of Christopher Crell the elder, in 1670 he settled in Kąsinowo in East Prussia as minister and as visitor to the whole of Silesia. He ended his life there, and his congregation was taken over by his son Paul.[86]

As a matter of course, the Socinian publications appearing in England provoked oral rebuttals as well as written replies by orthodox theologians. On the one hand these exchanges reinforced official enmity toward Socinianism, but on the other they added to the Socinians' notoriety and swelled the demand for the publications of the unregenerate heretics. The debate stimulated the growth of England's intellectual life and engaged her leading minds, while at the same time preoccupying the guardians of English law and order who sought to preserve the status quo and to expose "Socinian conspiracies." A government agent reported that "Mrs. Stucky, a Polander's wife," was harboring "young Crellius and his wife and other Socinians [in her home] and has meetings [of Socinian groups] there upon set days." This "wife" of Christopher Crell Jr.'s was actually his sister, both of them having been adopted by Mrs. Stucky. During this same period, one of his brothers, Samuel, was denied access to the stacks of the Bodleian Library at Oxford, "lest like Sandius [author of the famous *Bibliotheca anti-trinitariorum*] before him should there find material to adorn his cause."[37]

Benedictus Spinoza, 1632 - 1677

CHAPTER 10

THE SOCINIAN CONTRIBUTION TO WEST EUROPEAN THOUGHT

I. Socinianism and English thought

Socinianism contributed greatly to the stimulation of English thought; England's intellectual cream were on close terms with the Socinians. The philosopher John Locke, as mentioned earlier, met them in his early youth and again during his five-year exile in Holland. Locke's close contacts with English Socinians included Thomas Firmin and his group.[1] Locke's treatises and theological works bear a striking kinship with Socinian thought, revealing "the same lay disengagement from scholasticism, the same purpose of toleration tempered by prudence, the same interest in the minimising of essentials, and the same recurrence to Scripture, interpreted (that is to say, rationalised) by common sense rather than by profound exegesis."[2]

This kinship is patent in his *Letter on Toleration* and *The Reasonableness of Christianity*, which prompted orthodox writers to accuse him of Socinianism. Edwards, particularly bitter in his attacks on Locke, declared him "Socinianized all

Anthony Ashley Cooper - Shaftesbury, 1621 - 1683

over"[3] and, the more completely to alienate him from his readers, dubbed him the rabbi from Racovia.[4] He pointed out in his *Socinian Creed* that Locke, like Socinus, had completely rejected "innate ideas."[5]

In self-defense Locke, much like John Knowles, used the argument that he had never in his life read a single page from the works of Socinus or Crell — an assertion that modern research has refuted by establishing that his library contained a rich collection of Socinian authors, including the Polish Brethren Crell, Ruar, Schlichtyng, Smalcius, Wolzogen and Wiszowaty. He was in possession of *The Racovian Cathechism* and of a complete set of *Bibliotheca Fratrorum Polonorum*. Additionally he owned a copy of *Anonimi Dissertatio de pace et concordia ecclesiae* (which he ascribed to Hales, thereby perhaps partly justifying his claim about never having read Socinus), *The Brief History,* seventeen other Unitarian titles and three volumes of "Unitarian Tracts."[6]

That Locke was not merely ornamenting his library with these books is shown by his autograph notations in them as well as by references in his own books to works by Bidle and Crell.[7]

Living in a period of intolerance, Locke scrupulously avoided declaring the tenets of his faith or his view on the doctrine of the Trinity. When not challenged on the question, he simply passed it over in silence. When pressed to the wall with charges that his writings displayed Socinianism, "Locke candidly refrained from giving a clear answer, . . . undoubtedly because he was very sympathetic to the naturalistic Socinian and deistical interpretations."[8]

Locke's position on the role of reason in faith is unequivocal: "Whatsoever is Divine Revelation ought to overrule our opinions, prejudices, and interests. Whatsoever God hath revealed is certainly true. No doubt can be made of it. But whether it be a Divine Revelation or no, Reason must judge."[9]

When Locke would not recant his reasoning under critical pressure, an effort was made to intimidate him and to ban his ideas. "The Grand Jury of Middlesex handed down a presentment [in 1697] banning Locke's *Reasonableness of Christianity,* on the ground that it denied the Trinity, appealed to reason as the sole criterion of religious truth, gave rise to Arianism, Socinianism, atheism and Deism."[10] Similarly, in 1703

John Locke, 1632-1704

instructors at Oxford were forbidden to acquaint students with Locke's *Essay Concerning Human Understanding*.[11]

Locke displayed the tolerance characteristic of Socinians. The program sketched out in his *Letter on Toleration* does not differ basically from the views on church and state held by Socinian writers, particularly by Schlichtyng and Samuel Przypkowski.[12] In the interest of accuracy it must be stated that tolerance was also practiced by the Remonstrants, with whom Locke had close contact in Holland. Whether Locke acquired his tolerant attitude from the Polish Brethren he met there or from their hosts, probably will never be established: even as it will probably never be determined whether Rembrandt's famous "Polish Rider" sprang from Rembrandt's acquaintance with Polish Brethren studying in Leyden, where they moved among the local Mennonites who included Rembrandt himself in their number...

Locke's established conceptual kinship with Socinianism is incompatible with his protestations that he had never read any Socinian writings and that the idea of his *Reasonableness of Christianity* was entirely his own.

> Belief in the originality of one's ideas [writes Ogonowski] does not always accord with the actual state of affairs, as psychological studies of creativity have shown. Therefore, as regards *The Reasonableness of Christianity,* without calling into question the sincerity of Locke's statement, we must approach it with a certain skepticism, especially in the light of facts obtained from other sources which show that Locke was well read in Socinian literature.[13]

One cannot rule out the possibility that without being at all aware of it Locke had in his youth absorbed Socinian thoughts from the Crells or that, for example, in reading a book by one of the Crells he had been under the misapprehension that its author was Hales.

> In any case... in light of the known facts it would be indefensible to assert that [Socinian literature] did not influence him indirectly: through the rational

Isaac Newton, 1642 - 1727

theologians of Oxford (the Tew Circle); through certain circles of Arminians [including Jean Le Clerc and Philip van Limborch] sympathetic to the Socinians, with whom Locke had been in constant contact since his stay in Holland in the [16]80's; or, finally, through English Unitarian families. The concepts of the Lockean religious philosophy — regardless of whether or not the philosopher did in fact forge it independently out of nothing more than Holy Writ — were crystallized in an atmosphere saturated for several dozen years with Socinian ideas.[14]

Among the outstanding English minds of the period which communed with the Socinians, or Unitarians, was Locke's friend, the great Physicist-mathematician Isaac Newton. Evidence for their intellectual intercourse is found in Newton's posthumously published work, *Two Notable Corruptions of Scripture,* which shows clearly that "For Newton, as for Locke and the Socinians, the scriptures were the primary and fundamental authority for Christian doctrine, but for him, as for his predecessors, the faculty of reason had its rightful place in the discovery of divine truth."[15]

This same accent is found in his surviving correspondence.

Let them make good sense of it who are able: for my part, I can make none. If it be said that we are not to determine what is Scripture, and what not, by our private judgement, I confess it in places not controversial, but in disputable places, I love to take up what I can best understand. It is the temper of the hot and superstitious part of mankind in matters of religion, ever to be fond of mysteries, and for that reason, to like best what they understand least.[16]

L.T. More, discussing Newton's metaphysical manuscripts (which in sheer bulk outweigh his mathematical and physical writings), lists the following subjects: the doctrine of the Trinity and its Biblical foundations; the controversy between Arius and Athanasius; the problem of the unity of God the Father and the

Son; the problem of worshipping Jesus; and the problem of the Holy Ghost as a divine person.[17] Taken together, Newton's manuscripts are regarded as "pronounced Unitarianism."[18]

The picture becomes still clearer when it is noted that "The catalogue of Newton's library shows that he possessed several works by Socinian writers, including Socinus and Crell, and a volume of 'Socinian Tracts' (1691)."[19]

Faustus Socinus had formulated the thesis that, in Ogonowski's words, "Time has an 'existence' independent of the Creator, has existed forever coequally with God, and passes in the same way for men as for God. With the creation of the world only the measurement of time began."[20]

Might not this thesis of Socinus' have inspired Newton's similar concept?

McLachlan regards Locke and Newton as precursors of the eighteenth century and as representatives of the "Age of Reason," displaying "a spirit and temper that closely links them with seventeenth century Socinianism." In his judgment "Both men exhibited the detachment and critical attitude of the lay mind, . . . a marked feature of continental Socinianism."[21]

There were many others too in this period who were writing in the Socinian-Unitarian spirit; the present study restricts itself to pointing out some to whose consciousness there are strong indications that Polish Socinianism reached and to whose intellectual formation it manifestly contributed.

The number of new Socinian publications fell off sharply with the passing away in 1697 of Thomas Firmin, who had sponsored most of them; the growth of a degree of tolerance within the Church of England now permitted some open discussion, and the writings of the Unitarians had begun to pale as the works of Locke, with their rationalism, had prefigured something still more far-reaching than Socinianism. Deism was about to be born.

II. From Socinianism to Deism

Identified as "a more serious danger [to established religion] than Socinianism or Unitarianism,"[22] the rise of Deism or Freethinking is ascribed by Wilbur to the materialistic views of the English social philosopher Thomas Hobbes (1588-1679), the rationalism of John Locke (1632-1704) and the completely new view of the world formulated by Isaac Newton (1642-1727).[23] Some writers hold the conviction that Deism, like Socinianism before it, was a manifestation of the seventeenth-century desire to rationalize religion by formulating its principles in a manner compatible with reason. This desire was intensified by the development in the seventeenth century of the natural sciences and by progress in the formulation of philosophical concepts, which roused hopes that science would decipher the secrets of nature and resolve religious questions.[24]

Initially Socinianism-Unitarianism had been regarded as the enemy of orthodox faith, but in the early years of the eighteenth century that role was taken over by Deism, especially after the publication of John Toland's book, *Christianity Not Mysterious*.[25] It was only logical that Locke, who had been declared a Socinian, following publication of his *Essay Concerning Human Understanding* at the end of the seventeeth century was in the first years of the eighteenth branded a Deist.[26]

Socinianism, says Yolton, had been "a religious movement which did not differ radically from the general deistical temper."[27] In 1728 Peter Brown wrote, "Our modern Deists, and Freethinkers and Atheists . . . are . . . the Natural Growth and Offsprings of Socinianism."[28]

The idea that Socinianism — by way of Deism, particularly in England — had paved the way for the Enlightenment, emerged nearly a half a century ago. The Socinian contribution to the development of theological thought was pointed out by Dutch and German scholars with Dilthey being especially prominent among the latter.[29] Among Polish scholars, one of the early pronouncements was that of Górski:

> We may view the products of the Enlightenment very critically, we may look upon it as an epoch either useful or harmful to the subsequent spiritual development of mankind, but however we may think of it, the fact that the Polish Arians contributed to the formation of the intellectual foundations of the Age of Enlightenment cannot but remain a significant event in the history of our culture.[30]

Łempicki's thesis, too, is notable:

> If Kant describes the Enlightenment as mankind's emergence from childhood, then one of the most important signs of its adult independence was a critical attitude toward religious dogma. This independence appears for the first time in truly decisive manner in the criticism of dogma carried out by the Socinians and Arminians. Since the efforts of the Socinians developed first of all in Polish soil, it can be boldly stated that thanks to the Polish Brethren Poland, which already in the age of humanism had forged bonds with the culture of the great world, became one of the important factors in the development of the world culture.[31]

Łempicki's thesis is approved by Stanisław Kot, who points out that Polish scholarship has until recently "not exploited the subject and claimed the Polish contribution to the momentous labors from which grew the European Enlightenment."[32] Kot's statement accords well with the estimates on the significance of Socinianism for the Enlightenment found in modern encyclopedias of various European nations. Ogonowski quotes the German *Die Religion in Geschichte und Gegenwart* and *Der grosse Brockhaus* and the Swiss *Schweizer Lexikon,* and mentions the Italian *Enciclopedia Italiana*, and then undertakes his own analysis of the evolution of English Deism with the purpose of establishing the actual influence of Socinianism. He concedes a very fundamental role to Toland, who "was branded a godless atheist — in better informed circles, a Socinian . . . Toland's thesis had already been implicit in the views of Faustus Socinus and had been formulated explicitly in Stegmann's treatise *De Judice,* written at the opening of the 1630's and published in Amsterdam in 1644."[33]

In the matter of miracles, "In *Christianity Not Mysterious* Toland's position . . . is identical with Locke's and probably with Newton's,"[34] although Newton's view was not quite so expressly stated; Toland saw religious mysteries much as did Crell,[35] and "Wiszowaty's position essentially did not differ from Stegmann's or Toland's."[36]

"The everlastingness of God and the creation of the world," says Ogonowski, "are truths which the Socinians had maintained since the 1630's could be apprehended without the aid of revelation."[37]

Ogonowski points out the identity of the positions held by Toland and the Socinians in the matter of religious mysteries, both in content (Jan—John—Crell, and Andrzej—Andrew—Wiszowaty) and form (Joachim Stegmann).[38]

In searching for the source of the striking ideological kinship between Toland and the Socinians, Ogonowski resists the temptations of regarding it as sufficient to point out the respective reflections of Wiszowaty and Toland on miracles: "It is difficult for us to resist the impression that this Irishman [John Toland] was well acquainted with *Religio rationalis,*"[39] he suggests, adding that

> It is unlikely that Toland, interested as he was in philosophico-religious questions, would not have looked into the Socinian treatises which, although anathemized by theologians, were widely distributed in the British Isles and roused curiousity not only in heterodox circles but also (forbidden fruit!) among the orthodox. Still more easily might Toland have run into these treatises during his stay in Holland in 1692-94.[40]

But in his search after Toland's inspiration Ogonowski also looks at him from another angle: "Toland called himself a pupil of Locke's and . . . in fact was. And when we recall that Locke's position on the relationship of faith to reason, and of reason to revelation, outlined in the *Essay Concerning Human Understanding,* is akin to the position of the Socinians, we can easily see that Toland might have successfully deduced his theses straight from Locke's philosophy, without any direct inspiration from the Socinians."[41]

The inescapable conclusion is that "English Deism was . . . (like Socinianism) a *religious* rationalism . . . And it is difficult not to see that in this respect Deism is a direct continuation of Socinianism. . . . Tindal — whose book *Christianity As Old As The Creation* (1730) represents an advanced phase of Deism — when he examines the role of reason in religion, speaks constantly in the language of Stegmann and Wiszowaty."[42]

It is impossible to determine the precise moment when thinkers at the turn of the eighteenth century shifted from the rationalization of Christianity to a decidedly Deistic stance. Imperceptibly some of the most outstanding representatives of English Deism — Toland, Tindal, Chubb and Morgan — metamorphosed. Where in their earlier works toward the end of the seventeenth century they had shown a Socinian attitude, in their later writings they were certainly Deists.[43]

Socinianism and Deism show common features (in varying degrees, depending on the views of the various representatives) on four basic questions: natural religion; the proper attitude toward the Old Testament; the problem of humanizing God; and ethics. Analysis shows both Socinianism and English Deism to have been founded on two basic premises: that every man's reason is his own highest authority in matters of religion, and that morality is the supreme value of religion.[44]

A close study of Deist writings fails to yield any acknowledgment that their authors borrowed heavily from the Socinian thinkers. But it must be borne in mind that at that time the works of the Socinians were banned, and acknowledgment of the Socinians as ideological antecedents would have been as unwise as unnecessary.

The closest approach to such an acknowledgment is made by Toland. On one occasion he placed as a motto on the title page of his translation of a French work by Le Clerc: "Tota ruit Babylon; disjecit Tecta Lutherus, Calvinus Muros, et Fundamenta Socinus." (An identical thought was expressed in nineteenth-century England by Cardinal Newman: "Luther did but a part of the work, Calvin another portion, Socinus finished it.")[45] On a second occasion the debt was intimated in Toland's book *Socinianism Truly Stated*, which presented a Socinian religious debate and cited some of their doctrinal material.[46]

Evidence for the Deists' Socinian legacy lies in the Deists' logical method. In their religious rationalism the Socinians were "the most far-reaching attempt at rationalizing religion within the Christian framework," and "the watchword of religion without mystery which Toland formulated toward the end of the seventeenth century in his treatise *Christianity Not Mysterious* . . . had been functioning in Socinian doctrine already in the thirties."[47]

"To put it briefly, the religious rationalism of the Socinians . . . had been to Toland's own day the current most nearly approximating (as far as views on *religio rationalis* are concerned) the later Deism. In this respect it could unquestionably have served the Deists as a source of inspiration."[48]

There is also the possibility, noted by Pomian and Ogonowski, of a negative inspiration from Socinianism, through the latter's attempt at basing Christianity on rational principles; an attempt that "demonstrated the absolute hopelessness — or so at least it was read by the eighteenth century — of such attempts"; "the Socinians showed how Christianity should not be rationalized."[49] The lesson was drawn by the early Enlightenment in the form of two conclusions:

> The first, most clearly formulated by Bayle (for whom, *nota bene,* the critique of Socinianism served as a point of departure), maintained that religion was by its very nature irrational and that all attempts at reconciling it with the requirements of rational thought were — as can be seen in the efforts of the Socinians — vain and in advance doomed to failure.
>
> The second conclusion served as building material for Deist concepts. The argument went as follows: the defeat of the Socinians does not prove at all that they had taken on an impossible task, but only that they had gone about it in the wrong way. For religion (and here the Socinians are quite right) is undoubtedly consistent with reason, as well as with morality, humanistically construed . . . . In order truly to rationalize Christianity, it is necessary to do what the Socinians had had insufficient nerve to do. It is necessary to break the bonds between the Gospels and the Old Testament, whose God — the God of Joshua, Samuel and David — recalls more a cruel tyrant than a Being who is supposed to be, and in fact is, the personification of the highest moral values. Jesus will,

of course, cease to be a Messiah, but in exchange he will become all the more venerable as one of the rare moral leaders of mankind: as the one who condemned the falsehood and moral hypocrisy of the Pharisees and pointed out to straying mankind the path that leads back to the pure springs of natural religion — that religion which, never-changing even as God the creator of nature, is equally accessible to men of all races and at all times.[50]

Górski, Kot, Pomian and others have expressed the conviction that Socinianism played a major role in "leading mankind out of its infancy." Ogonowski's probing analysis supplants the *conviction* with the definite *thesis* that the thought and labors of the Socinians played an important role in the formulation of the religious ideas of the Enlightenment.[51]

CHAPTER 11

POLAND: COLLAPSE AND RESURRECTION OF THOUGHT

I. Post-Reformation Poland

Within a short time following the disappearance of Socinianism from Poland, the ground in turn collapsed under the Polish Calvinists who had contributed in so decisive a degree to the banishment of the Polish Brethren.[1] The Reformation was done away with, with deleterious effect on the state of learning since the monastic colleges, founded as bulwarks of counter-reformation, upon attaining their ends lost their impetus and fossilized into antiquated scholasticism. (Indeed, it may well be the real significance of all the religious disputes since ancient times, that they posed weighty philosophical problems and prompted men to seek convincing answers; politically, the significance of the debates was virtually nil, as popes, emperors and kings frequently allied themselves with confirmed religious foes, including the Mohammedan Turks.) The existing climate of thought in Poland would not permit the currents of the

XVIII - century map of Poland

Grzegorz Piramowicz, 1735-1801

Stanisław Konarski, 1700 - 1773

Hugo Kołłątaj, 1750-1812

Stanisław Staszic, 1755-1826

Jan Śniadecki, 1756–1830

Enlightenment, delayed as they were in arriving, to take root, and "Nearly a hundred years after the appearance of Descartes' works, he was attacked in Poland by the Jesuit Jerzy [George] Gengell, rector of the Gdańsk college, who was regarded as a great scourge of heresy."[2]

Fortunately, new ideas cannot long be kept out. About the middle of the eighteenth century new concepts galvanized the livelier minds of Poland; soon the latter set about reforming Polish education. The lead in this effort was taken by the most enlightened among the secular clergy (Reverend Grzegorz Piramowicz) and by the Piarist order (Father Stanisław Konarski). Interestingly enough, the Jesuits sought to counter their efforts.[3]

Idle theorizing was replaced by experiment, and the fresh philosophical currents coming in from the West proceeded to supplant the moribund system of Aristotle. "Popular books poked fun at Aristotle and praised Kopernik, Galileo, Newton, Locke, Leibnitz."[4]

Due probably to Saxon influences accompanying the Saxon king at the Polish royal court, the first phase of the Polish Enlightenment was characterized by German influences, which however quickly yielded, with the accession of Stanisław August Poniatowski to the throne, to French influences, via members of the Commission for National Education who were in touch with the Encyclopedists and freethinkers of the west — with d'Alembert, Condillac, Rousseau.

Prominent names among the illuminati of this period were those of Kołłątaj, Staszic and the brothers Śniadecki.

II. Hugo Kołłątaj

Doctor of philosophy from Poland and of theology from Italy,[5] Kołłątaj upon his return to Poland set about emancipating scholarship and education, the chief object of his endeavors being the University at Kraków, where under his rectorship "Natural law, as understood in the spirit of the times, was introduced into the curriculum, and the entire program of scholarship and philosophy was based on the sensualist principles of Locke and

Condillac. This program likewise, naturally, invoked rationalist tenets as declaring the independence of reason from theology and revelation."[6]

Kołłątaj — known to posterity chiefly as one of the most distinguished participants in the political life of eighteenth-century Poland, which he strove to preserve against political destruction — has left two works: *Porządek filozoficzno-moralny (A Philosophico-Moral System)* and *Rozbiór krytyczny zasad historii o początkach rodu ludzkiego (A Critical Analysis of Historical Principles Concerning the Beginnings of Humankind)*. These two works constitute a revealing portrait of an exceptional mind.

The focal point of Kołłątaj's interests was man and his world, and this led him to study ethics, history and social philosophy. He perceived the flaws inhering in political systems based on the privileges of a restricted group and on its total power over others. Kołłątaj sought to work out a rational sociopolitical system based on the general order discernible in the natural world. He saw man as one link in a natural chain, subject to "the same laws that he shares in common with plants and animals." Man differs from his fellow creatures, in Kołłątaj's opinion, in possessing certain traits peculiar to himself: thought, speech and subjection to moral laws, "which bind him . . . much like the laws of physics, i.e. . . . constantly, immutably and necessarily."[7]

His analysis of moral law leads him to a balanced system of objective laws and obligations; from the physiocrats he adopted their tabular collation. In this way Kołłątaj arrived at the rights of personal freedom and property, and at a prohibition against violating these rights,[8] as well as the principle of abolishing class privileges and arbitrary abridgement of rights.

In his search for the causes of evil — when in the physico-moral order mankind ought to find happiness — Kołłątaj set out on a historical path and, failing to find reliable historical material pertaining to "the beginnings of humankind," ventured the hypothesis that "the earliest information at the disposal of historiography does not refer to the true beginnings of man, but to the fortuitous survivors of the calamitous flood that completely destroyed the flourishing . . . antideluvian civilization."[9]

That civilization was believed to have had institutions and an intellectual culture consonant with the physico-moral order.

> In it reigned a natural religion based on the philosophical hypothesis of Deism, requiring no priests or special churchly institution. The laws of this society were merely expressions of the natural laws discovered by philosophy ... All our knowledge of that society's laws, we owe to certain conjectures that can be woven out of the religious and philosophical ideas of the postdeluvians. The reasonable and true ideas survived with them in distorted form, and jumbled together with errors and superstitions. Thus, for example, the idea of the First Cause found expression in a cult of false gods. Without the prior concept of the true God, in Kołłątaj's judgment, it would have been impossible to create false gods.[10]

Hugo Kołłątaj was a Deist.

"Kołłątaj's Deism was a significant factor . . . in emancipating [Polish] philosophy from religion and theology. A salient feature of this version of Deism was its secularization of God — of that cause of causes laicized as a being whose existence . . . was attested by the evidence of the human mind."[11]

Kołłątaj played a very important role: he took the step, which had never been taken in Poland to this time, from religion to philosophy.

> Kołłątaj's philosophical anthropology . . . was . . . the most mature expression . . . of his aims and of his philosophical position in the history of Polish intellectual culture. Their guiding idea was the overcoming of the stagnation and decline of philosophy in Poland in the period of the Enlightenment, the building of a bridge between the period of Poland's cultural flowering under Humanism and the contemporary world of the eighteenth century . . . It was quite consciously that Kołłątaj made reference to Kopernik as a model of a scientist and

thinker. He emphasized as a chief trait of this model
... an independence of mind which reckoned only with
its own deepest sense of the truth.[12]

III. Stanisław Staszic

After his ordination as a priest, Staszic spent two years studying in Paris. Returning to Poland, he was for several years tutor to the sons of the former royal chancellor Andrzej Zamoyski. Much as over a century earlier John Locke, while tutoring the sons of Lord Shaftesbury, had in the latter's home met a number of interesting persons who had stirred his intellect (leading initially to his strange draft constitution for Shaftesbury's Carolina colony), so Staszic in the Zamoyski household came in contact with minds that assembled to prepare the political transformation of Poland.

Fruits of his Paris studies and of his discussions with the leading minds of the time were Staszic's books, *Uwagi nad życiem Jana Zamoyskiego (Observations on the Life of John Zamoyski)* and *Przestrogi dla Polski (Warnings to Poland)*. These books reveal an author intent on transforming the political system of his country and on

> seeking a political form appropriate to Poland as she was, as well as attempting to establish the relationship between the proposed system and the ideal ...
>
> Staszic's interest in an ideal system was associated with the typically Enlightenment question of natural law. In outlining the only just political system, Staszic made constant reference to the laws of nature. In this context they appeared as a set of norms and formulae which he used to appraise the social relations prevailing in the Poland of the nobility and to point out their "unnaturalness."[13]

Staszic saw his ideal in a republic "which up till now has had no correlate in reality. In this political system bonds of personal dependence between people shall be done away with. All will be subject to the law, in whose establishment they take a part. Hence they are . . . free and equal."[14]

Staszic refused to recognize as a republic a system in which only a privileged group enjoyed property and authority. He did not view as social equality an equality among the privileged class (here differing with Rousseau[15]), and virtually equated feudalism with slavery, contrasting merely the methods used to maintain subjection, including physical force, religion (and "the morality derived from it") and "the entire legal system."[16]

Here it is to religion that Staszic assigns primacy and, having ascribed religion to ignorance and fear, he holds that in the final analysis the purpose of religion is to effectively subject one man to another. "Without these superstitions," he concluded, "there could be no lasting slavery."[17]

But, this time like Rousseau, Staszic saw changes coming about, including "changes in the forms of the religious cult associated with advances in knowledge," as well as an influence of growing knowledge on social changes.[18] He ascribes to the growth of reason (by which he means knowledge) the power to neutralize the means by which people are kept in bondage: superstition, false morality, false justice, etc. Staszic sees men's hope for development in their "learning the 'true,' the 'natural,' i.e. the natural-law, principles of human coexistence, in their learning 'true' morality, justice, religion, etc. He treats the acquisition of this learning as a protracted process, in accord with his own epistemological assumption that all human knowledge derives exclusively from experience."[19]

Educated in the West, Staszic shows the distinct influence of western ideas. He displays the imprint of Locke's ideas when he ascribes the totality of man's knowledge to experience and treats man at the beginning of history as *tabula rasa*;[20] just as he shows signs of Deism when, in condemning formal religion (like Voltaire, who was strongly influenced in his views by the mathematics and physics of Newton) as transmitted to man for the purpose of maintaining him in subjection, he predicts the advent through increased knowledge of "true" religion.

IV. Jan Śniadecki

The mature Polish mind of the second half of the eighteenth century is represented by the brothers Jan and Jędrzej Śniadecki, of whom Jan in particular exerted an influence on the evolution of Polish thought. Doctor of natural sciences from the Kraków Academy and next on the staff of that institution, he was one of Kołłątaj's close collaborators in the reconstruction of the educational system.

Jan Śniadecki spent the years 1778-81 studying at Goettingen, Paris and Utrecht. From this period derived his contacts with Condorcet and his fellow mathematicians d'Alembert and Laplace. He returned home from Paris at the summons of the Commission for National Education to take over a Kraków chair of mathematics and astronomy. In 1787 he visited England, where he inspected astronomical observatories and probably developed a close acquaintance with Scottish and English philosophy.[21]

Śniadecki's education was mainly in mathematics, but he made notable contributions to philosophy, language and literature, history, education and politics. He placed a high value on a developed mind and desired Poland's intellectual improvement:

> We must ... open up their minds so that they may learn to discern the truth, for only the truth itself, being one and invariable, can unite them. Thus we must solicitously perfect free men in solid unequivocal studies redemptive of reason and affording a reliable view of the nature of the truth. It is necessary, further, that their hearts ... always find their own interest; therefore we must illuminate the mind for the guidance of the heart.[22]

Śniadecki was a patriot with a high regard for Kopernik and Kołłątaj; aware of the desperate plight of his intellectually decayed nation, he sacrificed an academic career in the West in order to reorganize his own country's educational system. Under the circumstances he could not afford to attempt developing a philosophical system of his own; he drew from Locke and from Condillac and other philosophers of the French Enlightenment, as well as from a number of Polish writers, chiefly Kołłątaj. Perhaps due to his free borrowing from a variety of thinkers, he was at different times classed as a sensualist, materialist or positivist.

"He does away with 'innate ideas' and revelation, defends experiment against authority, fights scholasticism and idealism . . . In the Enlightenment reality the 'materialist' collaborates with the 'positivist' in one and the same business of refuting religion as an explication of the world. The one questions the reality of any world other than the material . . . while the other simply renounces the search, without transmuting the renunciation into ontological doctrine."[23]

The French Revolution affected Śniadecki's views: hitherto close to the French and German Enlightenments, he now inclined toward the English school, "in which he discovered the ideal philosophy of moderation, free from the French and German extremes. In other words, this philosophy opened up a way to learning without endangering the social order."[24]

Śniadecki also learned to appreciate the value of religion as "the bulwark of custom and morality,"[25] thereby showing an affinity with Toland, who had reserved the right of freethinking to the educated minority, leaving aside the unenlightened masses, which he felt needed religious principles for their morality as well as for the social order.[26] The loss of national independence impelled Śniadecki still farther toward moderation; "he was the voice of extreme caution and of philosophical restraint."[27]

V. Poland's Enlightenment heritage

Hugo Kołłątaj (1750-1812), Stanisław Staszic (1755-1826) and Jan Śniadecki (1756-1830) were leading representatives of the Enlightenment when, after considerable delay, it at length reached Poland.

All three were imbued with western thought, which they had made their own during their studies in the West. All three show symptoms of Deism, although not necessarily construed in the same fashion.

All three — particularly Kołłątaj — did most of their writing only after Poland had ceased to exist in the political sense, hence after political action had ceased to be possible. But all three during the Great Seym actively participated in the effort to remake the Polish mind, to win the still only superficially enlightened bulk of the Seym to the idea of progress and reform.

The handiwork of the most enlightened individuals of the Polish Enlightenment was the May 3d (1791) Constitution, delayed offspring of the Western European Enlightenment.

CHAPTER 12

THE SECOND REFORMATION AND AMERICA

I. The American continent in the awareness of the Polish Brethren

That the American continent must by the sixteenth century already have entered into the awareness at least of Polish Brethren educated at the Jagiellonian University in Kraków is strongly suggested by a globe preserved at the University Museum, made around 1510. This is the earliest extant globe to show "America terra noviter reperta."[1] But the earliest surviving reference to America by a Polish Brother is found in Samuel Przypkowski's *Apologia prolixior tractatus de jure Christiani magistratus* of about 1660: "The inhabitants of the islands of the Atlantic Ocean found out in dealing with the Spaniards how much surrendering without resistance to the mercy of an enemy is worth."[2]

Przypkowski used the sad fate of the islanders to point his argument concerning the necessity of defense against invaders.

No further evidence of his interest in the New World is available.

The next known reference to America by the Polish Brethren (indicating their interest in proselytizing the new continents) is found in the letter, probably of 1654, from the Gdańsk Brother Jeremiasz Felbinger to John Bidle, urging Bidle to spread Socinian thought in America.[3]

The Brother from Gdańsk was probably unaware that in that very same year the first president of Harvard, Henry Dunster, was indicted on the grave charge of speaking out against infant baptism.[4] Whether that early American intellectual had any Socinian affiliations is unknown; but the similarity of his view with those of the Polish Arians of about a century earlier leaves open the possibility.

II. The "Socinian" affair of William Pynchon

The Polish Brother from Gdańsk could hardly have known, either, that as early as 1652 a co-founder of Massachusetts colony, William Pynchon, by hastily quitting the colony, had "avoided the distinction of being the first person to be prosecuted in Massachusetts for opinions expressed in print." The offending opinions had appeared in his book, *The Meritorious Price of Our Redemption*, which "the General Court of the colony ... detested and abhorred" for its containing "many ... opinions and assertions ... false, erronyous [sic], and hereticale [sic]."[5]

The court sentenced the book to be burned on the Boston commons,[6] and proceedings were instituted against the offending author.

Anticipating a harsh sentence, Pynchon took off for England and there devoted himself entirely to private theological studies. In 1655 he published a new edition of his earlier treatise, under the expanded title of *The Meritorious Price of Man's Redemption; or Christ's Satisfaction Discussed and Explained*. The new edition raised a major stir. Chewley, in a polemic entitled *Anti-Socinianism* (1656), discovered in Pynchon "a dangerous Socinian Sophister."[7]

McLachlan's view is that Pynchon

> was a representative of lay thought pondering the same problems as the layman Socinus had pondered years before and coming to humane and liberal conclusions about the nature of God which prevented his accepting the extreme Calvinist view of the atonement. Since he was a well-educated man he had probably read more than one Socinian author, copies of whose works may have reached the New England shores. Several times in the last book he published he mentions Socinian views and quotes the opinion of Socinus, in one place contrasting John Norton's arguments unfavourably with those of the heresiarch. But if he had never seen a Socinian treatise, his own works would form part of a new, radical current of theological opinion which was flowing in the mid-seventeenth century and found its chief expression in the writings of John Bidle. Pynchon was, at least in one respect, a Socinian without knowing it.[8]

For about a century following the Pynchon affair little if anything was to be heard in the colonies in the way of bold theological discussion, although there were detectable tectonic movements in the form of a growing "pressure for broader civil liberty and more religious freedom."[9]

At the turn of the eighteenth century "the writings of the more liberal thinkers in England were freely circulated and read in Massachusetts, and were quietly influencing colonial thought — the rational and broad-minded Chillingworth, Locke, Milton, Baxter, Jeremy Taylor, Hutcheson, Tillotson; and the figures in the Trinitarian Controversy in the Church . . . all these mellowed the hard soil of the old Calvinism."[10]

III. The break-down of American religious orthodoxy

Due to the influx into America of polemical and other writings by European thinkers of the Enlightenment, the religious views of educated colonists began to change, and "Leading ministers began to be alarmed, as appears from the annual Convention sermons." The preaching of Cotton Mather was part of the ensuing period of religious fanaticism known as the "Great Awakening."[11] This in turn prompted to action the clergy concentrated about Harvard and Yale.

George Whitefield, co-founder of the Methodist Church, arrived from England with the intent of strengthening colonial orthodoxy. From the pulpit he thundered against the more educated New England clergy, terming them "dumb dogs, half devils and half beasts, spiritually blind, and leading people to hell,"[12] clearly indicating that he included in these descriptions the theologians at Harvard and Yale.

There followed a struggle between orthodox and progressive theologians, the latter banning Whitefield from academic pulpits and the former accusing them of Arminianism, Arianism and Socinianism[13] — which did nothing to slow the disintegration of orthodoxy. That process went slowly and all but imperceptibly and, as an American historian has well remarked, "it can best be treated only as it appears in the persons of the outstanding representative individuals."[14]

IV. The advent of American Unitarianism

A doctor of theology at Harvard University, the Reverend Ebenezer Gay, who "as early as 1740 took a decided stand with regard to the Trinity,"[15] is frequently called "the father of American Unitarianism."

Next was the Reverend Lemuel Briant, during his lifetime called an Arminian and Socinian, whom President John Adams (himself a Unitarian) established beyond any doubt as having been an early Unitarian.[16] History reveals a number of long forgotten men: the liberal minister Charles Chauncy, a doctor of theology from the University of Edinburgh who before the American Revolution was vocal in his demand for the independence of the colonies; and Jonathan Mayhew, Harvard alumnus whom the Boston divines, aware that he did not believe in the Trinity, would not ordain, forcing the ceremony to be performed outside of Boston, but with the participation of his friend the Reverend Ebenezer Gay. Mayhew

> was familiar with the writings of such English liberal writers as Milton, Locke, Clarke . . . and was by temperament a radical, who spoke his views without disguise or equivocation. In 1745, two years after his ordination, he published a volume of sermons in which he strongly urged the duty of free inquiry and of private judgment in matters of religion, and opposed the use of creeds, especially the Athanasian, as tests. The volume was soon reprinted in England, and won him warm approval from prominent clergymen there. The result was that several of them . . . recommended him to the University of Aberdeen for the degree of Doctor of Divinity, which was conferred in 1749, when he was only thirty years of age.[17]

In 1755 Mayhew published a volume of his sermons, in which he taught the unity of God and denied the existence of the Holy Trinity, describing that doctrine as contradicting reason, Holy Scripture and itself.[18] The publication of Mayhew's sermons prompted an American edition of Thomas Emlyn's *Humble Inquiry* (1756), which is credited with causing the omission of the Trinity from the *Shorter Catechism* published that same year.

Mayhew was also tremendously active in the political life of the colonies in the period preceding the Revolution; he died in 1766 without seeing his country come into independence, but nevertheless he is regarded as the father of religious freedom in Massachusetts and as a founding father of the political freedom of all the states.

Mayhew's religious views were accepted by his Boston congregation, which thereby became the earliest Unitarian community in America.[19]

V. The emergence of the Unitarian Church in America

When the events of the Revolution caused part of the colonial population to move to Canada, the remaining Boston congregation invited a Harvard-educated theologian, James Freeman, to become its pastor. Freeman modified the liturgy of his church, openly making it Unitarian; with the agreement of his parish, "the first Episcopal Church in New England became the first Unitarian Church in America." At the same time, Freeman's church adopted the *Reformed Prayer Book* prepared by Lindsey in London for his Essex Street Chapel.[20]

Salem, Massachusetts, became the second oldest avowedly Unitarian center, with Freeman's fellow Harvard student William Bentley as minister. It is interesting to note the correspondence between interdenominational and sociopolitical boundaries:

> There was enough difference between these two and their colleagues ... to show a certain degree of coolness towards them. This lack of cordiality was not a matter of theology alone: Freeman was minister of the Stone Chapel, or King's Chapel, with its Anglican tradition; and Bentley, of the East Church in Salem, was a Jeffersonian when most of his colleagues were Federalists.[21]

VI. Tightening bonds between English and American Unitarianism

This period brought closer ties between American and English Unitarians. A lively correspondence developed between Freeman and Lindsey, who sent the Harvard University Library copies of works by himself and by Joseph Priestley, the discoverer of oxygen. It was only after 1776 that the collection of Socinian and Unitarian works began to be enriched with English publications. The attitude of American Unitarians toward English Unitarians was profoundly enhanced by the awareness that during the Revolution the latter had backed the colonists. Among others, a Unitarian minister in Ireland, William Hazlitt, father of the famous English essayist and critic of the same name, had fought for better treatment of American prisoners, thereby of course incurring the displeasure of patriotic Britons.[22]

In 1783 the Reverend Hazlitt left with his family for America to minister to the growing Unitarian church. But his views turned out to be too radical for American religious liberals. This made it difficult for him to find a permanent congregation, the more so as he would invariably answer attempts at persuasion with the statement that "he would sooner die in a ditch than submit to human authority in matters of faith."[23] Consequently Hazlitt spent years circuit-preaching or substitute-ministering.

Perhaps because of that very fact his influence encompassed practically all the then existing centers of Unitarianism, and "his achievement was considerable; he laid the foundations of Unitarianism in the United States."[24] An American historian notes: "Freeman was much influenced by the Reverend William Hazlitt, an English Socinian or Unitarian, and a friend of both [the radical British clergyman Richard] Price and Priestley."[25]

Freeman expressed his appreciation of Hazlitt's value to American Unitarianism with the words: "I bless the day when that honest man first landed in this country."[26]

Personal contacts between English and American Unitarians had dated from Lindsey's establishment of the first avowedly Unitarian church in London. One of the participants in the inaugural service in the Essex Street Chapel had been Benjamin Franklin, in London on colonial business; this had been on April 17, 1774. Unitarian Franklin "had already formed a friendship with Lindsey, and worshipped here as long as he remained in England."[27] To appreciate the latter statement, one must realize that Franklin spent many years in London. During this period — as early as 1764, in fact — he formed a friendship with Priestley[28] (who, shunned by churchmen, royalists, and his fellows in the Royal Society on account of his progressive political and philosophical views, in 1794 moved to Franklin's Pennsylvania, where he spent his last ten years[29]).

VII. The elite nature of American Unitarianism

Unitarianism in America, as well as abroad, never became a mass movement, confuting William Hazlitt's prediction, in an article entitled "The State of Rational Religion in America," that within thirty years all of Massachusetts would be Unitarian.[30]

In estimating the future growth of Unitarianism, Thomas Jefferson made the same mistake when he wrote: "I rejoice that in this blessed country of free inquiry and belief, which has surrendered its conscience to neither kings nor priests, the genuine doctrine of only one God is reviving, and I trust that there is not a *young man* [Jefferson's emphasis] now living in the United States who will not die a Unitarian."[31]

Instead of drawing all Americans to it, Unitarianism selectively attracted the cultured element, which due to their intellect and character occupied to a very large proportion the highest positions in American society, especially in the most difficult period of the nation's early independence. Noted American Unitarians have included John Adams (second president of the United States), Thomas Jefferson (third president), James Madison (fourth president), John Quincy Adams (sixth president), Benjamin Franklin (nominated to be first president but declining for reasons of advanced age), Millard Fillmore (thirteenth president), William Howard Taft (twenty-seventh president, and chief justice of the Supreme Court from 1921 to 1930), and two-time presidential candidate Adlai Stevenson.

VIII. The significance of Unitarianism and Deism in critical periods of American history

Especially during the working out of the concept of independence (Declaration of Independence, 1776) and during the struggle to ratify the Constitution of 1789, the Unitarians (together with Deists such as Thomas Paine and George Washington) played an enormously important role. They often possessed good educations (although not necessarily formal educations — Dr. Franklin never attended school in his life, though he was honored with degrees from four educational institutions), and equally important, they had that tolerant attitude characteristic of Unitarians. This second attribute must have been tremendously important to a country people with groups of heterogeneous cultural backgrounds, with only a rudimentary sense of belonging to an American community, and worse yet, with still smoldering interdenominational antagonisms. An eloquent illustration of the prevailing state of affairs is supplied by a passage from a book by an Englishman, Andrew Burnaby, entitled *Travels through the Middle Settlements in North America in the Years 1759-60:*

> Fire and water are not more heterogeneous than the different colonies in North America. Nothing can exceed the jealousy and emulation which they possess in regard to each other. The inhabitants of Pennsylvania and New Yrok have an inexhaustible source of animosity, in their jealousy for the trade of the Jerseys. Massachusetts-Bay and Rhode Island are not less interested in that of Connecticut. The West Indies are a common subject of emulation to them all. Even the limits and boundaries of each colony are a constant source of litigation. In short, such is the difference of character, of manners, of religion, of interest of the different colonies that I think if I am not wholly ignorant of the human mind, were they left to themselves, there would even be a civil war, from one end of the colony to the other; while the Indians and Negroes would, with better reason, impatiently watch the opportunity for exterminating them all together.[32]

That the passage of sixty years did not suffice to transform American society, to obliterate the divisiveness within it, to emancipate it from hostility toward culturally differing groups, is indicated by a mob foray against an Ursuline convent in Charlestown, Massachusetts, in 1834. In the course of the seven-hour-long night raid, the nuns and children were dragged out of the convent into a field, and the buildings were ransacked, plundered and burned to the ground. No one in the assembled crowd of spectators went to the aid of the victims; none of the offenders was ever brought to trial; neither the convent nor injured individuals ever received any compensation.[33]

The raid was a product and symptom of religious bigotry. One can readily imagine how still more intolerant American society must have been half a century earlier during its early independence. Had American society adopted the tolerant attitude of the Unitarians, there would never have been hostile acts of a chauvinistic nature directed against Catholics or other religious groups, such as occurred again in July of 1869 in San Jose, California, when a Methodist-Episcopal church was burned down, "apparently out of hatred for Chinese in the area."[34] Probably an East-Orthodox chapel in the historical Fort Ross, California, would not have been destroyed, in 1970, by "fire of undetermined nature"; neither a synagogue in Santa Clara, California, would have become a victim of conflagration, in February of 1979.

The Unitarians and the kindred Deists were during critical periods a priceless source of enlightened and unprejudiced thought, as well as of humane feeling arising from a desire for general wellbeing, leaving to each individual absolute freedom of worship and of religious practice. Thus, as an American historian has succinctly put it, "When the crisis [the Revolutionary War] came, Jefferson, Paine, John Adams, Washington, Franklin, Madison and many lesser lights were to be reckoned among either the Unitarians or the Deists."[35]

IX. The role of Unitarianism in the abolition of slavery and the spread of democratic thought

As has been said, Unitarianism in America began as an elite movement; and so it has remained. It is often called "the church of university professors," suggesting in it the preponderance of minds in which reflection predominates over emotion.

"We have," writes a Unitarian author, "no creed or interpretation of the Bible to which all must give their assent as a condition of church membership."[36]

Their numerically small ranks produced powerful opponents

of slavery (for which reason they were removed from university and college professorships[37]) at a time when other churches either "remained neutral on the subject" or even defended slavery, while at the same time "banning card-playing and dancing."[38]

"The revolutions of the last century," it has been written, "were Unitarian revolutions ... Theologically Unitarianism has always been weak and timid, but on the moral and human side its strength has been repeatedly proved ... in America, the Unitarian organization, small as it was, did more to emancipate the slaves than all the other Churches combined."[39]

Unitarianism also produced Theodore Parker (1810-60), "a fiery preacher for prison reform [therein echoing Socinus], the rights of factory workers, and the slave..."[40] It was from Parker that Abraham Lincoln, modifying the latter's definition of democracy as "government of all, by all, for all," took his own "government of the people, by the people, for the people."[41]

All in all, American Unitarianism, though an insignificant movement numerically, exerted a vastly disproportionate influence on the formation of social philosophy in the United States.

X. American Unitarianism as a product of European Socinianism and Unitarianism

William Pynchon, the first documented exponent of Socinian thought in America, acquired the reputation of a Socinian, and "Chewney believed that Pynchon was 'acquainted with Socinian John'..." However, Chewney's *belief* in itself is insufficient to establish the Socinian antecedents of Pynchon's views, and moreover there is uncertainty as to the identity of this "Socinian John" — was he Bidle, or Goodwin?[42]

Similarly, there is no evidence of Socinian works having actually been read in America in the seventeenth or eighteenth centuries. On the other hand, it seems well-nigh impossible that they did not reach the western shores of the Atlantic, that they were never to be found among the belongings of laymen or divines emigrating from England and Holland.

It is established beyond doubt that in the first half of the eighteenth century (about 1738) two Socinians, the brothers Steven and Joseph Crell, sons of Samuel already mentioned, arrived in America. It seems hard to believe that the great-grandsons of Jan Crell, rector of the Raków Academy in the 1620's, decendants of an unbroken line of Socinian theologians, should not have brought over with them to America — if only as family heirlooms — some books or other writings of their ancestors.

But Steven and Joseph Crell settled in Georgia, not in a Massachusetts receptive to new religious ideas. It is known that one of them became a justice of the peace and the other went into agriculture; their marriages produced no male issue, and all trace of their daughters has been lost. To date, no Sociniana that they might have left have been discovered.[43]

A well-known and permanent product of contacts with foreign Socinians is the United Protestant Religious Society of New York, since 1805 affiliated with the Unitarian movement. The founder of the Society was Dr. Francis A. van der Kemp, a former Mennonite preacher in Leyden who arrived in America in 1788. His Socinianism is ascribed to his early close relations with surviving Polish Brethren in Holland.[44]

However, the influence of European Unitarianism — and hence of Polish Socinianism — on American thought becomes indisputably apparent only after the formation of close relations between Freeman and Lindsay, and between Franklin and Priestley; and this influence was greatly enhanced by the arrival in America of William Hazlitt in 1783. Hazlitt's work helped his American brethren refine their views, may frequently have decided individuals to join the movement, and certainly consolidated a force that providentially neutralized religious fanaticisms which might otherwise have threatened the survival of the young nation.

American Unitarianism, through Hazlitt and other links with English Unitarianism, and as a descendant of Polish Socinianism, played a saving role at two of the most critical junctures in the history of the United States: during their formation as an independent political unit, and during the period when their unity was seriously being threatened over the question of human bondage.

CHAPTER 13

CONCLUSIONS

I. The revealed kinships

Our study of the continually mutating American constitution and of the successive Polish constitutions has revealed kinships in their ordering of the several branches of government, in accordance with their authors' aim of assuring the effective functioning of government while at the same time preserving the liberties of the citizens.

All the constitutions that have been discussed, with the exception of Kościuszko's and that of April, 1935, show a mechanism of checks and balances:

1. between two legislative chambers;
2. between the several branches of government;
3. and between the governed and their governors, whose respective interests do not always coincide.

In point of fact, the American Constitution that took shape from the several-month-long efforts of the Philadelphia

Convention in 1787 did not fully develop the third item; this was satisfactorily acquitted only with the appending of the Bill of Rights, i.e. of the first ten amendments.

II. The circumstances surrounding the framing of the constitutions

The delegates of the various states (except Rhode Island, which did not participate) assembled at Philadelphia supposedly "for the sole and express purpose of revising the Articles of Confederation and reporting to Congress and the several Legislatures such alterations and provisions therein as shall, when agreed to in Congress, and confirmed by the States, render the Federal Constitution adequate to the exigencies of Government, and preservation of the Union."[1]

Instead of merely amending the Articles of Confederation, the assembled delegates exceeded their authority by framing a completely new constitution. To keep the nature of their labors secret, they never called their meeting a "Constitutional" Convention; and in order to prevent the garrulous Franklin from giving them away, some member of the Convention was assigned to accompany him constantly during the deliberations. Madison was convinced to his dying day that but for these measures of strict secrecy, the Constitution would never have come about.[2]

This same conspiratorial element was present in the working out of at least three Polish constitutions. The Constitution of May 3, 1791 was written out at private meetings into which trusted persons were gradually admitted. Had it been discussed from first to last at open meetings of the Seym, it would never have seen the light of day. Even the manner of its ratification was not exactly above-board.

It was a similar case with Kościuszko's acts of law-making. They had been planned in secret by political emigres in Dresden and had simply been presented to the Polish people as binding laws which must be obeyed.

The same element of secrecy again characterizes the drafting of the Polish Constitution of April, 1935. The manner of its ratification differs from that of the American Constitution, in that while the latter's ratification by the requisite nine states was achieved legally after intensive propaganda, discussion and compromise, the Polish Constitution was enacted via the bypassing of the law. It is, of course, another matter that in Poland there was no room for compromise: only one side or the other could win the victory, and that victory would without fail have gone to the government's Seym opposition, thus spelling defeat for the constitutional proposal.

III. Early social kinships

The American Revolution was guided by intellectuals the decided majority of whom we would today call progressives: Benjamin Franklin, Patrick Henry, Samuel Adams, Thomas Jefferson, Thomas Paine.

In Poland the disastrous national uprisings had convinced men of education that national independence could never be won by the landed gentry alone, even if the latter were reinforced by the growing intelligentsia. The necessity of enlisting all the classes of society in the struggle had been grasped by Kościuszko, who had been confirmed in this view — acquired in France from Rousseau — by his participation in the American war of independence.

Other leaders too — Dembowski in the 1840's and Sierakowski in the 1860's — sought to enlist the masses. But it was only the turn of the twentieth century that brought a definite program aimed at educating the people to a national and social awareness that prepared them for participation in the struggle.

In America, while part of the population took up arms, a fairly large group of Loyalists (about a third of the population) favored continued subjection to London and even gave their services to the British Army. With the defeat of the British these Loyalists, who included many great landowners, lost their property.

Poland had her own loyalists: groups whose existence had suggested to the occupying powers during World War I the idea of forming a Council of Regency. Some of these loyalists, like the American patriot Hamilton, dreamed of a monarchy.

In America the imminence of armed conflict with British

forces prompted the Massachusetts colonists to organize a militia.³ In Poland, the Polish Socialist Party — particularly its revolutionary wing — during the opening years of the present century made ready for armed struggle. In 1908 the Związek Walki Czynnej (an officer cadre) was formed, pledged "in the event of national uprising [to] recognize the Polish Socialist Party as the leadership of any military actions."⁴

One of the few early leaders of the independence movement present at the Constitutional Convention in Philadelphia was Benjamin Franklin — an idealist who sought the welfare not only of his own country but of the entire world, and who had written: "God grant that not only the love of liberty but a thorough knowledge of the rights of man may pervade all the nations of the earth, so that a philosopher may set his foot anywhere on its surface and say, 'This is my country!' "⁵

Franklin's attitude won him friends all over the world; his position in Europe was appraised by John Adams as "more universal than that of Leibnitz or Newton, Frederic or Voltaire, and his character more beloved and esteemed than any or all of them."⁶ Franklin's special moral and intellectual position contributed to his success in diplomatic missions. His influence proved equally providential in national politics; he had a gift for mollifying passions and healing divisiveness. Perhaps the only time his talent failed him was when his own natural son joined the Loyalists.⁷

Poland too had leaders who saw their own independence movement as part of a broader world movement and dreamed of resolving mankind's problems in a world scale.

In America the competition for social influence began during the Revolution itself, in the midst of military operations, and influence over the masses gradually shifted away from men "like Thomas Jefferson who desired to accomplish democratic and humanitarian reforms along with independence"⁸ to others "like Adams and George Washington who wished to see independence achieved with comparatively little social change in America, but whose ranks were thinned by the loss of their former allies, now Loyalists."⁹

When it came to remaking the basic law of the land, the men called to the task were those who could be counted on to avoid unsettling, radical changes. Most prominent among these were Washington, Madison and Hamilton: the first two, large landowners; the third, the extremely gifted natural son of a wealthy Scottish merchant in the West Indies. This was truly an assemblage of "demi-gods;" but these were men of an entirely different stamp than the ones who had made the revolution.

The collapse of the Austro-Hungarian Empire in November, 1918, signaled to Polish nationalists and radicals an opportunity to take power, and the Lublin government arose. But with the appearance on the scene of an individual capable of gathering together and uniting the divergent political forces of the country, the Lublin radicals surrendered power to Piłsudski, who under existing chaotic circumstances did not want to introduce radical changes (although he did preserve the decrees of the Lublin government improving the conditions of the workers.) No doubt a significant factor was awareness of the revolution underway across the unsettled eastern border, and fear of further devastation and anarchy if Russia's revolution were to spill over into the territories under Piłsudski's jurisdiction.

Similar factors were at play in the early history of the United States, whose viability was threatened by rebellions such as that led by Captain Shays.

A curious detail to be found in both eighteenth-century America and twentieth-century Poland is the use of the form of address "Citizen." American leftists, including Jefferson, went through this phase, which formed in fact the sole expression of their Platonic sympathy for the French Revolution.[10] In Poland, "Citizen" was used in Piłsudski's Legions, even in reference to the Commandant himself; but it never penetrated into the ranks of the subsequently organized regular army. It was anachronistic, as was Stanisław Thugutt's circular by which, as minister of internal affairs in 1918-19, he attempted to replace "Pan" (Mister) with "Obywatel" (Citizen) and to strip the national eagle of its crown,[11] as under the early Piasts.

A second interesting phenomenon appears in both countries. The former officers of Washington's army associated themselves into a "Society of the Cincinnati" at the suggestion of the Prussian general "Baron" von Steuben. Intended by its charter to preserve the bonds among the former comrades in arms, the organization soon threatened to give rise to a new hereditary aristocracy and to a dictatorship based on the latter. In the words of an American historian, the Society "embarrassed George Washington, distressed John Adams, alarmed Thomas Jefferson, amused Benjamin Franklin, and in some way stirred the lives of nearly all leading Americans."[12] Washington had no desire to be dictator and would not accede to pressures that he make himself one; he regarded dictatorship as unnecessary and harmful, as it could split the country and plant the seeds of endless coups.

In Poland the Constitutional Seym of 1919-21 took much the same attitude toward Piłsudski and his former officers as was taken in America toward the "Cincinnati," especially following Piłsudski's Kiev expedition of that period. The Constitution of March, 1921, preserved this when, reckoning with the possibility that Piłsudski might become president, it forbade the president from exercising the powers of commander-in-chief in wartime [even as it in reality deprived the president of all other powers].

IV. The common sources of similar mechanisms

The appearance, in the constitutions of two geographically distant countries, of a strikingly similar system of checks and balances at three different levels cannot but suggest a kinship of descent. A first surmise might be that the Polish Constitution of 1791 and its successors took their cue from the U.S. Constitution ratified in 1789. After all, in politics no less than in industry, it is fairly common to steal ideas. It is known that one of the chief framers of the U.S. Constitution, James Madison, "wrote to his friend Thomas Jefferson in Paris and asked him to supply books on the constitutions and public laws of the several confederacies which have existed and he dedicated toilsome days and nights to mastering the history of the great experiments in federal governments from remote antiquity to his own time."[13] Thus "Jefferson became an encyclopedia of historical precedents for the federative system government, studying the Union of Utrecht, the governments of the Helvetic body, Denmark, Sweden and Poland . . ."[14]

The search for models to follow, and even for foreign

assistance in framing a political system, was no novelty. On the eve of the first partition of Poland, "the anti-[Bar] Confederation Poles ... sent a member of the Diet [Michal Wielhorski] to ask the socialist *philosophe* Mably and the *antiphilosophe* Rousseau to draw up tentative constitutions for a new Poland. Mably submitted his recommendations in 1770-71; Rousseau finished his *Constitution of Poland* in April, 1772 — two months after the first partition treaty had been signed."[12]

In the search for external influences on American constitutional thought, we find Jefferson writing on May 30, 1790, to his son-in-law "on the subject of his political education": "In Political Economy, I think Smith's Wealth of Nations the best book extant; in the science of government, Montesquieu's Spirit of Laws is generally recommended ... Locke's little book on government is perfect as far as it goes."[16]

As a result of certain kinships in the cultural evolution of the two nations, the Polish Constitution of May 3, 1791 adopted a division of powers according to this same Montesquieu whom Jefferson encouraged his son-in-law to peruse; and this Constitution was promulgated by Stanisław August Poniatowski, King "by the grace of God *and the will of the people* [our emphasis]," the same people from whose consent governments "derive their just power": clear echoes of Locke's social concept and of Rousseau's views as expressed in *The Social Contract.*

The Polish Constitution of 1791, drawn up in haste out of a well-founded fear of improved Russo-Prussian relations, provided only a general framework. More parts were to have come, and the fact that work on them was underway is indicated by a letter from Kołłątaj to Jan Śniadecki in which the former reported that

> "In preparation is a draft law that will not only bring pleasure to enlightened Europe but moreover genuine benefit to our country. Father Ossowski is writing an economic constitution ... The first chapter will contain a law instituting and guaranteeing all rights of property, the second a law securing protection and honor to all manners of labor ..."

The projected law was based on the teachings of

> Adam Smith ... Still a third basic law was planned: to the political Constitution of May 3d and the economic constitution was to be added a "moral constitution," no doubt a Polish analog of the American and French declarations of the rights of man.[17]

There is not the slightest doubt that both Poland, in creating her Constitution of 1791, and America, in inaugurating hers in 1789, were being borne along on the same intellectual wave of the Enlightenment. Just how profoundly both countries in the second half of the eighteenth century were under the influence of the Enlightenment, is shown in the kinships between the two respective constitutions that have been pointed out. But is not the best proof of Enlightenment influence — particularly of Rousseau's — the very fact of the written constitutions themselves, whose ratification by representatives of the "people" (in the case of the U.S., by the legislatures of the several states) made them actual "social contracts"?

A further part of this same Enlightenment wave was the series of acts jointly constituting the Kościuszko Constitution. These were the work of the framers of the May 3d Constitution, who — no longer held back by the inertia of both chambers of the Seym — took several additional steps toward the realization of the ideal of human freedom.

Enlightenment influences continue apparent in the constitution of the Kingdom of Poland during the 1830-31 Uprising. Montesquieu is recognizably present, as are civil rights. Remodeled during the insurrection against the Russian Empire, in the midst of internal power struggles, it did not seek to realize any political ideal, and perhaps its closest kinship with the American Constitution resides in its elasticity — in its amendability, although in the U.S. the amendments could not have been introduced (as in Poland under that constitution) in the form of routine laws.

A distinct Enlightenment influence is still preserved in the Polish Constitution of March, 1921. This document was a reflection of constitutional concepts that had developed in nineteenth-century Europe and had reached Poland in their French redaction, whose prime concern was not so much in balancing the powers of the three branches of government as in preventing the chief executive from transforming himself into the head of state. Such a concern obviously favored constitutional guarantees of broad civil freedoms.

A heightened kinship with the U.S. Constitution was introduced by the Polish Constitution of April, 1935, in its formal break "with the mechanical, universal and absolute equality propagated by the Declaration of the Rights of Man ... of 1789." This statement is not quite the paradox it may seem to be. The "mechanically" construed equality was in the United States expressed not in the U.S. Constitution (as so many erroneously believe) but in the Declaration of Independence of 1776. The U.S. Constitution itself did not touch on the matter of equality and out of political necessity reconciled itself even to slavery, not to mention that it ignored the rights of Indians, thus in the eyes of conscientious critics earning the epithet of "a covenant with death and an agreement with hell."[18] What it did do, however, was to create an executive authority well supplied with coercive powers; furthermore, the powers provided by the Constitution were subsequently expanded without major upheavals, in accordance with the view of a Polish theoretician that

> A written constitution is always an imprecise representation of the actual people and government. It contains hidden powers that with time emerge and require recognition. Besides the written law there exists an unwritten law that supplements and corrects the former. Since the first task of politics is to assist the recognition of developing laws, the duty of politics is to protect hitherto latent law. Hence politics cannot hang timorously onto the written word or allow itself to be thwarted by the written law. As an example we may mention the difference between English parliamentary acts and political practice....[19]

Poland lacked that elastic approach to her political problems; consequently a change of constitution was required. The Constitution of April, 1935, no longer declared, as had that of March, 1921, that "supreme authority in the Polish Republic resides with the people." Instead it contains the statement that "The Polish state is the common good of all citizens" (which in itself constitutes no title to power for "all citizens," just as ownership of common stock in a business confers no automatic directorial powers over the business). Right after that we find: "Resurrected through the labor and self-sacrificing struggle of its finest sons, it shall be passed down from generation to generation."

When to the above is added the fact of voting rights in senatorial elections being reserved to citizens of demonstrated personal merit (as established by a decoration), a picture emerges of the Polish Senate as essentially bearing a tremendous similarity to the early United States Senate, which was conceived as an elite body. Hamilton urged that senators be given life tenure. The U.S. Senate was to exist apart from the masses and without direct dependence on them; it was to "consist," according to John Dickinson, "of the most distinguished characters, distinguised for their rank in life and their weight of property, and bearing as strong a likeness to the British House of Lords as possible."[20]

Without efficient authorities equipped with strong power of compulsion, the United States would never have risen to the status of a great power. The Polish Constitution of April, 1935, sought to make Poland, if not a great power, at least one of the lesser ones.

The parliamentary reporter whose accounts were taken seriously because they presented only that which had a chance of passing the censor,[21] noted: "the leaders of the Nonpartisan Bloc assure us that high circles have given their consent for the new constitution to bear the name of Józef Piłsudski."[22] And properly so, for it was in fact his political testament — very likely not one that fulfilled all the dreams of his youth, but in his own view the only realistic testament ... All the more a tragic one.

V. The genealogy of the Enlightenment

Having traced the actual causes of the emancipation of the American people and the sources of their political concepts, it is impossible not to note the fundamental role of the Enlightenment — the same Enlightenment that had so decisive an impact on the history of the Polish constitutions.

In searching out the roots of the Enlightenment, one is struck by the revolutionary role that was played by Mikołaj Kopernik.

> The geocentric theory had fitted reasonably well a theology which supposed that all things had been created for the use of man. But now men felt tossed about on a minor planet whose history was reduced to a "mere local item in the news of the universe." What could "heaven" mean when "up" and "down" had lost all sense, when each would become the other in half a day? "No attack on Christianity," wrote Jerome Wolf to Tycho Brahe in 1575, "is more dangerous than the infinite size and depth of the heavens" — though Copernicus had not taught the infinity of the universe. When men stopped to ponder the implications of the new system they must have wondered at the assumption that the Creator of this immense and orderly cosmos had sent His Son to die on this middling planet. All the lovely poetry of Christianity seemed to "go up in smoke" (as Goethe was to put it) at the touch of the Polish clergymen. The heliocentric astronomy compelled men to reconceive God in less provincial, less anthropomorphic terms; it gave theology the strongest challenge in the history of religion. *Hence the Copernican revolution was far profounder than the Reformation* [our emphasis]; it made the differences between Catholic and Protestant dogmas seem trivial; it pointed beyond the Reformation to the Enlightenment, from Erasmus and Luther to Voltaire, and even beyond Voltaire to the pessimistic agnosticism of a nineteenth century that would add the Darwinian to the Copernican [revolution].[23]

Angus Armitage associates Kopernik with mankind's embarkation upon a new, scientific course,[24] and the late Bertrand Russell assigned to him the role of the first

LAVRENTII
Grimalii Goslicii
DE OPTIMO SENATORE
LIBRI DVO.

In quibus Magistratuum officia, Ciuium uita beata, Rerumpub. fœlicitas explicantur.

Opvs planè aureum, summorum Philosophorum & Legislatorum doctrina refertum, omnibus Respu. ritè administrare cupientibus, non modo utile, sed apprimè necessarium.

Accessit locuples rerum toto Opere memorabilium Index.

CVM PRIVILEGIO,
VENETIIS, Apud Iordanum Zilettum,
M D LXVIII.

The title page of *De Optimo Senatore* by Wawrzyniec Goslicki revolutionizer of science.[25] Historians of science will note the affinity between Kopernik's ideas and those of the ancient Greek astronomer Aristarchus. Russell suggests that Kopernik was acquainted with the ancient theories, but that his discovery of Aristarchus merely strengthened his own conviction concerning the heliocentric view. "Otherwise, the effect of [the Aristarchan] hypothesis on subsequent astronomy was practically nil."[26]

In any case, nothing can alter Kopernik's epochal role in leading men's minds onto a path of logical reasoning based on sound observation. It is no more important whether Aristarchus or Kopernik was the first to come forward with the idea than whether Kopernik or Gresham first authored the economic law "called 'Gresham's Law' after a later discoverer, Sir Thomas Gresham";[27] just as nothing is altered by the fact that certain ideas in Frycz-Modrzewski's *Commentariorum de republica emendata* [1551] "were later announced as their own by Beccaria, Filangieri and Bentham,"[28] or that the Spanish translator of Modrzewski's work, Justinianus, stated "that such a work has not been seen in Europe in a thousand years."[29] What *is* important is that this virtual hermit on the Baltic coast, born and educated on the banks of the Vistula, succeeded in breaking down the barriers of medieval superstition and creating — or adopting — a theory similar to (if not identical with) one held by an enlightened Greek in the third century before Christ.

It bears eloquent testimony to the cultural level that Poland had attained by the sixteenth century that within ten years of its publication Kopernik's theory was accepted by the Krakow Academy, while being long rejected by high official authorities elsewhere.[30]

During the Reformation, educated Poles joined and advanced the current of Reformation thought. Its Polish precursor at the turn of the sixteenth century had been Biernat of Lublin; Frycz-Modrzewski, Jan Łaski and Piotr Giezek had joined it, and the Second Reformation in Poland had seen the publications of dozens of polemicists. In a period of schism when western Christendom shrank from no means to break down or extirpate heresy, Poland was conspicuous by her humanitarianism.

During the same period a Catholic priest, Wawrzyniec Goślicki, well known for his tolerance and for his authorship of

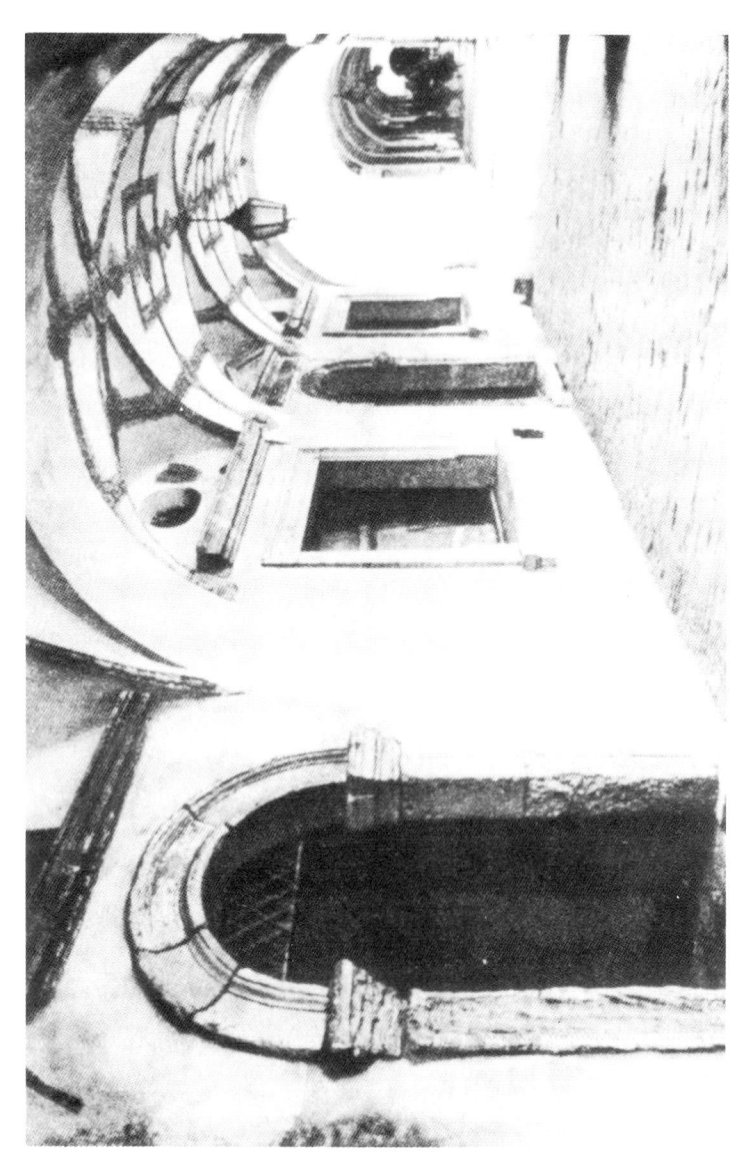

The arcades in Zamosc

De optimo senatore, returned from the West — from a Venice then famous for liquidating champions of the Reformation by placing them, weighted with stones, on a plank between two gondolas in the Adriatic and then separating the boats.[31] The Catholic Jan Zamoyski (1542-1605) also returned from Italy, to require in an Academy founded by himself, scientific truths instead of futile pseudo-philosophical arguments.[32]

The Polish version of western culture developed along two paths simultaneously. As Faustus Socinus (1539-1604) was discovering in Poland a center of the Reformed Church whose views were just about as well developed as his own; as the Polish Brethren's system of schools was developing with the Raków Academy (the "Sarmatian Athens") at its head; as the Raków press was issuing works that exerted an influence on west European thought — at the same time the Zamość Academy, without dwelling on articles of faith or knocking down dogmas, was teaching young men to think, and its press was producing works such as *Dialectica Ciceronis* by a lecturer at the Academy, Adam Burski (c. 1560-1611), the first Polish philosopher to urge the use of the inductive method and experiment in the quest for knowledge.

The existence of two centers of progressive thought, at Raków and at the town of Zamość founded by Jan Zamoyski, might have had a redemptive influence, through their fostering of tolerance and reason, on the intellectual development of Poland, and indirectly of the entire civilized world; Poland might have become a land of Lockes, Newtons, Humes and Voltaires. But instead there prevailed the interests of the Catholic Church, which was reluctant to lose its easternmost European bastion together with all the opportunities that it presented for influencing the East; and a secular interest in preserving the single church as a unifying element for an ethnically heterogeneous society. These considerations prompted the elimination of the Reformation from Poland; first to go were the Polish Brethren, the most advanced of the intellectual movements.

The destruction of the Socinian community in Poland does not indicate any particular ruthlessness characteristic of the Roman Catholic Church or of the influential classes in Poland. We find the same ruthlessness in the history of all the other countries that experienced the Reformation, which included virtually all of Europe; in England Catholic heads fell under Henry VIII, and Protestant heads under his daughter "Bloody" Mary. One can hardly wonder at the sudden demise of the tolerance once so typical of Poles, when one considers that Thomas More, who had advocated full religious tolerance as part of his *Utopia*,[33] on finding himself in power changed his attitude beyond all recognition. "Sir Thomas More, the scourge of heretics, . . . mercilessly advocated their death . . . More had the same problem as the religious reformers who had been his victims: he had conscientious convictions that unshakeably motivated his conduct."[34]

Poland went to religious orthodoxy for much the same reasons as England did. "As long as England believed that its national security . . . depended upon the maintenance of a single religion by law established, as long as complete conformity was thought to be indispensable for the support of that religion . . . there could be no forbearance . . ."[35]

The same motive also guided the Spanish Inquisition. "The aim was to unify Spain,"[36] concludes an American cultural historian, adding: "For good or ill, Spain chose to remain medieval, while Europe, by the commercial, typographical, intellectual, and Protestant revolutions, rushed into modernity."[37] All this notwithstanding, in his view, "the universities suffered less in Catholic than in Protestant countries in this cataclysmic [sixteenth] century."[38]

Poland in the seventeenth century excluded herself for the next century and more from further participation in the development of western European thought. The writings of the Polish Brethren saved their thought for humanity and not only were not forgotten, but helped give rise to a liberal Socinian-Unitarian center in Britain, which in turn led to the founding of American Unitarianism. A second, no less important consequence was that Socinianism and Unitarianism in England contributed to the rise of Deism, which led to the Enlightenment.

Polish minds took no direct part in the creation of the European Enlightenment. The Enlightenment was brought to Poland, along with knowledge acquired abroad, most prominently by Staszic, by the brothers Śniadecki and above all by Kołłątaj. These men developed the ideas which they had brought back with them and invested them in the effort to make up the century and more of Poland's relapse into the intellectual middle ages. The culminating monument to their labors, particularly of the illuminati gathered about Kołłątaj, was the Constitution of May 3, 1791.

Americans had not contributed to the flowering of the Enlightenment either. The Enlightenment was imported into America from Europe too, and it was this Enlightenment that gave America the foundations for her emancipation and the philosophical groundwork for her Declaration of Independence and Constitution.

Herein resides the key to the kinship between the American and Polish constitutions: they all derive from a common conceptual heritage; and a crucial part of that heritage is Socinianism, a "movement of the human mind."[39]

Polish Arianism-Socinianism-Unitarianism — a numerically insignificant movement — has been associated over a period of four centuries with the names of bold thinkers and scientific discoverers. It is not pure accident that the earliest roots of the movement lead straight back to the Antitrinitarian writings of Servetus, the sixteenth-century discoverer of the pulmonary circulation of the blood;[40] and that through Jan Crell, Samuel Przypkowski and Faustus Socinus — the first advocates before Locke of religious tolerance and of separation of church and state — the movement leads forward to Grotius, Spinoza, Locke, Milton, Newton, Voltaire, Helvetius, Holbach, Priestley and Hazlitt. "Rousseau was ... a Unitarian," says Durant,[41] as were the economist Ricardo, and Franklin, Jefferson, Madison, the presidents Adams, and the poet-philosopher Emerson.

Socinianism-Unitarianism, as a current of thought, has always been characterized — Mickiewicz notwithstanding — by an absence of dogma, and hence by a state of constant conceptual unrest whose intensity rose in contacts with differing concepts. Where that contact ceased — in Transylvania, for example — there followed an ossification of thought. In Transylvania the living process of thought was replaced by virtual dogma; liturgy and hierarchy took root, and the Unitarian Church in Transylvania became merely one more orthodox church. The

Jean Jacques Rousseau, 1712 - 1778

Thomas Jefferson, 1743 - 1826

Jan Zamoyski, 1542-1605

Transylvanian church had not been that way during the period when it had carried on its lively dispute with its Polish brethren, preserved in the jointly published anthology *De falsa et vera Unius Dei cognitione* (1567).

But it was not only Polish *Reformation* thought that shared in generating the Enlightenment. A major contribution to the eighteenth-century Enlightenment was made by Wawrzyniec Goślicki, royal secretary and in advanced age the Catholic Bishop of Poznań, in his political treatise *De optimo senatore,* published in Venice in 1568, and first translated into English (although not published) in 1585. J.A. Teslar, in an article on this treatise's relations to English literature, states the view that Goślicki's treatise was

> a sequel to [royal chancellor and hetman] Jan Zamoyski's book *De Senatu Romano* (1563) printed five years earlier. It their subject matter the two works are complementary: Zamoyski's is a learned dissertation on the Roman Senate, with textual allusions to the Polish Senate; Goślicki's presents, against an analysis of the political systems of states ancient and modern — chiefly of the Polish Republic — the role of the Senate in mediating between the king and the parliament— . . . in defending equally against "absolutum dominium," or tyranny by one individual, and against tyranny by parliament, or by the many.[42]

Fillipowicz's studies of Goślicki resulted in the Polish ambassador's lecture at the annual meeting of the American Society of International Law in April, 1932. Subsquently considerable attention has been devoted to Goślicki's treatise by Coleman and Haight. Coleman shows Goślicki to have been

> an ancestor in demonstrably direct line of the Fathers of the American Declaration of Independence and the American Constitution. Back of Thomas Jefferson and Tom Paine, the Fathers familiar to everyone, were such figures as Blackstone and Helvetius, Montesquieu and Jean-Jacques Rousseau, John Locke

THE
Accomplished Senator.

In TWO BOOKS.

Written Originally in LATIN,

By LAURENCE GRIMALD GOZLISKI, *Senator* and *Chancellor* of POLAND, and *Bishop* of POSNA or POZEN.

Done into ENGLISH, from the Edition Printed at *VENICE*, in the Year 1568.

By MR. OLDISWORTH.

Omnis in Hoc Uno variis Discordia cessit Ordinibus. —— Claudian.

LONDON:
Printed for the AUTHOR, in the Year 1733.

The title page of The Accomplished Senator

and Algernon Sidney. Sidney . . . is perhaps the most important of all in this "family tree," for he was not only the archsmiter of Stuartian Divine Right-ology but the one who supplies a clue to "Fathers" more remote than himself.[43]

In his development of Filipowicz's thesis, Coleman points out that Goślicki's treatise was a source of inspiration to Bellarmine, author of the definition of democratic government. Bellarmine was in turn pounced upon, with bitter criticism and apotheosis of royal power as deriving "directly from God" (contrary to popular belief, not a medieval European concept), by Sir Robert Filmer, who was sharply rebutted by Sidney, who took up and popularized the views expressed by Goślicki in his treatise — the same views that had inspired Cardinal Bellarmine.[44]

Haight quotes as key passages from Goślicki:

> The King can do no public act of government without the advice and authority of the State . . . The King of Poland, in the administration of his Government, is obliged to make the law the sole guide and rule of his conduct. He cannot govern according to his own will and pleasure, nor make war or peace without *the advice and consent of the senate* [our emphasis] . . .[45]

Haight describes the oath of office tendered in pre-partition Poland as a precursor of such later oaths in America. The oath of office was intended, in Goślicki's words, as "a sure covering and defense for the public, against all attempts upon its laws, liberties and happiness;" Goślicki emphasized that the judges and officials bound by the oath were subordinate to the law, thereby underlining the rule of law in the Polish system. "Goślicki's 'reign of law,' under which 'both the rulers and the ruled have to obey the law,' is identical with the ideas of Frycz-Modrzewski and the American concept of 'government of law.' "[46]

Commenting further on Goślicki's views, Haight remarks that "Legal order is according to Goślicki a necessary element of every state, the other two being: a definite territory, and a population. In this approach, Goślicki was first, and preceded by nine years the ideas of Jean Bodin."[47]

Haight notes Goślicki's observation that "differences and contentions will often arise between king and people; whilst one party is pressing forward, and aiming at too much power, and the other is falling back into an excess of liberty."[48]

Goślicki sees an enormously important role for the senator, who, "in his proper post, and by the very nature of his office, is really a judge and arbiter between the quiet and peaceable, and the violent and unruly; between liberty and servitude, between king and people."[49]

Goślicki condemns the tendency in rulers to govern by force, against the will of their peoples. Rulers, to him, are given authority "not for their own, but for the people's sake."[50]

An idea of Goślicki's that impressed the English and is enshrined in basic American concepts is that "Sometimes a people, justly provoked and irritated by the tyranny and usurpations of their kings, take upon themselves the undoubted right of vindicating their own liberties; and by a well-formed conspiracy or by open arms, shake off the yoke, drive out their lords and masters, and take the government entirely into their own hands."[51]

It is difficult to resist the idea that Goślicki's treatise must have been familiar to John Locke, who combatted Sir Robert Filmer's apotheosis of absolute monarchy and wrote in his *Second Treatise* on civil government:

> Wherever law ends tyranny begins . . . And whosoever in authority exceeds the power given him by the law, and makes use of the force he has under his command to compass that upon the subject which the law allows not ceases in that to be a magistrate; and, acting without authority, may be opposed as any other man who by force invades the right of another.[52]

The history of the English translations of Goślicki's book, three of which were published in 1598, 1607 and 1733, attests the book's persistent interest to English-language readers; and if the book was, as Teslar shows incontrovertibly in his article "A

Polish Political Treatise in Shakespeare's Hands," familiar to a man of the theater, it could hardly have gone unnoticed by other educated men interested in political questions.

The translations of Goślicki's book were presumably known in America as well, as copies of all three English translations that were published are to be found in the possession of major American book collections.[53] Hence it seems likely that the founders of the United States drew on the ideas of a Pole who had lived over two centuries earlier.

At times a progressive idea will shrink back in apparent fear or retreat before a counter-idea, only to return again later, perhaps transformed. Thus Locke's famous concept of the newborn mind being without ideas, referred to by him as *tabula rasa*,[54] had already appeared in the works of Burski, who himself had picked it up from Cicero.[55] That Locke borrowed from Goślicki and the Socinians is beyond dispute, just as it is known that Jefferson borrowed from Locke.

> Adams observed [that] Jefferson said nothing new in composing the [Declaration of Independence]. He planned the document in two main parts. In the first he restated the familiar compact theory of John Locke who had held that governments were formed to protect the rights of life, liberty and property, but Jefferson gave the theory a more humane twist by referring instead to the rights of "life, liberty and the pursuit of happiness."[56]

Rousseau had adopted Locke's doctrine of majority rule, translating it into his "collective will," just as Marx was later (following Ricardo's lead) to take possession of Locke's observation that value derives from invested labor, and use it in his own theory.[57]

The United States Constitution contains Goślicki's "advice and consent of the Senate;" his oath of office; his concept (identical with Frycz-Modrzewski's) of a "reign of law"; and Goślicki's view that "the Senator . . . is . . . a judge and arbiter . . . between liberty and servitude, between king and people." The United States Constitution realizes Goślicki's view of government as "made not for [its own], but for the people's sake."

Together with the ideas of the Catholic Goslicki, principles of the Polish Brethren found their way into the American Constitution: the separation of church and state, freedom of conscience, and the imposition of no cruel or excessive punishments.

When circumstances permitted and required it, the ideas of Goslicki and the Polish Brethren returned to Poland Documentation for their repatriation is provided by the successive constitutions of Poland.

NOTES

Foreword

1. Marian Kukiel, *Dzieje Polski porozbiorowe : 1795-1921*, 39.
2. "United States," *Funk & Wagnalls Standard Encyclopedia, 1931, XXIV.*
3. John F. Kennedy, *A Nation of Immigrants*, 36.
4. Edward Channing, *A History of the United States*, I, 170.
5. John Lutz, a private letter dated January 8, 1969.
6. "Amerykańsko-polski Komitet Pomocy," *Wielka Encyklopedia Powszechna PWN*, I.
7. Merian C. Cooper, (Brig. Gen. USAF, Ret., formerly Lieut. Col., Polish Air Force, Commander Kosciuszko Squadron [7th], "How I Happened To Go To Poland," *Poland*, (an occasional publication, March 1972), Mark J. Mażyński, ed., 15-6.

Chapter I

1. Samuel Eliot Morison, *The Oxford History of the American People*, 7.
2. Rachel Louise Carson, *The Sea Around Us*, 106.
3. Peter Farb, *Man's Rise to Civilization*, 237-8.
4. Henrietta Merz, *Pale Ink*, 158.
5. Herman Palsson and Magnus Magnusson, *The Vinland Sagas: The Norse Discovery of America.* Also, Helge Marcus Ingstad, *Land under the Pole Star: A Voyage to the Norse Settlements and the Saga of the People that Vanished*, 116-71.
6. Morison, *The European Discovery of America: the Northern Voyages: 500-1000*, 58-60.
7. *Ibid.*, 90.
8. "Jan z Kolna," *Wielka Encyklopedia Powszechna*, V.
9. Morison, *European Discovery*, 36.
10. T. Harry Williams, Richard N. Current and Frank Freidel, *A History of the United States [to 1877]*, 12.
11. "United States," *Funk & Wagnalls*, XXIV.
12. Williams *et al.*, 101.
13. *Ibid.*, 60.
14. John C. Miller, *Origins of the American Revolution*, 4.
15. James A. Williamson, *The Evolution of England: a Commentary on the Facts*, 257.
16. Morison, *Oxford History*, 134.
17. Williams *et al.*, 66.
18. Ray Allen Billington, *American History before 1877*, 25-6.
19. *Ibid.*, 33-7.
20. *Ibid.*, 53-61.
21. *Ibid.*, 70-1.
22. Catherine Drinker Bowen, *Miracle at Philadelphia: the Story of the Constitutional Convention, May to September, 1787*, 5.

23. Williams *et al.*, 181.
24. *Ibid.*
25. Allan Nevins and Henry Steele Commager, *America: The Story of a Free People*, 101.
26. *Ibid., 101-2.*
27. Bowen, 20.
28. Williams *et al.*, 179.
29. Bowen, 20.
30. *Ibid.*
31. *Ibid.*, 14.
32. *Ibid.*, 4.
33. William H. Young, *Ogg and Ray's Introduction to American Government*, 22-3.
34. Joyce Appleby, "The Jefferson-Adams Rupture and the First French Translation of John Adams' 'Defence,' " *The American Historical Review*, LXXIII, No. 4 (April, 1968), 1091.
35. Young, 39-42.
36. Emmette S. Redford *et al.*, *Politics and Government in the United States*, 94.
37. *Ibid.*, 352.
38. Young, 347-8.
39. Redford *et al.*, 94.
40. Young, 30.
41. Redford *et al.*, 95.
42. Young, 356.
43. *Ibid.*, 602-4.
44. Marian D. Irish and James W. Prothro, *The Politics of American Democracy*, 371.
45. Young, 346.
46. Sam Houston Johnson, "My Brother Lyndon," *Look*, 33, No. 25., (December 16, 1969), 54.
47. Young, 43.

Chapter II

1. Paweł Zaremba, *Historia Polski*, I, 20.
2. W.G. Sumner and A.G. Keller, *The Science of Society*, I, 704; Will Durant, *The Story of Civilization*, Vol. I: *Our Oriental Heritage*, 23-4.
3. A.R. Cowan, *A Guide to World History*, 18.
4. Herbert Spencer, *The Principles of Sociology*, III, 316.
5. Stanisław Kutrzeba, *Historia ustroju Polski:Korona*, 39.
6. Wiehczysław Wagner, "Laurentius Grimaldus Goslicius and His Age: Modern Constitutional Law Ideas in the XVI Century," *The Polish Review*, III, No. 1-2 (Winter-Spring, 1958), 37-42.
7. *Ibid.*
8. Helmut von Moltke, *Vermischte Schriften*, II, 121., cited by Wacław Lednicki, *Life and Culture of Poland*, 5.

9. Marceli Handelsman, ed., *Konstytucje polskie: 1791-1921*, 7.
10. Adam Pragier, "Z historii wolnomularstwa polskiego," *Na antenie*, VI, (April 21, 1968), VII.
11. "Revolution in Poland," *The Newport Mercury*, (July 30, 1791), quoted in *The Polish Review*, III, No. 17. (May 3rd, 1943), 4-6.
12. Eugene Kusielewicz, "Niemcewicz in America," *The Polish Review*, V., No. 1 (Winter 1960), 70.
13. *The Newport Mercury*, quoted in *The Polish Review*, III, No. 17 (May 3rd, 1943), 4-6.
14. Handelsman, 12-3.
15. *Ibid.*, 56-8.
16. *Kentucky Gazette*, September 1, 1791, quoted in *The Polish Review*, III, No. 17 (May 3rd, 1943), 5.
17. William John Rose, *Poland Old and New*, 77.
18. Will and Ariel Durant, Vol. X: *Rousseau and Revolution*, 487-8.
19. Robert von Mohl, *Enzyklopaedie der Staatswissenschaften*, 157, cited by Franciszek Kasparek, *Prawo polityczne ogólne z uwzględnieniem Austryjackiego: razem ze wstępną nauką o państwie*, II, 144.
20. Leonard R. Sayles and George Strauss, *Human Behavior in Organizations*, 296.
21. Andrzej Mycielski, *Polskie prawo polityczne*, 40-1.
22. Charles Louis de Secondat Montesquieu, *The Spirit of the Laws*, Book II, 60, cited by Redford *et al.*, 67-8.
23. U.S. *Const.*, art. I, sec. 1.
24. Polish *Constitution* (1791), art. VI.
25. U.S. *Const.*, art. I, sec. 2.
26. Pol. *Const.* (1791), art. VII; Regional Seyms Act (1791).
27. U.S. *Const.*, art. I, sec. 7.
28. Pol. *Const.* (1791), art. VI.
29. U.S. *Const.*, art. I, sec. 3.
30. Pol. *Const.* (1791), art. VII.
31. U.S. *Const.*, art. I, sec. 3.
32. Pol. *Const.* (1791), art. VI.
33. U.S. *Const.*, art. I, sec. 3
34. Pol. *Const.* (1791), art. VI.
35. *Ibid.*
36. John F. Kennedy, *Profiles in Courage*, 21-2.
37. U.S. *Const.*, art. I, sec. 8.
38. Pol. *Const.* (1791), art. VII.
39. U.S. *Const.*, art. I, sec. 3.
40. Pol. *Const.* (1791), art. VII.
41. U.S. *Const.*, art. I, sec. 2.
42. *Ibid.*, sec. 3.
43. *Ibid.*
44. Pol. *Const.* (1791), art. VII.
45. U.S. *Const.*, art. II, sec. 1.
46. Pol. *Const.* (1791), art. VII.

47. U.S. *Const.*, art. II, sec. 2.
48. Pol. *Const.* (1791), art. VII.
49. U.S. *Const.*, art. II, sec. 3.
50. Pol. *Const.* (1791), art. VII.
51. U.S. *Const.*, art. II, sec. 3.
52. Pol. *Const.* (1791), art. VII.
53. U.S. *Const.*, art. II, sec. 3.
54. Pol. *Const.* (1791), art. VII.
55. U.S. *Const.*, art. II, sec. 2.
56. Pol. *Const.* (1791), art. VII.
57. *Ibid.*, art. XI.
58. U.S. *Const.*, art. II, sec. 2.
59. Pol. *Const.* (1791), art. VII.
60. U.S. *Const.*, art. II, sec. 3.
61. *Ibid.*, sec. 1.
62. Pol. *Const.* (1791), art. VII.
63. U.S. *Const.*, art. II, sec. 2.
64. Pol. *Const.* (1791), art. VII.
65. U.S. *Const.*, art. I, sec. 8.
66. Pol. *Const.* (1791), art. VII.
67. *Ibid.*, art. XI.
68. U.S. *Const.*, art. II, sec. 1.
69. Pol. *Const.* (1791), art. VII.
70. U.S. *Const.*, art. II, sec. 2.
71. Pol. *Const.* (1791), art. VIII.
72. *Ibid.*, art. VI.
73. *Ibid.*, art. VII.
74. U.S. *Const.*, preamble.
75. Pol. *Const.* (1791), art. V.
76. *Ibid.*, preamble.
77. U.S. *Const.*, preamble.
78. Pol. *Const.* (1791), preamble.
79. U.S. *Const.*, art. I, sec. 9.
80. Pol. *Const.* (1791), art. II.
81. *Free Royal Cities Act* (1791), art. II., pars. 4 and 8.
82. U.S. *Const.*, art. I, sec. 9.
83. Pol. *Const.* (1791), art. II.
84. U.S. *Const.*, art. I, sec. 9.
85. Pol. *Const.* (1791), art. IV.
86. Williams *et al.*, 148; Redford *et al.*, 605.
87. Arnold Toynbee, "Peace, Power, Race in America," *Look,* 33, No. 6 (March 18, 1969), 26.
88. William Loren Katz, "Let's Set Black History Straight," *Reader's Digest,* (July 1969), 60.
89. Henry Wilder Foote, *The Religion of Thomas Jefferson,* 16.
90. U.S. *Const.*, art. I, sec. 9.
91. *Free Royal Cities Act* (1791), art. II, par. 1.

92. Pol. *Const.* (1791), art. II.
93. U.S. *Const.*, amend. VIII.
94. *Free Royal Cities Act* (1791), art. II, par. 1.
95. U.S. *Const.*, amend. I.
96. Pol. *Const.* (1791), art. I.
97. *Free Royal Cities Act* (1791), art. I, par. 10.
98. U.S. *Const.*, art. V.
99. Pol. *Const.* (1791), art. VI.

Chapter III

1. Kutrzeba, 396-7.
2. Kasparek, *Prawo polityczne ogólne*, II, 289.
3. Kutrzeba, 396.
4. Handelsman, 12.
5. Kutrzeba, 397.
6. Will and Ariel Durant, Vol. X: *Rousseau and Revolution*, 491.
7. Act of July, 1794.
8. Kukiel, *Dzieje*, 24.
9. R.F. Leslie, *The Polish Question: Poland's Place in Modern History*, 15.
10. Adam Próchnik, *Kim był Tadeusz Kościuszko*, 7, quoted in Marian M. Drozdowski, *Rewolucja Amerykańska w polskiej myśli historycznej*, 148.
11. Jan Górski, "Kościuszko Tradition," *Polish Perspectives*, XI, No. 2., 20.
12. Henryk Mościcki, in *Dzwon wolności 1776-1926 - W rocznicę narodzin Stanów Zjednoczonych Ameryki*, [Collective work], 35, quoted in Drozdowski, *Rewolucja Amerykańska w polskiej myśli historycznej*, 151.
13. Jan Górski, "Kościuszko Tradition", 20-2.
14. Kukiel, *Dzieje*, 27.
15. Marian Kukiel, "Wojna o Kościuszkę," *Na antenie*, VI, No. 61 [April 14-21, 1958], p.V.
16. Jerzy Szacki, "Mochnacki: Rewolucja i tradycja," *Myśli i ludzie: Filozofia polska*, Vol. II, *Filozofia nowożytna i współczesna*, Dr. Bronisław Baczko, ed., 207-8.
17. "150 lat niepodległości amerykańskiej," Editorial. *Czas*, No. 150 [5 July 1926], cited by Drozdowski, *Rewolucja Amerykańska w polskiej myśli historycznej*, 157.
18. Redford *et al.*, 91.

Chapter IV

1. Kukiel, *Dzieje*, 33.
2. J. Christopher Herold, *The Mind of Napoleon: a Selection from his Written and Spoken Words Edited and Translated by J. Christopher Herold*, 184.
3. Handelsman, 13.
4. Szymon Askenzy, *Rosja - Polska*, 66-7.

5. Michał Rostworowski, *Diariusz sejmu z 1830-31 r.*, 125.
6. Government Act of January 29, 1831, art. 4.
7. Oath Act of February 8, 1831, art. 2.
8. Government Act of August 17, 1831., art. 1-2.
9. Oath Act of February 8, 1831, art. 1.
10. National Colors Act of February 7, 1831, art. 1.
11. Powers of the Supreme Commander Act of January 24, 1831, art. 1.
12. Representation for Lithuania and Volhynia Act of May 11-19, 1831, preamble.
13. Handelsman, 124-34.
14. Legislative Procedures Act of January 22, 1831, art. 1.
15. Government Act of August 17, 1831, art. 5.
16. Legislative Procedures Act of January 22, 1831, art. 2.
17. *Ibid.*, art. 3.
18. Pol. *Const.* (1815), art. 151.
19. Government Act of January 29, 1831, art. 11.
20. Legislative Procedures Act of January 22, 1831, art. 4.
21. Government Act of January 29, 1831, art. 9.
22. Government Act of August 17, 1831, art. 2.
23. Government Act of August 17, 1831, art. 1.
24. Pol. *Const.* (1815), art. 151.
25. *Ibid.*, art. 11.
26. Representation for Lithuania and Volhynia Act of May 11-9, 1831, art. 4.
27. U.S. *Const.*, art. I, sec. 9.
28. Pol. *Const.* (1815), art. 18.
29. *Ibid.*, art. 16.
30. U.S. *Const.*, amend. I.
31. *Ibid.*, VIII.
32. Pol. *Const.* (1815), art. 22.
33. U.S. *Const.*, amend. VI.
34. Pol. *Const.* (1815), art. 21.
35. U.S. *Const.*, amend. VI.
36. Pol. *Const.* (1815), art. 20.
37. U.S. *Const.*, amend. V.
38. Pol. *Const.* (1815), art. 26.
39. U.S. *Const.*, amend. V.
40. Pol. *Const.* (1815), art. 23.
41. U.S. *Const.*, amend. XIV.
42. *Ibid.*, art. I, sec. 2.
43. Pol. *Const.* (1815), art. 33.
44. U.S. *Const.*, art. II, sec. 1.
44. *Ibid.*, art. I, sec. 9.
46. Pol. *Const.* (1815), art. 24.
47. U.S. *Const.*, art. III, sec. 3.
48. Pol. *Const.* (1815), art. 159.
49. U.S. *Const.*, art. VI.
50. Pol. *Const.* (1815), art. 158.

51. Oath Act of February 8, 1831, art. 2.
52. U.S. *Const.*, preamble.
53. Government Act of August 17, 1831, art. 2.

Chapter V

1. Barbara Tuchman, *The Guns of August*, 361-2.
2. Kukiel, *Dzieje*, 530.
3. T.N. Page, "Report by T.N. Page, U.S. Ambassador to Italy, to the Secretary of State," *U.S.F.R.: 1917*, Supplement 1., (January 21, 1917), 22.
4. James W. Gerard, *My Four Years in Germany*, 130.
5. James B. Scott, *Official Statements of War Aims and Peace Proposals*, 258.
6. "Manifest of the Provisional People's Government of the Polish Republic" (November 7, 1918), quoted in Manfred Kridl, Władysław Malinowski and Józef Wittlin, eds., *For Your Freedom and Ours*, 220-1.
7. Józef Piłsudski, *Pisma wybrane*, 195.
8. Kukiel, *Dzieje*, 547.
9. Decree Concerning the Supreme Representative Authorities of the Polish Republic, of November 22, 1918, quoted in Handelsman, 143-4.
10. Pol. *Const.* (1921), art. 1.
11. *Ibid.*, art. 2.
12. *Ibid.*, chpt. V.
13. *Ibid.*, art. 2.
14. *Ibid.*, art. 10.
15. *Ibid.*, art. 3.
16. *Ibid.*, art. 43.
17. *Ibid.*, art. 51.
18. *Ibid.*
19. *Ibid.*, art. 59.
20. *Ibid.*, art. 64.
21. *Ibid.*, art. 75.
22. *Ibid.*, art. 84.
23. *Ibid.*, art. 85.
24. *Ibid.*, art. 77.
25. *Ibid.*, art. 66.
26. *Ibid.*, art. 73.
27. U.S. *Const.*, art. VI.
28. Pol. *Const.* (1921), art. 38.
29. U.S. *Const.*, art. I-III.
30. Pol. *Const.* (1921), art. 2.
31. Kennedy, *Profiles*, 21-4.
32. *Ibid.*, 22.
33. U.S. *Const.*, amend. XVII.
34. Pol. *Const.* (1921), art. 36.
35. Kennedy, *Profiles*, 24.
36. U.S. *Const.*, art. I, sec. 5.

37. Pol. *Const.* (1921), art. 19.
38. U.S. *Const.*, art. I, sec. 5.
39. Pol. *Const.* (1921), art. 29.
40. U.S. *Const.*, art. I, sec. 6.
41. Pol. *Const.* (1921), art. 21.
42. U.S. *Const.*, art. I, sec. 6.
43. Pol. *Const.* (1921), art. 24.
44. U.S. *Const.*, art. I, sec. 6.
45. Pol. *Const.* (1921), art. 17.
46. U.S. *Const.*, art. I, sec. 7.
47. Pol. *Const.* (1921), art. 35.
48. U.S. *Const.*, art. I, sec. 2.
49. Pol. *Const.* (1921), art. 11.
50. U.S. *Const.*, art. I, sec. 2.
51. Pol. *Const.* (1921), art. 13.
52. U.S. *Const.*, art. I, sec. 2.
53. Pol. *Const.* (1921), art. 13.
54. U.S. *Const.*, amend. XIX.
55. Pol. *Const.* (1921), art. 13.
56. U.S. *Const.*, art. II, sec. 3.
57. *Ibid.*, art. I, sec. 7.
58. Pol. *Const.* (1921), art. 10.
59. U.S. *Const.*, art. I, sec. 2.
60. Pol. *Const.* (1921), art. 51.
61. U.S. *Const.*, art. I, sec. 2
62. Pol. *Const.* (1921), art. 28.
63. U.S. *Const.*, art. II, sec. 1.
64. Pol. *Const.* (1921), art. 43.
65. U.S. *Const.*, amend. XII.
66. Pol. *Const.* (1921), art. 39.
67. U.S. *Const.*, art. II, sec. 1.
68. Pol. *Const.* (1921), art. 54.
69. U.S. *Const.*, art. II, sec. 2.
70. Pol. *Const.* (1921), arts. 45 and 58.
71. U.S. *Const.*, art. II, sec. 2.
72. Pol. *Const.* (1921), art. 45.
73. U.S. *Const.*, art. II, sec. 2.
74. Pol. *Const.* (1921), art. 46.
75. U.S. *Const.*, art. II, sec. 3.
76. Pol. *Const.* (1921), art. 48.
77. U.S. *Const.*, art. II, sec. 2.
78. Pol. *Const.* (1921), art. 48.
79. Young, 593.
80. U.S. *Const.*, art. II, sec. 2.
81. Pol. *Const.* (1921), art. 49.
82. *Ibid.*, arts. 49 and 50.
83. U.S. *Const.*, art. II, sec. 3.

84. Pol. *Const.* (1921), art. 25.
85. U.S. *Const.*, art. II, sec. 3.
86. Pol. *Const.* (1921), art. 25.
87. *Ibid.*, art. 44.
88. U.S. *Const.*, art. II, sec. 2.
89. Pol. *Const.* (1921), art. 47.
90. U.S. *Const.*, art. II, sec. 1.
91. Pol. *Const.* (1921), art. 52.
92. U.S. *Const.*, art. III, sec. 2.
93. Pol. *Const.* (1921), art. 83.
94. U.S. *Const.*, art. III, sec. 1.
95. Pol. *Const.* (1921), art. 78.
96. U.S. *Const.*, art. II, sec. 2.
97. Pol. *Const.* (1921), art. 76.
98. U.S. *Const.*, art. I, sec. 9.
99. Pol. *Const.* (1921), art. 96.
100. U.S. *Const.*, amend. I.
101. Pol. *Const.* (1921), art. 104.
102. U.S. *Const.*, amend. I.
103. Pol. *Const.* (1921), arts. 105 and 108.
104. U.S. *Const.*, amend. I.
105. Pol. *Const.* (1921), art. 107.
106. U.S. *Const.*, amend. XIII.
107. Pol. *Const.* (1921), art. 101.
108. *Ibid.*, art. 111.
109. U.S. *Const.*, amend. I.
110. Pol. *Const.* (1921), art. 114.
111. *Ibid.*, art. 116.
112. U.S. *Const.*, art. I, sec. 9.
113. Pol. *Const.* (1921), art. 97.
114. U.S. *Const.*, amend. IV.
115. Pol. *Const.* (1921), art. 100.
116. U.S. *Const.*, amend. V.
117. Pol. *Const.* (1921), art. 99.
118. U.S. *Const.*, amend. VI.
119. Pol. *Const.* (1921), art. 98.
120. U.S. *Const.*, amend. V.
121. Pol. *Const.* (1921), art. 83.
122. U.S. *Const.*, amend. VIII.
123. Pol. *Const.* (1921), art. 98.
124. U.S. *Const.*, art. I, sec. 9.
125. Young, 82.
126. Pol. *Const.* (1921), art. 124.
127. U.S. *Const.*, art. I, sec. 8.
128. Pol. *Const.* (1921), art. 123.
129. Piłsudski, 456.

Chapter VI

1. Robert L. Heilbroner, *The Worldly Philosophers: the Lives, Times and Ideas of the Great Economic Thinkers*, 129.
2. January Grzędziński, *Maj 1926*, 89, 101
3. Piłsudski, 417.
4. Pol. *Const.* (1921), art. 26. (amend. in August, 1926).
5. *Ibid.*, art. 44. (amend. in August, 1926).
6. Bernard Singer, *Od Witosa do Sławka*, 187.
7. *Ibid.*, 158.
8. *Ibid.*, 145.
9. *Ibid.*, 214.
10. *Ibid.*, 144.
11. Kazimierz Sosnkowski, *O Józefie Piłsudskim*, 63.
12. Singer, 188-9.
13. Stanisław Stroński, *The Two Polish Constitutions of 1921 and 1935*, 4-5.
14. Stanisław Car, preface to *Constitution of the Republic of Poland (April 23rd 1935)*, 9.
15. *Ibid.*, 10.
16. Pol. *Const.* (1935), art. 7.
17. Car, 10.
18. *Ibid.*
19. *Ibid.*, 8.
20. U.S. *Const.*, art. VI.
21. Pol. *Const.* (1935), art. 49, par. 2.
22. Circular of the President of the Council of Ministers, July 15, 1936.
23. U.S. *Const.*, art. I, sec. 5.
24. Pol. *Const.* (1935), art. 41.
25. U.S. *Const.*, art. VI.
26. Pol. *Const.* (1935), art. 39, pars. 1 and 2.
27. U.S. *Const.*, art. I, sec. 6.
28. Pol. *Const.* (1935), art. 40.
29. U.S. *Const.*, art. I, sec. 6.
30. Pol. *Const.* (1935), art. 41.
31. U.S. *Const.*, art. I, sec. 5.
32. Pol. *Const.* (1935), art. 38, par. 1.
33. U.S. *Const.*, art. I, sec. 5.
34. Pol. *Const.* (1935), art. 38, par. 4.
35. U.S. *Const.*, art. I, sec. 2.
36. Voting Regulations for the Seym (1935).
37. U.S. *Const.*, art. I, sec. 2.
38. Voting Regulations for the Seym (1935).
39. U.S. *Const.*, amend. XIX.
40. Voting Regulations for the Seym (1935).
41. U.S. *Const.*, art. II, sec. 3.
42. *Ibid.*, art, I, sec. 7.
43. Pol. *Const.* (1935), art. 50, par. 1.

44. U.S. *Const.*, art. I, sec. 2.
45. Pol. *Const.* (1935), art. 34, par. 1.
46. U.S. *Const.*, art. I, sec. 7.
47. Pol. *Const.* (1935), art. 53, par. 2.
48. U.S. *Const.*, art. I, sec. 7.
49. Pol. *Const.* (1935), art. 46, par. 2.b.
50. U.S. *Const.*, art. II, sec. 2.
51. Pol. *Const.* (1935), art. 46, par. 2.a.
52. U.S. *Const.*, amend. XVII.
53. Pol. *Const.* (1935), art. 47, par. 1.
54. Voting Regulations for the Senate (1935).
55. U.S. *Const.*, art. II, sec. 1. and amend. XII.
56. Pol. *Const.* (1935), arts. 16-8, and Election Regulations for the Presidency (1935).
57. U.S. *Const.*, art. II, sec. 1.
58. Pol. *Const.* (1935), art. 19.
59. U.S. *Const.*, art. II, sec. 1.
60. Pol. *Const.* (1935), art. 19.
61. Young, 29-30.
62. **U.S. *Const.*, art. II, sec. 2.**
63. Pol. *Const.* (1935), arts. 12-3.
64. Car, 9.
65. Myers v. United States, 272 U.S. 52 (1926).
66. Pol. *Const.* (1935), art. 13, par. 2.c.
67. U.S. *Const.*, art. II, sec. 2.
68. Pol. *Const.* (1935), art. 65, par. 1.
69. U.S. *Const.*, art. II, sec. 2.
70. Pol. *Const.* (1935), art. 12.d.
71. U.S. *Const.*, art. II, sec. 3.
72. Pol. *Const.* (1935), art. 12.e.
73. U.S. *Const.*, art. II, sec. 2.
74. Pol. *Const.* (1935), art. 12.e.
75. U.S. *Const.*, art. II, sec. 2.
76. Young, 602-5
77. *Ibid.*
78. Pol. *Const.* (1935), arts. 12.g. and 52.
79. U.S. *Const.*, art. II, sec. 3.
80. Pol. *Const.* (1935), art. 12.b,c.
81. U.S. *Const.*, art. I, sec. 7.
82. Pol. *Const.* (1935), art. 54, par. 1.
83. *Ibid.*, pars. 2-3.
84. *Ibid.*, arts. 55-7.
85. *Ibid.*, art. 56.
86. *Ibid.*, art. 79.
87. *Ibid.*, art. 14.
88. U.S. *Const.*, art. II, sec. 2.
89. Pol. *Const.* (1935), art. 13.j.

90. U.S. *Const.*, art. I, sec. 3.
91. Pol. *Const.* (1935), art. 23.
92. Young, 356.
93. *Ibid.*, 357.
94. *Ibid.*, 356.
95. *Ibid.*
96. Pol. *Const.* (1935), art. 25, par. 1.
97. *Ibid.*, par. 4.
98. *Ibid.*, par. 5.
99. Redford *et al.*, 298.
100. U.S. *Const.*, art. II, sec. 3.; Redford *et al.*, 298.
101. Pol. *Const.* (1935), art. 45.
102. U.S. *Const.*, art. III, sec. 2.
103. Pol. *Const.* (1935), art. 70.
104. U.S. *Const.*, art. III, sec. 1.
105. Pol. *Const.* (1935), art. 65.
106. *Ibid.*, art. 66.
107. U.S. *Const.*, amend. I.
108. Pol. *Const.* (1935), art. 5, pars. 2-3.
109. U.S. *Const.*, art. I, sec. 9.
110. Pol. *Const.* (1935), art. 68, par. 1.
111. U.S. *Const.*, art. I, sec. 9.
112. Pol. *Const.* (1935), art. 68, par. 4.
113. U.S. *Const.*, art. I, sec. 9.
114. Pol. *Const.* (1935), art. 68, par. 4
115. U.S. *Const.*, art. III, sec. 2.
116. Pol. *Const.* (1935), art. 68, par. 4.
117. U.S. *Const.*, amend. IV.
118. Pol. *Const.* (1935), art. 68, par. 3.
119. U.S. *Const.*, amend. IV.
120. Pol. *Const.* (1935), art. 68, par. 2.
121. *Ibid.*, par. 3.
122. U.S. *Const.*, amend. XIX.
123. Pol. *Const.* (1935), art. 7., par. 2.
124. U.S. *Const.*, amend. XIV., sec. 1.
125. Young, 93.
126. Pol. *Const.* (1935), art. 7, par. 1.
127. *Ibid.*, par. 2.
128. *Ibid.*
129. U.S. *Const.*, art. I, sec. 8.
130. Pol. *Const.* (1935), art. 10, par. 2.
131. *Ibid.*, art. 80.
132. Car, 9.
133. Piłsudski, 417.
134. *Ibid.*, 381-2.
135. *Ibid.*, 412.
136. *Ibid.*, 412

137. Paweł Hostowiec (Jerzy Stempowski), Introduction to Singer, *Od Witosa*, 10.
138. *Time: The Weekly Newsmagazine*, Vol. 94, No. 1 (July 4, 1969), 14.
139. Pol. *Const.* (1935), art. 5, par. 3.
140. *Ibid.*, art. 68, par. 4.
141. U.S. *Const.*, art. II, sec. 9.
142. Young, 119.
143. Pol. *Const.* (1935), art. 24.
144. Stroński, 5.
145. *Ibid.*, 7.
146. Arthur Bliss Lane, *I Saw Poland Betrayed.*
147. Bolesław Bierut, *O konstytucji Polskiej Rzeczypospolitej Ludowej*, 35.

Chapter VII

1. Farb, 129-30.
2. Young, 30.
3. Abraham J. Katsh, "Judaism and American Ideals," in *Bar Mitzvah*, Abraham J. Katsh, ed., 129.
4. *Ibid.*, 131.
5. *Ibid.*
6. Joseph Felicijan, *The Genesis of the Contractual Theory and The Installation of the Dukes of Carinthia*, 7.
7. *Ibid.*, 10.
8. Tytus Filipowicz, "The Accomplished Senator," *Proceedings of the American Society of International Law at Its Twenty-sixth Annual Meeting Held at Washington, D.C., April 28-30, 1932*, 241.
9. Miller, 25
10. Paul Tillich, *The Interpretation of History*, 50.
11. Gore Vidal, *Reflections Upon a Sinking Ship*, 104.
12. Vine Deloria, Jr., *Custer Died For Your Sins*, 177.
13. Ray Allen Billington, Bert James Loewenberg and Samuel Hugh Brockunier, *The United States: American Democracy in World Perspective*, 35-6.
14. Williams *et al.*, 42.
15. Morison, *Oxford History*, 95.
16. Billington *et al.*, 36-7.
17. *Ibid.*, 37-8.
18. *Ibid.*, 38.
19. *Ibid.*, 39.
20. *Ibid.*
21. *Ibid.*, 42.
22. *Ibid.*, 42-4.
23. Williams *et al.*, 95.
24. Billington *et al.*, 45.
25. Charles Beard and Mary Beard, *The Rise of American Civilization*, 439.

26. Williams et al., 130.
27. Beard and Beard, 448-9.

Chapter VIII

1. Piłsudski, 292.
2. Will Durant, Vol. VI: *The Reformation*, 629.
3. Stanisław Kot, "Polska Złotego Wieku wobec kultury zachodniej," *Kultura staropolska*, 682, cited by Lednicki, 107.
4. Leslie Stephen, *History of English Thought in the Eighteenth Century*, I, 262, cited by Will and Ariel Durant, Vol. IX, *The Age of Voltaire*, 122.
5. R.R. Palmer, ed., *Rand McNally Atlas of World History*, 64.
6. Andrzej Lubieniecki, *Polonoeutychia*, cited by Stanislas Kot, *Socinianism in Poland: The Social and Political Ideas of the Polish Antitrinitarians in the Sixteenth and Seventeenth Centuries*, xiv.
7. Earl Morse Wilbur, *A History of Unitarianism: Socinianism and Its Antecedents*, 282.
8. Ludwik Ehrlich, *Pisma wybrane Pawła Włodkowica - Works of Paul Wladimiri (A Selection)*, I, x.
9. Angus Armitage, *The World of Copernicus (Sun Stand Thou Still)*, 56-7.
10. *Ibid.*, 99.
11. Durant, Vol. VI: *The Reformation*, 629.
12. Antonina Jelicz, *Życie codzienne w średniowiecznym Krakowie (wiek XIII-XV)*, 139.
13. Aleksander Brueckner, *Różnowiercy polscy*, 51.
14. Earl Morse Wilbur, *Our Unitarian Heritage*, 104.
15. Will Durant, Vol. VI: *The Reformation*, 630.
16. Herbert John McLachlan, *Socinianism in Seventeenth Century England*, 2.n.
17. *Ibid.*
18. Tadeusz Czacki, *O litewskich i polskich prawach*, I, 118.
   Stanislaus Lubieniecius, *Historia Reformationis Polonicae*, 213, quoted by Wilbur, *Socinianism and Its Antecedents*, 283.
19. Łukasz Górnicki, *Dzieje w Koronie Polskiej*, 5.
20. Andreas F. Modrevius, *Sylvae Guatuor*, 81, cited by Wilbur, *Socinianism and Its Antecedents*, 284.
21. Stanislas Kot, *Socinianism in Poland*, xii.
22. *Ibid.*
23. *Ibid.*, xiii.
24. Wilbur, *Socinianism and Its Antecedents*, 291.
25. Wilbur, *Unitarian Heritage*, 146.
26. Wilbur, *Socinianism and Its Antecedents*, 255-6.
27. Edward Darling, "Francis David and King John Sigismund: Architects of Religious Liberty," *The Register-Leader of the Unitarian Universalist Association*, Vol. 150, No. 3 (March, 1968), 4.
28. *Ibid.*

30. McLachlan, 10.
31. Kot, *Socinianism in Poland*, 198.
32. *Ibid.*, 116.
33. Friedrich Samuel Bock, *Historia Antitrinitariorum, Maxime Socinianismi Et Socinianorum, Ex Fontibus, Magnamque Partum Monumentis Et Documentis Msscctis Recenscutur*, 645.
34. Gottfried Lengnich, *Geschichte der Preussischen Lande Koeniglich-Polnischen Antheils*, VI, 102.
35. Tadeusz Żelenski (Boy), *Marysieńka Sobieska*, 106.
36. Wilbur, *Unitarian Heritage*. 174.
37. Thomas Rees, ed., *The Racovian Catechism, with notes and illustrations . . . to which is prefixed a sketch of the history of Unitarianism in Poland and the adjacent countries*, quoted in McLachlan, *Socinianism*, 12.n.
38. McLachlan, *Socinianism*, 12.
39. Charles Beard, *The Reformation of the Sixteenth Century in Its Relation to Modern Thought and Knowledge*, 277.
40. Władysław Tatarkiewicz, *Historia filozofii*, Vol. II: *Filozofia nowozytna do roku 1830*, 181.
41. Kot, *Socinianism in Poland*, 197.
42. Samuel Przypkowski, *Cogitationes Sacrae*, quoted in Kot, *Socinianism*, 185-6.
43. *Ibid.*
44. Andrew Wiszowaty and Joachim Stegmann, preface to *The Racovian Catechism*, quoted in McLachlan, 16.n.
45. Faustus Socinus, *Opera Omnia*, I, 700, quoted in McLachlan, 16.
46. *Ibid.*, 373, quoted in McLachlan, 16.
47. Hugo Grotius, prolegomena of *De Jure Belli Et Pacis*, book I, chaps. 2-3; book II, chp. i, cited by Kot, *Socinianism*, 140-2.
48. Socinus, *Opera*, i, 476, cited by McLachlan, 15.

Chapter IX

1. Wilbur, *Socinianism and its Antecedents*, 480.
2. *Ibid.*, 520-1
3. Theodor Wotschke, "Die Unitarische Gemeinde in Meseritz-Bobelwitz," *Zeitschrift der Historischen Geselschaft fuer die Provinz Posen*, XXVI (1911), 203, quoted in Wilbur, *Socinanism and Its Antecedents*, 521.
4. Adam Mickiewicz, *Dzieła*, Vol. II: *Literatura słowiańska, wykłady lozańskie, pisma historyczne*. Tadeusz Pini, ed., 144.
5. Tatarkiewicz, *Ibid.*, Vol. III: *Filozofia XIX wieku i współczesna*, 196.
6. Ludwik, Chmaj, *Bracia Polscy: ludzie, idee, wplywy*, 319.
7. *Ibid.*, 319-45.
8. McLachlan, 19.
9. Pierre Bayle, *Dictionnaire historique et critique*, "Socin," cited in McLachlan, 19.n.
10. McLachlan, 19.

265

11. *Ibid.,* 20.
12. *Ibid.*
13. *Ibid.,* 21.
14. *Ibid.,* 22.
15. Bayle, *Dictionnaire,* "Socin," quoted in McLachlan, 19.n.
16. McLachlan, 23.
17. Wilbur, *Socinianism and Its Antecedents,* 567.
18. Kot, *Socinianism in Poland,* 206.
19. Wilbur, *Socinianism and Its Antecedents,* 504-5.
20. G.G. Zeltner, *Historia Crypto-Socinianismi Altorfinae quondam Acadamiae et M. Ruari Episolarum centuriae due,* 1196, cited by McLachlan, 26.
21. Martin Ruar, *Epistolarum Selectarum centuriae due,* 379, quoted in McLachlan, 27.
22. McLachlan, *Ibid.*
23. Ruar, *Epistolarum Selectarum,* ii, 56, 60, cited by McLachlan, 28.
24. McLachlan, *31.*
25. *Ibid.,* 33.
26. *Ibid.,* 33.n.
27. *Ibid.,* 40.n.
28. *Ibid.,* 41.
29. David Wilkins, *Concilia Magnae Britaniae et Hiberniae, a Synodo Verlamiensi . . . Accedunt constitutiones et alia historiam Ecclesiae Anglicanae spectantia,* iv, 548, cited by McLachlan, 42.
30. McLachlan, 42.
31. Bayle, *Dictionnaire,* 173, cited by McLachlan, 43.n.
32. McLachlan, 43.
33. Robert Wallace, *Antitrinitarian Biography; or Sketches of Lives and Writings of Distinguished Antitrinitarians, from the Reformation to the Close of the Seventeenth Century: to which is Prefixed a History of Unitarianism in England,* iii, 158, cited by McLachlan, 103.
34. Wallace, *Ibid.,* cited by McLachlan, 103.n.
35. Christopher Sandius (Sand), *Bibliotheca Antitrinitariorum,* 117, cited by McLachlan, 111.
36. McLachlan, 116.
37. Wilbur, *A History of Unitarianism in Transylvania, England and America,* 148.
38. Thomas Carlyle, *Oliver Cromwell's Letters and Speeches,* i, 215, quoted in McLachlan, 160.n.
39. McLachlan, 156.
40. Paul Best, *Mysteries Discovered. Or a Mercuriall Picture: pointing out the way from Babylon to the Holy City, for the good of all such as, during the Night of generall Errour and Apostacy, 2 Thes. 2, 3. Revelat. 3, 10. have been so long misled with Rome's hobgoblins. By me Paul Best, Prisoner in the Gatehouse, Westminster. 1647.,* quoted in McLachlan, 159.
41. Columbia University, *The Works of John Milton,* xviii, 572, cited by McLachlan, 161.

42. Anthony Wood, *Athenae Oxonienses. An Exact History of all the Writers and Bishops Who Have Had Their Education in the Most Ancient and Famous University of Oxford, from the Fifteenth Year of King Henry the Seventh, A.D. 1500 to the Author's Death in November 1695,* II, 300, cited by McLachlan, 169.
43. *A Short Account of the Life of John Bidle,* 5, cited by McLachlan, 170.
44. J.H. Hanford, "The Date of Milton's De Doctrina Christiana," *Studies in Philosophy,* XVII, 309-19, cited by McLachlan, 190.
45. John Masson, *Life of John Milton,* iv, 423, cited by McLachlan, 190.
46. McLachlan, 190-1
47. Joshua Toulmin, *Memoires of the Life of Faustus Socinus,* 260, cited by McLachlan, 191.
48. Wallace, iii, 25, cited by McLachlan, 90.
49. McLachlan, 92.
50. Sandius, 157, cited by McLachlan, 183.
51. Jeremias Felbinger, a letter to John Bidle, dated August 24, 1654, cited by John Bidle, *A Twofold Catechism: The One simply called A Scripture-Catechism; The Other, A brief Scripture Catechism for Children. Therein the chiefest points of the Christian Religion, being Question-wise proposed, resolve themselves by pertinent Answers taken word for word out of the Scripture, without either Consequences or Comments. Composed for their sakes that would fain be meer Christians, and not of this or that Sect, inasmuch as all the Sects of Christians, by what names soever distinguished, have either more or less departed from the simplicity and truth of the Scripture,* 210.
52. McLachlan, 160.
53. *Ibid.,* 177-8.
54. *Ibid.,* 253.
55. Wood, II, 306, cited by McLachlan, 215.
56. Wood, II, 305-6, cited by McLachlan, 215.
57. McLachlan, 216.
58. *The Life of Mr. Thomas Firmin, Late Citizen of London,* 15-6, cited by McLachlan, 295.
59. *The Life of Mr. Thomas Firmin, Late Citizen of London,* 10, quoted in McLachlan, 296.
60. *The Life of Mr. Thomas Firmin, Late Citizen of London,* 48, cited by McLachlan, 295-6.
61. McLachlan, 301.
62. *Ibid.,* 288.
63. *Ibid.*
64. *Ibid.,* 277, 289.
65. Wilbur, *A History of Unitarianism in Transylvania, England, and America,* 496.
66. McLachlan, 264.n.
67. *Ibid.,* 280.
68. John Knowles, *A Modest Plea for Private Mens Preachings,* 20, quoted in McLachlan, 264.

69. Knowles, preface to *A Modest Plea*, quoted in McLachlan, 264-5.
70. McLachlan, 276.
71. *Ibid.*, 285-6.
72. Knowles, *An Answer to Mr. Ferguson's Book, Intituled Justification, Wherein he is friendly reprov'd, fully silenc'd, and clearly instructed. Whereunto is added, A Compendium, or brief Discourse concerning the Ends and Intents of Christ's Death and Passion, consider'd as a Ransom. By John Knowles, a servant of Jesus Christ*, 165, quoted in McLachlan, 281.
73. McLachlan, 285.
74. *Ibid.*, 259-60.
75. *Ibid.*, 302.n.
76. Alexander Gordon, "Heads of English Unitarian History. With Appended Lectures on Baxter and Priestly," *The Christian Life,* xviii, 399, cited by McLachlan, 314.
77. McLachlan, 316.
78. *Ibid.*, 291.
79. Thomas Sydenham, *Processus integri morbis fere omnibus curandis*, I, 428, cited by McLachlan, 289.
80. Wallace, III, 483-4, cited by McLachlan, 289.
81. T. Birch, *Life of Dr. John Tillotson*, 292.
82. Wilbur, *Socinianism and Its Antecedents*, 577.
83. John Edwards, *The Socinian Creed*, 214, quoted in McLachlan, 290.
84. McLachlan, 29.n.
85. *Ibid.*, 293.
86. Wilbur, *Socinianism and Its Antecedents*, 518.
87. *Ibid.*, 498.

Chapter X

1. Henry Richard Fox Bourne, *The Life of John Locke*, I, 310-11, cited by McLachlan, 326.
2. Gordon, *Heads of English Unitarian History*, 31, quoted in McLachlan, 326.
3. John Edwards, *Socinianism Unmasked. A Discourse Showing the Unreasonableness of a Late Writer's Opinion Concerning the Necessity of Only One Article of Christian Faith; and of His Other Assertions in His Late Book, Entitled, The Reasonableness of Christianity . . . and in His Vindication of It. With a Brief Reply to Another (Professed) Socinian Writer*, 50, quoted in McLachlan, 327.n.
4. Zbigniew Ogonowski, *Socynianizm a oświecenie: Studia nad myślą filozoficzno-religijną arian w Polsce XVIII wieku*, 562.
5. John W. Yolton, *John Locke and the Way of Ideas*, 62.
6. McLachlan, 326.
7. King Lord, *The Life of John Locke*, II, 103, 188-94, cited by McLachlan, 327.
8. Yolton, 10.
9. John Locke, *An Essey Concerning Human Understanding*, Alexander Campbell Fraser, ed., Book II, chap. 1, par. 2.

10. John Gailhard, *The Blasphemous Socinian Heresie Disproved and confuted . . . with Animadversions Upon a Late Book Called Christianity Not Mysterious. Humbly Dedicated to Both Houses of Parliament*, 82-3.
11. Yolton, 11.
12. Ogonowski, "Antytrynitaryzm w Polsce - wiara i rozum," *Myśli i ludzie: Filozofia polska*, Vol. II, *Filozofia nowożytna i współczesna*, Bronisław Baczko, ed., 126-7.
13. Ogonowski, *Socynianizm*, 562.
14. *Ibid.*, 563-4
15. McLachlan, 330.
16. [Isaac Newton, Sir] *Two Letters of Sir Issac Newton to Mr. Le Clerc . . . The Former Containing a Dissertation Upon the Reading of the Greek Text I, John, V.7., the Latter Upon that of I. Timothy, III.16.*
17. [Louise Trenchard More] *Issac Newton, a Biography by Louise Trenchard More*, chap. xvi. and especially pp. 640-3, cited by McLachlan, 331.
18. Louise Trenchard More, 643, quoted in McLachlan, 331.
19. McLachlan, 331.n.
20. Ogonowski, "Antytrynitaryzm," 110.
21. McLachlan, 331.
22. Wilbur, *Socinianism and Its Antecedents*, 234.
23. *Ibid.*, 251.
24. Yolton, 169.
25. *Ibid.*, 170.
26. *Ibid.*, 171.
27. *Ibid.*, 174.
28. Peter Brown, *Procedure, Extent and Limit of Human Understanding*, 40, quoted in Yolton, 174.
29. Wilhelm Dilthey, *Das natuerliche System des Geisteswissenschaften*, 129-44.
30. Konrad Górski, "Arianie polscy," *Encyklopedia Świat i Życie*, I, quoted in Ogonowski, *Socynianizm*, 456.
31. Zygmunt Łempicki, *Renesans, Oświecenie, Romantyzm*, 85, quoted in Ogonowski, *Socynianizm*, 453.
32. Kot, *Ideologia polityczna i społeczna Braci Polskich zwanych Arianami*, 147, quoted in Ogonowski, *Socynianizm*, 457.
33. Ogonowski, *Socynianizm*, 474.
34. *Ibid.*, 482.
35. *Ibid.*, 491.
36. *Ibid.*, 497.
37. *Ibid.*
38. *Ibid.*, 499.
39. *Ibid.*
40. *Ibid.*, 499-500.
41. *Ibid.*, 500.
42. *Ibid.*, 504.
43. *Ibid.*, 505.
44. *Ibid.*, 540.

45. John Henry Newman, Cardinal, *An Essey on the Development of Christian Doctrine*, 112.
46. Ogonowski, *Socynianizm*, 544.
47. *Ibid.*, 541-2.
48. *Ibid.*, 542.
49. *Ibid.*
50. Ogonowski, "*Antytrynitaryzm,*" 122.
51. Ogonowski, *Socynianizm*, 564.

Chapter XI

1. J. Umiński, "The Counter-Reformation in Poland," *Cambridge History of Poland*, Otto Halecki, ed., 412.
2. Tatarkiewicz, II, 254.
3. *Ibid.*, 255.
4. *Ibid.*
5. Henryk Hinz, "Kołłątaj - Ład fizyczno-moralny a historia," *Myśli i ludzie: Filozofia polska*, Vol. 11, 131-3.
6. *Ibid.*, 134.
7. Hugo Kołłątaj, *Porządek fizyczno-moralny oraz Pomysły do dzieła Porządek fizyczno-moralny*, 27, quoted in Hinz, "Kołłątaj - Ład fizyczno-moralny a historia," 132.
8. Hinz, *Ibid.*
9. *Ibid.*, 144.
10. *Ibid.*, 145.
11. *Ibid.*, 153.
12. *Ibid.*, 156.
13. Barbara Szacka, "Staszic - Synteza dziejów ludzkości," *Myśli i ludzie: Filozofia polska*, Vol. II, 160.
14. *Ibid.*, 162.
15. *Ibid.*, 167.
16. *Ibid.*, 168.
17. *Ibid.*
18. *Ibid.*, 169.
19. *Ibid.*, 173.
20. *Ibid.*, 163.
21. Jerzy Szacki, "Jan Śniadecki - Nauka i edukacja narodowa," *Myśli i ludzie: Filozofia polska*, Vol. II, 180.
22. Jan Śniadecki, *Rozprawa o nauk matematycznych początku, znaczeniu i wpływie na oświecenie powszechne*, quoted in Szacki, "Jan Śniadecki -Nauka i edukacja narodowa," 182.
23. Szacki, 186.
24. *Ibid.*, 188-9.
25. *Ibid.*, 188.
26. Friedrich Albert Lange, *The History of Materialism and Criticism of Its Importance*, I, 325.
27. Tatarkiewicz, II, 256.

Chapter XII

1. Edward Hartwig, *Kraków*, part: "Objaśnienia ilustracji," 2.
2. Samuel Przypkowski, *Apologia Christiani magistratus prolixior tractatus de jure*, 753, quoted in Kot, *Ideologia polityczna i społeczna Braci Polskich*, 199.
3. Felbinger, *Ibid.*
4. Leonard Williams Levy, *Origins of the Fifth Amendment*, 399.
5. *Ibid.*
6. *Records of the Governor and Company of the Massachusetts Bay*, III, 215, cited by McLachlan, 235.
7. Nicholas Cheyney, *Anti-Socinianism*, quoted in McLachlan, 238.
8. McLachlan, 238-9.
9. Wilbur, *A History of Unitarianism in Transylvania, England, and America*, 382.
10. *Ibid.*
11. *Ibid.*, 383.
12. *Ibid.*, 384.
13. Josiah Quincy, History of Harvard University, ii, Chpt. xxii, cited by Wilbur, *A History of Unitarianism in Transylvania, England, and America*, 384.
14. Wilbur, *Ibid.*, 385.
15. *Ibid.*
16. *Ibid.*, 386.
17. *Ibid.*, 387-8.
18. *Ibid.*, 388.
19. *Ibid.*, 389.
20. F.W. Greenwood, *History of King's Chapel*, 139, cited by Wilbur, *Ibid.*, 391.
21. Conrad Wright, *The Beginnings of Unitarianism in America*, 210.
22. "Dark, Rugged and Cordial," *The Times Literary Supplement*, (August 29, 1968), 917.
23. *Ibid.*
24. *Ibid.*
25. Wright, 213.
26. Thomas Belsham, *Memoirs of the Late Rev. Theophilus Lindsay Including a Brief Analysis of His Works Together with Anecdots and Letters of Eminent Persons, his Friends and Correspondents, also a General View of the Progress of the Unitarian Doctrine in England and America*, 240.n.
27. Wilbur, *A History of Unitarianism in Transylvania, England, and America*, 285.
28. Foote, 69.
29. Will Durant, Vol. IX, *The Age of Voltaire*, 530.
30. "Dark, Rugged and Cordial," *Ibid.*
31. Foote, 75-6.
32. Andrew Burnaby, "Travels Through the Middle Settlements in North America in the Years 1759-60," quoted in Williams *et al.*, *The United States to 1877*, 122.

33. Irving Mark, Eugene L. Schwaab, eds., "Who Among Us Is Safe?", *The World of History*, Courtland Canby, Nancy E. Gross, eds., 105.
34. Daniel K. Stern, "The Mercury - 1869: Editor Called Chinese-Haters Our 'Enemies'," *San Jose Mercury-News*, (San Jose, California, March 2, 1969), 2F.
35. Charles Beard, Mary Beard, 449.
36. Jack Mendelsohn, Jr., "A Different Kind of Language," *The Unitarian Universalist Pocket Guide*, Henry Barron Scholefield, ed., 13.
37. Morison, Oxford History, 514.
38. *Ibid.*
39. Moncure Daniel Conway, "From Deism to Agnosticism," The Free Review, I, 1, quoted in Warren Sylvester Smith, *The London Heretics: 1870-1914*, 251.
40. Morison, *Oxford History*, 526.
41. *Ibid.*, 527.
42. McLachlan, 238.
43. Wilbur, *A History of Unitarianism in Transylvania, England, and America*, 379.
44. *Ibid.*

Chapter XIII

1. Congressional resolution of February 21, 1787, cited by Stefan Lorant, *The Glorious Burden: The American Presidency*, 14.
2. Lorant, 16.
3. Williams *et al.*, 138.
4. Ignacy Daszyński, *Pamiętniki*, Vol. II, 43.
5. Bowen, 17.
6. *Ibid.*
7. *Ibid.*
8. Williams *et al.*, 145.
9. *Ibid.*
10. *Ibid.*, 206.
11. Singer, 71-2.
12. Edwin A. Hoey, "A 'New and Strange Order of Men'," *American Heritage*, XIX, No. 5 (August, 1968).
13. Fawn M. Brodie, *Thomas Jefferson: An Intimate History*, 112.
14. Charles Beard, ed., *The Enduring Federalist*, 23.
15. Will and Ariel Durant, Vol. X: *Rousseau and Revolution*, 482; Frances Winwar, *Jean-Jacques Rousseau: Conscience of an Era*, 333.
16. Charles Beard, ed., *The Writings of Thomas Jefferson*, VIII, 31-2.
17. Kukiel, *Dzieje porozbiorowe*, 26.
18. John Rosenberg, "Toward A New Civil War Revisionism," *The American Scholar*, (Spring 1969), 263.
19. Kasparek, I, 16-7.
20. Kennedy, *Profiles*, 22.
21. Hostowiec, Introduction to Singer, *Od Witosa*, 14.

22. Singer, 232.
23. Will Durant, Vol. VI. *The Reformation*, 863.
24. Armitage, 91.
25. Bertrand Russell, *A History of Western Philosphy*, 452, 535.
26. *Ibid.*
27. Armitage, 91.
28. Kasparek, I, 165.
29. *Ibid.*
30. Konstanty Żantuan, "Olbracht Laski in Elisabethan England - an Episode in the History of Culture," *The Polish Review*, XIII, No. 4 (Autumn 1968), 18.
31. Wilbur, *Unitarian Heritage*, 69.
32. Kazimierz Leśniak, "Burski - Pochwała dialektyki stoickiej," *Myśli i ludzie: Filozofia polska*, Vol. II, 69.
33. Thomas More, *Utopia*, Bk. II.
34. Levy, 69.
35. *Ibid.*, 107-8.
36. Will Durant, Vol. VI: *The Reformation*, 209.
37. *Ibid.*, 220.
38. *Ibid.*, 778.
39. McLachlan, 336.
40. Wilbur, *Socinianism and Its Antecedents*, 146-8.
41. Will and Ariel Durant, Vol. X: *Rousseau and Revolution*, 163
42. J.A. Teslar, "Polski traktat polityczny w rękach Szekspira," *Wiadomości*, No. 768-9 (18-25 December 1960), 3-4.
43. Arthur P. Coleman, "Laurentius Grimaldus Goslicius and His Age," part II, *The Polish Review*, Vol. III, No. 1-2 [Winter-Spring 1958], 43.
44. *Ibid.*
45. Laurentius Grimaldus Goslicius, *De Optimo Senatore*, 51, quoted in Charles S. Haight, "Laurentius Grimaldus Goslicius," part III, *The Polish Review*, Vol. III, No. 1-2 (Winter-Spring 1958), 50.
46. Goslicius, 51, quoted in Haight, 51.
47. Haight, 53.
48. Goslicius, 149, quoted in Haight, 53.
49. Goslicius, 150, quoted in Haight, 53-4.
50. Goslicius, 32, quoted in Haight, 56.
51. Goslicius, 32-3, quoted in Haight, 49.
52. Locke, *Of Civil Government Second Treatise*, 169.
53. Coleman, 42-3.
54. Locke, *An Essey Concerning Human Understanding*, Bk. II, Chap. I, par. 2.
55. Leśniak, 81.
56. Williams *et al.*, 143-4.
57. Russell Kirk, Introduction to Locke, *Second Treatise*, xi.

BIBLIOGRAPHY
of sources referred to in the text

"Amerykańsko-polski Komitet Pomocy," *Wielka Encyklopedia Powszechna PWN*, I.
Appleby, Joyce. "The Jefferson-Adams Rupture and the First French Translation of John Adams' 'Defence' " *The American Historical Review*, LXXIII (April, 1968), 1084-91.
Armitage, Angus. *The World of Copernicus (Sun, Stand Thou Still)*. New York, 1952.
A Short Account of the Life of John Bidle. London, n.d.
Askenazy, Szymon. *Rosja - Polska*. Lwów, 1907.

Bayle, Pierre. "Socin" in *Dictionnaire historique et critique*. Rotterdam, 1695-7.
Beard, Charles., ed. *The Enduring Federalist*. Edited and analysed by Charles Austin Beard. Doubleday, 1948.
— — — — — — — *The Reformation of the Sixteenth Century in its Relation to Modern Thought and Knowledge*. London, 1921.
Beard, Charles, Beard, Mary. *The Rise of American Civilization*. 3 V. New York, 1966.
Belsham, Thomas. *Memoirs of the Late Rev. Theophilus Lindsay Including a Brief Analysis of His Works Together with Anecdotes and Letters of Eminent Persons, His Friends and Correspondents, also a General View of the Progress of the Unitarian Doctrine in England and America*. London, 1812.
Best, Paul. *A Letter of Advice unto the Ministers Assembled at Westminster, with Several Parcels of Queries*. London, 1646.
— — — — *Mysteries Discovered. Or, a Mercurial Picture: Pointing out the Way from Babylong to the Holy City, for the Good of all such as during that Night of general Errour and Apostacy, 2 Thes. 2,3. Revelat. 3, 10 have been so long misled by Rome's hobgoblin. By me Paul Best, Prisoner in the Gatehouse, Westminster, 1647*.
Bierut, Bolesław. *O konstytucji Polskiej Rzeczypospolitej Ludowej*. Warszawa, 1952.
Billington, Ray Allen. *American History Before 1877*. New Jersey, 1961.
Billington, Ray Allen; Loewenberg, Bert James; and Brockunier, Samuel Hugh. *The United States: American Democracy in World Perspective*. New York -Toronto, 1947.
Birch, T.: *Life of Dr. John Tillotson*. London, 1753.
Bock, Friedrich Samuel. *Historia antitrinitariorum, maxime Socinianismi et Socinianorum, ex fontibus, magnamque partum monumentis et documentis msscctis, recenscutur*. 2 V. Regiomonti. 1774-84.
Bourne, Henry Richard Fox. *The Life of John Locke*. New York, 1876.
Bowen, Catherine Drinker. *Miracle at Philadelphia: the Story of the Constitutional Convention, May to September, 1787*. Boston - Toronto, 1966.

Brodie, Fawn M. *Thomas Jefferson: An Intimate History.* Toronto - New York - London, 1975.
Brown, Peter. *Procedure, Extent and Limit of Human Understanding.* London, 1728.
Brueckner, Aleksander. *Różnowiercy polscy.* Warszawa, 1962.
Burnaby, Andrew. "Travels through the Middle Settlements in North America in the Years 1759-60", quoted in Williams *et al., A History of the United States to 1877.* New York, 1965.
Car, Stanisław. Preface to *Constitution of the Republic of Poland (April 23rd 1935).* Warsaw, 1935.
Carlyle, Thomas. *Oliver Cromwell's Letters and Speeches.* London, 1897.
Carson, Rachel Louise. *The Sea Around Us.* New York, 1968.
Channing, Edward. *A History of the United States.* 6 V. Macmillan, 1905.
Chmaj, Ludwik. *Bracia Polscy: ludzie, idee, wpływy, propaganda Braci Polskich w Paryżu XVII wieku.* Warszawa, 1957.
Coleman, Arthur P. "Laurentius Grimaldus Goslicius and his Age," Part II, *The Polish Review,* Vol. III. No. 1-2 (Winter-Spring, 1958) pp. 42-7.
Conway, Moncure Daniel. "From Deism to Agnosticism," *The Free Review,* Vol. 1, No. 1 (October, 1893), p. 12.
Cooper, Merian C. "How I happened to go to Poland" *Poland* (occassional publication, Los Angeles, March 1972), pp. 15-6.
Cowan, A.R. *A Guide to World History.* London, 1923.
Czacki, Tadeusz. *O litewskich i polskich prawach.* Warszawa, 1801.
"Dark, Rugged and Cordial" A review of a book by Ernest J. Moyne, u.t. "The Journal of Margaret Hazlitt," *The Times Literary Supplement,* (August 29, 1969).
Darling, Edward. "Francis David and King John Sigismund: Architects of Religious Liberty," *The Register-Leader of the Unitarian Universalists Association,* Vol. 150, No. 3 (March 1968), pp. 3-7.
Daszyński, Ignacy. *Pamiętniki.* 2 V. Kraków, 1926.
Deloria, Vine, Jr. *Custer Died for Your Sins.* Toronto, 1969.
Drozdowski, Marian M. *Rewolucja Amerykańska w polskiej myśli historycznej.* Warszawa, 1976.
Durant, Will. *The Story of Civilization.* Vol. I: *Our Oriental Heritage.* New York, 1954.
— — — — — — *The Story of Civilization.* Vol. VI: *The Reformation.* New York, 1957.
Durant, Will, and Durant, Ariel. *The Story of Civilization.* Vol. IX: *The Age of Voltaire.* New York, 1965.
— — — — — — — *The Story of Civilization.* Vol. X: *Rousseau and Revolution.* New York, 1967.
Edwards, John. *The Socinian Creed.* London, 1696.
— — — — — — *Socinianism unmasked. A discourse showing the unreasonableness of a late writer's opinion concerning the necessity of only one article of Christian faith; and of his other assertions in his late book entitled The Reasonableness of Christianity . . . and in his Vindication of it. With a brief reply to another (professed) Socinian writer.* London, 1696.

Edwards, Thomas. *Gangraena: or, A catalogue and discovery of many of the errours, heresies, blasphemies and pernicious practices of the sectaries of this time, vented and acted in England in these last four years.* London, 1646.
Ehrlich, Ludwik. *Pisma wybrane Pawła Włodkowica. Works of Paul Wladimiri (A selection).* Instytut Wydawniczy "Pax", 1965.
Farb, Peter. *Man's Rise to Civilization: as shown by the Indians of North America from primeval times to the coming of the industrial state.* New York, 1969.
Felbinger, Jeremias. Letter to John Bidle, dated August 24, 1654, quoted in John Bidle, *Twofold Catechism.*
Felicijan, Joseph. *The Genesis of the Contractual Theory and The Installation of the Dukes of Carinthia.* Klagenfurt, 1967.
Filipowicz, Tytus. "The Accomplished Senator," *Proceedings of the American Society of International Law at its Twenty-sixth Annual Meeting Held at Washington, D.C., April 28-30, 1932.,* pp. 234-41.
Foote, Henry Wilder. *The Religion of Thomas Jefferson.* Boston, 1960.

Gailhard, John. *The blasphemous Socinian heresie disproved and confuted . . . with animadversions upon a late book called Christianity not Mysterious. Humbly dedicated to both houses of Parliament.* London, 1697.
Gerard, James W. *My Four Years in Germany.* New York, 1918.
Goslicius, Lavrentius Grimaldus (Grzymała-Goślicki, Wawrzyniec). *Lavrentii Grimaldii Goslicii De Optimo Senatore Libri Duo.* Venetiis, MDLXVIII.
Górnicki, Łukasz. *Dzieje w Koronie Polskiej.* Kraków, 1637.
Górski, Jan. "Kościuszko Tradition," *Polish Perspectives,* Vol. XI, No. 2. (February 1968), pp. 16-20.
Górski, Konrad. "Arianie polscy," *Encyklopedia Świat i Życie.* n.d.
Greenwood, Francis William Pitt. *A history of King's Chapel, the first Episcopal Church in New England: comprising notices of the introduction of Episocopacy into the northern colonies.* Boston, 1833.
Grotius, Hugo. *Prolegomena of De jure belli et pacis.* Amsterdam, 1625.
Grzędziński, January. *Maj 1926.* Paryż, 1965.

Haight, Charles S. "Laurentius Grimaldus Goslicius," part III, *The Polish Review,* Vol. III, No. 1-2 (Winter-Spring 1958), pp. 47-57.
Handelsman, Marceli, ed. *Konstytucje polskie.* Warszawa, 1926.
Hanford, J.H. "The Date of Milton's De Doctrina Christiana," *Studies in Philosophy,* Vol. XVII (1920).
Hartwig, Edward. "Objaśnienia ilustracji," *Kraków.* Warszawa, 1969.
Heilbroner, Robert L. *The Worldly Philosophers: the Lives, Times and Ideas of the Great Economic Thinkers.* New York, 1966.
Herold, J. Christopher. *The Mind of Napoleon, a Selection from His Written and Spoken Words. Edited and Translated by J. Christopher Herold.* New York and London, 1961.
Hinz, Henryk. "Kołłątaj: Ład fizyczno-moralny a historia," *Filozofia polska:* II. *Filozofia nowożytna i współczesna.* Dr. Bronisław Baczko, ed., Warszawa, 1967.

Hoey, Edwin A. "A New and Strange Order of Men," *American Heritage*, Vol. XIX, No. 5 (August 1968).
Hostowiec, Paweł (Stempowski, Jerzy). "Słowo wstępne" in *Od Witosa do Sławka*, by Singer, Bernard. Paryż, 1962.

Ingstad, Helge Marcus. *Land under the Pole Star; a voyage to the Norse settlements of Greenland and the Saga of the people that vanished.* Translated from the Norwegian by Naomi Walford. New York, 1966.
Irish, Marian D., and Prothro, James W. *The Politics of American Democracy.* Englewood Cliffs, New Jersey, 1965.

Jelicz, Antonina. *Zycie codzienne w średniowiecznym Krakowie.* Warszawa, 1965.
Johnson, Sam Houston. "My Brother Lyndon," *Look*, Vol. 33 No. 25 (Dec. 16, 1969), pp. 43-6, and 51-4.

Kasparek, Franciszek. *Prawo polityczne ogólne z uwzględnieniem Austriackiego: Razem ze wstępna nauką o państwie.* 2 Vol. Kraków, 1877.
Katsh, Abraham I. *"Judaism and American Ideals," Bar Mitzvah.* New York City, 1955.
Katz, William Loren. (An interview with.) "Let's Set Black History Straight," *Reader's Digest*, (July 1969), pp. 59-63.
Kennedy, John F. *A Nation of Immigrants.* New York, 1964.
— — — — — — *Profiles in Courage.* New York, 1960.
Kirk, Russell. "Introduction, " *Of Civil Government Second Treatise*, by Locke, John. Chicago, 1962.
Knowles, John. *A Modest Plea for Private Mens Preaching.* 1648.
— — — — — — *An Answer to Mr. Ferguson's Book, Entitled Justification Only upon a Satisfaction, Wherein He Is Friendly Reprov'd, Fully Silenc'd, and Clearly Instructed. Whereunto Is Added, A Compendium, or Brief Discourse Concerning the Ends and Intents of Christ's Death and Passion, Consider'd as a Ransom. By John Knowles, a Servant of Jesus Christ.* 1668.
Kołłątaj, Hugo. *Porządek fizyczno-moralny oraz Pomysły do dzieła Porządek fizyczno-moralny.* Warszawa, 1811.
Kot, Stanislas. *Socinianism in Poland: The Social and Political Ideas of the Polish Antitrinitarians in the Sixteenth and Seventeenth Centuries.* Boston, 1957.
Kot, Stanisław. *Ideologia polityca i społeczna Braci Polskich zwanych Arianami.* Warszawa, 1932.
Kridl, Manfred; Malinowski Władysław; and Wittlin Józef, Eds. *For Your Freedom and Ours*, New York, 1943.
Kukiel, Marian. *Dzieje Polski porozbiorowe: 1795-1921*, London, 1961
— — — — — — "Wojna o Kościuszkę," Na antenie, VI, No. 61 (14/21 kwietnia 1968), pp. 5-6.
Kusielewicz, Eugene. "Niemcewicz in America," *The Polish Review*, Vol. V., No. 1 (Winter, 1960), pp. 69-79.
Kutrzeba, Stanisław. *Historia ustroju Polski: Korona.* Warszawa, 1949.

Lane, Arthur Bliss. *I Saw Poland betrayed.* Indianapolis, 1948.
Lange, Friedrich Albert. *The History of Materialism and Criticism of its Present Importance.* New York, 1925.
Lednicki, Wacław. *Life and Culture in Poland: As reflected in Polish Literature.* New York, 1944.
Lengnich, Gottfried. *Geschichte der Preussischen Lande Koeniglich-Polnischen Antheils.* Danzig, 1755.
Leslie, R.F. *The Polish Question: Poland's Place in Modern History.* London, 1964.
Leśniak, Kazimierz. "Burski - Pochwała dialektyki stoickiej," *Filozofia polska: II. Filozofia nowożytna i współczesna.* Dr. Bronisław Baczko, ed., Warszawa, 1967.
Levy, Leonard Williams. *Origins of the Fifth Amendment.* New York, 1968.
Locke, John. *An Essey Concerning Human Understanding.* Alexander Campbell Fraser, ed., Oxford, 1894.
— — — — — — *Of Civil Government Second Treatise.* Chicago, 1962.
Lorant, Stefan. *The Glorious Burden: The American Presidency.* New York, Evanston and London, 1969.
Lord, King. *The Life of John Locke, with Extracts from his Correspondence, Journals, and Common Place Books.* 2 V. 1830.
Lubieniecius, Stanislaus (Lubieniecki, Stanisław). *Historia Reformationis Polonicae.* Freistadii, 1685.
Lubieniecki, Andrzej. *Polonoeutychia.* Lwów, 1843.

Łempicki, Zygmunt. *Renesans, Oświecenie, Romantyzm.* Warszawa - Lwów, 1923.

Mark, Irving, and Schwaab, Eug. L., eds., "Who Among us is Safe?" From "The Faith of our Fathers: An Anthology of Americana," in *The World of History.* Courtland Canby and Nancy E. Gross, eds., for The Society of American Historians, Inc., New York, 1954.
Masson, John. *Life of John Milton.* Cambridge, 1859.
McLachlan, Herbert John. *Socinianism in Seventeenth Century England.* Oxford University Press, 1951.
Mendelsohn, Jack, Jr. "A Different Kind of Language," *The Unitarian-Universalist Pocket Guide,* Henry Barron Scholefield, ed., Boston, 1965.
Merz, Henrietta. *Pale Ink: Two Ancient Records of Chinese Exploration in America.* Chicago, 1953.
Mickiewicz, Adam. *Dzieła:* II. *Literatura słowiańska, wykłady lozańskie, pisma historyczne.* Tadeusz Pini, ed., Lwów - Warszawa - New York, n.d.
Miller, John Chester. *Origins of the American Revolution.* Boston, 1943.
Modrevius, Andreas F. (Modrzewski, Andrzej Frycz), *Sylvae quatuor. Racoviae, 1590.*
Montesquieu, Charles Luis de Secondat. *The Spirit of the Laws.* New York, 1949.
More, Luis Trenchard. *Life of Sir Isaac Newton.* New York, 1934.
More, Thomas, Sir. *Utopia.* H.V.S. Ogden, ed., New York, 1949.

Morison, Samuel Eliot. *The European Discovery of America: the Northern Voyages, A.D. 500-1600.* Oxford University Press, 1971.

— — — — — — — *The Oxford History of the American People.* Oxford University Press, 1965.

Mościcki, Henryk. *Dzwon wolności 1776-1926 - W rocznice narodzin Stanów Zjednoczonych Ameryki.* Collective work. Warszawa, 1926.

Mycielski, Andrzej. *Polskie prawo polityczne.* Kraków, 1946.

Nevins, Allan, and Commager, Henry Steele. *America — The Story of a Free People.* Oxford University Press, 1943.

Newton, Isaac, Sir. *Two Letters of Sir Isaac Newton to Mr. Le Clerc . . . The*

Ogonowski, Zbigniew. "Antytrynitaryzm w Polsce," *Filozofia polska:* II. *Filozofia nowożytna i współczesna.* Dr. Bronisław Baczko, ed., Warszawa, 1967.

— — — — — — — *Socynianizm a Oświecenie: Studia nad myślą filozoficzną arian w Polsce XVII wieku.* Warszawa, 1966.

Page, T.N. "Report by T.N. Page, U.S. Ambassador to Italy, to the Secretary of State," *U.S.F.R.: 1917,* Supplement 1., January 21, 1917.

Palmer, R.R., ed., *Atlas of World History.* New York-Chicago-San Francisco, 1957.

Palsson, Herman, and Magnusson, Magnus. *The Vinland Sagas: The Norse Discovery of America.* New York University Press, 1966.

Piłsudski, Józef. *Pisma wybrane.* Edinburgh, 1943.

Pragier, A. "Z historii wolnomularstwa polskiego," *Na antenie,* VI (April 21, 1968), p. VII.

Próchnik, Adam, *Kim był Tadeusz Kościuszko.* Łódź, 1930.

Przypkowski, Samuel. *Apologia prolixior tractatus de jure Christiani magistratus.* n.d.

— — — — — — — *Cogitationes sacrae . . . nec non tractatus varii momenti, praecipue De jure Christiani magistratus. Eleutheropoli (Amsterdam),* 1692.

— — — — — — — *Dissertatio de Pace, etc., or, a Discourse touching the Peace and Concord of the Church.* London, 1653.

— — — — — — — *The Life of that Incomparable Man, Faustus Socinus Senensis, described by a Polonian Knight. Whereunto is added An Excellent Discourse, which the same Author would have had premised to the Works of Socinus, together with the Catalogue of these Works.* Translated by John Bidle. London, 1653.

Quincy, Josiah. *History of Harvard University.* n.d.

Records of the Governor and Company of the Massachusetts Bay. Boston, 1854.
Redford, Emmette S; Truman, David B.; Hacker, Andrew; Westin, Alan F.; and Wood, Robert C. *Politics and Government in the United States.* New York-Chicago-Burlingame, 1965.
Rees, Thomas, ed. *The Racovian Catechism, with notes and illustrations . . . to which is prefixed a sketch of the history of Unitarianism in Poland and the adjacent countries.* London, 1818.
"Revolution in Poland," *The Newport Mercury.* Editorial. July 30, 1791.
Rose, William John. *Poland Old and New.* London, 1948.
Rosenberg, John. "Toward a New Civil War Revisionism," *The American Scholar,* Spring 1969.
Rostworowski, Michał. *Diariusz sejmu z 1830-31.* Warszawa, 1919.
Ruar, Martin. *Epistolarum selectarum centuriae duae.* London, 1729.
Russell, Bertrand. *A History of Western Philosophy.* New York, 1945.

Sandius (Sand), Christopher. *Bibliotheca Antitrinitariorum.* Freistadii-Amsterdam, 1684.
Sarolea, Charles. *Letters on Polish Affairs.* Edinburgh, 1922.
Sayles, Leonard P., and Strauss, George. *Human Behaviour in Organizations.* Englewood Cliffs, New Jersey, 1966.
Scholefield, Harry B., ed. *A Pocket Guide to Unitarianism.* Boston, 1961.
Scott, James B. *Official Statements of War Aims and Peace Proposals.* Washington, 1921.
Singer, Bernard. *Od Witosa do Sławka.* Paryz, 1965.
Socinus, Faustus. *Opera omnia.* (In Bibliotheca Fratrum Polonorum.) Irenopolis-London, 1656.
Sosnkowski, Kazimierz. *O Józefie Piłsudskim.* London, 1961.
Spencer, Herbert. *The Principles of Sociology.* 3 V. New York, 1910.
Stephen, Leslie. *History of English Thought in the Eighteenth Century.* 2 V. London, 1902.
Stern, Daniel K. "The Mercury - 1869: Editor Called Chinese-Haters Our 'Enemies' " *San Jose Mercury-News (San Jose, California, March 2, 1969.)*
"Sto pięcdziesiąt [150] lat niepodległości amerykańskiej," Czas. Editorial. No. 150 (5 July, 1926.)
Stroński, Stanisław. *The Two Polish Constitutions of 1921 and 1935.* Glasgow, 1944.
Sumner, W.G., and Keller, A.G. *The Science of Society.* 3 V. New Haven, 1928.
Sydenham, Thomas. *Processus integri in morbis fere omnibus curandis.* London, n.d.
Szacka, Barbara. "Staszic: Synteza dziejów ludzkości," *Filozofia polska:* II. *Filozofia nowożytna i współczesna.* Dr. Bronisław Baczko, ed., Warszawa, 1967.
Szacki, Jerzy. "Jan Śniadecki: Nauka i edukacja narodowa," *Filozofia polska:* II. *Filozofia nowożytna i współczesna.* Warszawa, 1967.

"Mochnacki: Rewolucja i tradycja," *Filozofia polska: Filozofia nowozytna i współczesna.* Warszawa, 1967

Sniadecki, Jan. *O nauk matematycznych poczatku, znaczeniu i wpływie na oświecenie powszechne.* Kraków, 1781.

Tatarkiewicz, Władysław. *Historia Filozofii.* II. *Filozofia nowozytna do roku 1830.* Warszawa, 1958.

— — — — — — — *Historia filozofii.* III. *Filozofia XIX wieku i współczesna.* Warszawa, 1958.

Teslar, Józef Andrzej. "Polski traktat polityczny w rękach Szekspira," *Wiadomości,* No. 768/9 (Dec. 18-25, 1960).

The Life of Mr. Thomas Firmin, late Citizen of London. London, 1698.

Tillich, Paul. *The Interpretation of History.* New York, 1936.

Time: The Weekly Newsmagazine. Editorial. Vol. 94., No. 1 (July 4, 1969), 14.

Toulmin, Joshua. *Memoires of the Life of Faustus Socinus.* London, 1777.

Toynbee, Arnold. "Peace, Power, Race in America," *Look,* Vol. XXXIII, No. 6. (March 18, 1969), 26.

Tuchman, Barbara. *The Guns of August.* New York, 1962.

Umiński, J. "The Counter-Reformation in Poland," *Cambridge History of Poland* pp. 392-415., Cambridge, 1950.

"United States," *Funk and Wagnalls New Standard Encyclopedia of Universal Knowledge,* Vol. XXIV.

Vidal, Gore. *Reflection Upon a Sinking Ship.* Boston-Toronto, 1969.

Wagner, Wieńczysław. "Laurentius Grimaldus Goslicius and His Age: Modern Constitutional Law Ideas in the XVI Century," *The Polish Review,* Vol. III, No. 1-2 (Winter-Spring 1958), pp. 37-42.

Wallace, Robert. *Antitrinitarian Biography; or Sketches of Lives and Writings of Distinguished Antitrinitarians, from the Reformation to the Close of the Seventeenth Century: to which is prefixed a History of Unitarianism in England. 3 V.,* London, 1850.

Wilbur, Earl Morse. *A History of Unitarianism in Transylvania, England, and America.* Cambridge, Massachusetts, 1952.

— — — — — — — *A History of Unitarianism: Socinianism and Its Antecedents.* Cambridge, Massachusetts, 1945.

— — — — — — — *Our Unitarian Heritage.* Boston, 1925.

Wilkins, David. *Concilia Magnae Britaniae et Hiberniae, a Synodo Verlamiensi . . . at Londinensem . . . Accedunt constitutiones et alia ad historiam Ecclesiae Anglicanae spectantia.* Londini, 1737.

Williams, T. Harry; Current, Richard N.; and Freidel, Frank. *A History of the United States to 1877.* New York, 1965.

Williamson, James A. *The Evolution of England: a Commentary on the Facts.* Oxford at the Clarendon Press, 1945.

Winwar, Frances. *Jean-Jacques Rousseau: Conscience of an Era.* New York, 1961.

Wiszowaty, Andrew and Stegmann, Joachim. Preface to *Racovian Catechism.* Irenopoli: post annum Domini 1569 (Amsterdam, 1665).

Wood, Anthony. *Athenae oxonienses. An Exact History of all the Writers and Bishops Who have had Their Eduction in the Most Ancient and Famous University of Oxford, from the Fifteenth Year of King Henry the Seventh, A.D. 1500 to the Author's Death in November 1695.* Oxford, 1721.

Wotschke, Theodor. "Die Unitarische Gemeinde in Meseritz-Bobelwitz," *Zeitschrift der Historischen Geselschaft fuer die Provinz Posen,* Vol. XXVI, (1911).

Wright, Conrad. *The Beginnings of Unitarianism in America.* Boston, 1955.

Yolton, John W. *John Locke and the Way of Ideas.* Oxford University Press, 1956.

Young, William H. *Ogg and Ray's Introduction to American Government.* New York, 1962.

Zaremba, Paweł. *Historia Polski.* 2 V. Paryż, 1961.

Zeltner, G.G. *Historia Crypto-Socinianismi Altorfinae Quondam Academiae et M. Ruari Epistolarum Centuriae Duae.* Leipzig, 1727.

Żantuan, Konstanty. "Olbracht Łaski in Elisabethan England - an Episode in the History of Culture," *The Polish Review,* Vol. XIII, No. 4., (Autumn 1968).

Żeleński, Tadeusz (Boy). *Marysieńka Sobieska.* Lwów-Warszawa, 1938.

INDEX

Adams, John, President of the United States, 16, 131, 132, 216, 220, 222, 228, 230, 241
Adams, John Quincy, President of the United States, 220, 241
Adams, Samuel, 9, 16, 227, 241
advice and consent of the senate, 106, 247, 249, 107, 108, 113, 116
Albon de, 16
Alciata, 150
Aleksander, King of Poland, in 1505 gave origin to Polish parliamentarism, 29
American press, and account of events of May 3d 1791 in Poland, 40
American Revolution, participation of the Poles in, XII; its influence on Poland, 65, 66, 227, 131, 132
American Unitarianism, 216-24
Anabaptism, 151
Anabaptists, in Bohemia, 142; their thought in Poland, 143
Antitrinitarianism, in Poland 145, 151; in Eastern England, 166
April (1935) Constitution, 101; its basic provisions, 102-3; kinships with the United States Constitution, 103-13, 226-7, 232, 234
Arciszewski, Tomasz, Polish socialist, freedom fighter, member of the Lublin Government, in November 1918, 82
Arianism, progressive theologians in the Colonies accused of, 216
Arians, followers of Arius; derogatory name for the Polish Bretheren, 150, 165
Aristarchus of Samos, 237
Aristotle, 204
Arius, presbiter in Alexandria (c. 318 A.D.), who gave origin to the heresy known as Arianism, 150
Arminianism, progressive theologians in the Colonies accused of, 216
Arminians, 189, 192
Armitage, Angus, historian of science, 235
Articles of Confederation (1777), necessary changes in, 226
Athanasian Creed, 178, 179, 217
Athanasius, criticised by Bidle, 173; controversy with Arius, 189
August (1926) Novels, 99-100

Bancroft, George, 4
Banneker, Banjamin, 53
Baptism of Poland (A.D. 966), 27, 133
Bar Confederation (1768-72), 231
Bertram, John, 128
Baxter, Richard, 215
Bayle, Pierre, 163, 164, 167, 195
Beard, Charles, 155
Beccaria, Cesare Bonesana, 237
Bellarmine, Robert, Cardinal, 247
Bentham, Jeremy, 237
Bentley, William, 218
Beseler, Hans von, German Governor General in Warsaw, 81
Best, Paul, English translator of Polish Brethren's works, 169, 170, 171, 172, 178

Betham-Holweg, Chancellor of the German Reich, disturbed by President Wilson's official pronouncement of January 22, 1917, 80
Biandrata (Blandrata), Georgio, 143, 150, 151
Bidle, John, English translator of Polish Brethren's works, fighter for religious freedom, 170, 171, 172, 173, 174, 176, 177, 178, 180, 181, 185, 186, 214, 215, 223
Biernat of Lublin, 143, 156, 237
Bierut, Boleslaw, 117
"Bill of Rights", 19, 54, 91, 92, 93, 125, 226
Black, Hugo, Justice of the Supreme Court of the United States, 115
Blackstone, William, 123, 245
"Blue Division" (Army Division formed of Polish-Americans in 1918), XIII
Bodin, Jean, 124, 248
Bohemian Brethren, expelled from their own country, 143
Bona, Queen of Poland (wife of King Zygmunt I), 135, 150
"Boston Masacre", 9
"Boston Tea Party", 10
Boy-Żeleński, Tadeusz, M.D., translator, author, 153
Brahe, Tycho, 126, 235
Briant, Lemuel, 216
Brown, Peter, 191
Budny, Szymon, thinker and writer, who contributed to the formation of the Polish Brethren's doctrines, 152, 165
Burke, Edmund, 41
Burnaby, Andrew, 221
Burnet, English Bishop, 179
Burski, Adam, philosopher, lecturer at Zamosc Academy, 239, 249

Calvin (Calvinus), John, 145, 150, 194
Calvinists, in Poland 143; Synod in Secemin, 145; contributed to the banishment of the Polish Brethren, 197; refugees from Poland in 1681, helped by a Socinian, Thomas Firmin, 175
Car, Stanislaw, 101, 102
Cardinal Laws (1793), 58, 59
Carl Gustav, King of Sweden, 153, 154
Carswell, Judge-nominate to the Supreme Court of the United States, 122
Catherine, Empress of Russia, 41
Charles II, King of England, 180
Chauncy, Charles, 216
"checks and balances", 21, 225, 230
Chewley, 214
Chewney, 223
Chillingworth, 215
Chubb, Thomas, 194
Church, Frank, Senator of Idaho, 115
Cicero, 249
"circular letters", 9

"Citizen", 229
Clarke, 217
Clerc, Jean Le, 189, 194
Cloppenburg, 163
Colden, Cadwallader, 128
Coleman, Arthur P., 245, 247
Columbus, Christopher, 4, 122
Condillac, Etienne Bonnot de, 204, 205, 210
Condorcet, Jean Antoine de, 208
Constitution of July 18, 1952, 117
Constitution of Kingdom of Poland during the 1830-1 Uprising, kinships with the United States Constitution, 75-8, 232
Constitution of the United States, 17; its basic provisions, 19-24; kinships with May 3d Constitution 1791, 41-56; with Kościuszko Constitution (1794), 65-7; with Constitution of Kingdom of Poland at the time of the November (1830-1) Uprising, 74-8; with March (1921) Constitution, 86-95; with April (1935) Constitution, 103-13; 233; 226, 230, 233, 249
Cooper, James Fenimore, XIII
Cooper, John, 174, 175, 177, 178
Cooper, Merian C. in WWI LTC in the Polish Air Force, in WWII General USAF, XIII
Copernican concept, 131
Copernican revolution, 235
Copernicus, Nicolaus (Mikolaj Kopernik) 126, 135
Cottrell, Ja., 172
Council of Constance (1414-8), 141
Council of Constantinople (A.D. 381), 156
Council of Torda (1568), 151
Crell, Christopher, Jr., 178, 179, 181
Crell, Christopher the elder (known also as Crell, Krzysztof or Crellius, Christopher the elder or Crellius-Spinowski, Krzysztof), 166, 175, 177, 178, 179, 180
Crell, Jan, (known also as Crellius, Jan), 163, 169, 175, 180, 185, 190, 192, 224, 241
Crell, Joseph, 224
Crell, Paul, 179, 180
Crell, Samuel, 178, 179, 181, 224
Crell, Steven, 224
Crellius, Christopher the elder (known also as Crellius—or Crell—Krzysztof, Crellius-Spinowski, Krzysztof or Crell, Christopher the elder), 166, 175, 177, 178, 179, 180
Crellius, Jan (known also as Crell, Jan), 163, 169, 175, 180, 185, 190, 192, 224, 241
Cromwell, Oliver, 169, 171, 177
Curtius, Philosophy Doctor, XIII
Cushing, Chief Justice of the Massachusetts Supreme Court, 53
Czartoryski, Adam Jerzy, 72
Czartoryski, Adam Kazimierz, 31
Czechowic, Marcin, thinker and writer, who contributed to the formation of the Polish Brethren's doctrines, 152

Czechs, the Poles received Christianity from, 135
Czernin, Ottokar, Austro-Hungarian Minister of Foreign Affairs, 80
Darwinian revolution, 235
Daszyński, Ignacy, 82, 83
David, Francis, 151
Declaration of Independence (1776), 11, 12; the role of Unitarians and Deists during the working out of the concept of independence, 220; 233, 245
Declaration of the Rights of Man and the Citizen of 1789, 102, 233
Deganavidah, Indian saintly prophet, 122
Deism, 131-2, 190, 191, 193, 194, 195, 204, 206, 207, 211
Deists, 132, 191, 194, 220, 222
Deloria, Vine, Jr., 125
Dembowski, Edward, 227
Descartes, Rene, 165, 204
Dickinson, John, 234
Diderot, Denis, 16
Dilthey, Wilhelm, 191
Downarowicz, Medard, 82
Dugard, William, 171
Dunster, Henry, president of Harvard University, 214
Durant, Will, 241
Dutch Anabaptists, 166
Dutch Collegiants, 163, 179-80
Dutch Mennonites, 163; forced to migrate to Poland, 166; 187
Dutch Remonstrants, 163, 175, 178, 187
Edwards, John, 180, 183
Elisabeth I, Queen of England, 166
Emerson, Ralph Waldo, 161, 241
Emlyn, Thomas, 217
Enlightenment, 125, 126, 127, 128, 129, 130, 131, 192, 195, 204, 210, 215, 232, 234, 235, 241
Erasmus, Desiderius of Rotterdam, 135, 235
Eriksson, Leif, 4
Essen, Minister of Saxony to Warsaw, 31
Eve, Paul Fitzsimmons, M.D., XIII
Farrington, John, 173
Felbinger, Jeremias, 172, 214
Felicijan, Joseph, 123
Filangieri, Geatano, 237
Filipowicz, Tytus, 124, 245, 247
Fillmore, Millard, 220
Filmer, Robert sir, 247, 248
Firmin, Thomas, 174, 175, 176, 177, 178, 179, 180, 183, 190,
Franklin, Benjamin, 16, 22, 33, 128, 132, 219, 220, 221, 222, 224, 226, 227, 230, 241
Frederick II, King of Prussia, 228
Frederick Augustus I, King of Saxony, Grand Duke of Warsaw, 70

Free Royal Cities Act (April 1791), 31
Freeman, James, 218, 219, 224
Freethinking, 190
French Revolution, 33, 66, 229
Frycz-Modrzewski (Modrzewski-Frycz), Andrzej, thinker, political writer, King's Secretary, 145, 237, 247
Fuller, Thomas, 166

Galileo, Galilei, 126, 204
Gandhi, Mohandas Karamchand, 145
Gay, Ebenzer, "Father of American Unitarianism", 216, 217
Geisteran, Jan, 163
Gengell, Jerzy George, 204
Gentile, Giovanni Valentino, 150, 151
George II, King of England, London Parliament dominated by adherents of, 8
Gerard, James, American Ambassador in Germany, 80
Giezek, Piotr, Polish Thinker who by avowing an Antitrinitarian credo led to the creation of the Lesser Reformed Church, which eventually became Socinian and, finally, Unitarian Church, 145, 237
Goethe, Johan Wolfgang von, 235
Goodwin, John, 223
Goslicius, Laurentius Grimaldus (Goślicki, Wawrzyniec Grzymała), thinker, writer, King's Secretary, Catholic Bishop, 124, 135, 237, 245, 247, 248, 249, 250
Goślicki, Wawrzyniec Grzymała, as above
Government Act of August 17, 1831, 73
Government Act of January 29, 1831, 72
"government of law", 247
Górnicki, Łukasz, 145
Górski, Konrad, 191, 196
Grand Duchy of Lithuania, 40, 41, 140
Grand Duchy of Warsaw, 70-1, 74
"Great Awakening", 216
"Great Peace" in the 1570's, 122
"Gresham Law", 237
Gresham, Thomas sir, 237
Grimaldi, Mateo, professor at the University of Padua, 145
Grotius, Hugo, 157, 163, 165, 241
Guines de, 4
Gumplowicz, Ludwik, 28

Habsburgs, the, 151
Haight, Charles S., 245, 247, 248
Hales, Alexander of, 185, 187, 189
Hamilton, Alexander, 15, 16, 20, 227, 229
Handelsman, Marceli, professor at the University of Warsaw, 61
Harvard University, 214, 216
Haynes, Hopton, 178

Haynsworth, Judge-nominate to the Supreme Court of the United States, 22
Hazzlitt, William, 219, 220, 224, 241
Hedworth, Henry, 174, 175, 177, 178, 179, 180
Helvetic body, 231
Helvetius, Claude Adrien, 241, 245
Henry VIII, King of England, 240
Henry, Patrick, 16, 227
Heriolfsson, Bjarne, 4
Hiawatha, 122
Higginson, Stephen, 14
Hobbes, Thomas, 191
Holbach, Paul Henry Dietrich, 241
Hugo, Cardinal, 143
Huguenots, in 1680 helped by a Socinian, Firmin, 175
Hussite Wars, the memory of, 142
Hutcheson, Francis, 215

Ibrahim Ibn Jacob, 27
"Intolarable Acts", 10
Irish Protestants, in 1688-9 helped by a Socinian, Firmin, 175
Iroquois League, 122
Izabela, daughter of King Zygmunt I and Queen Bona, 143; 151

Jagiellonian University (Kraków Academy), 203, 208, 213
James I, King of England, 162, 166, 167
Jan Kazimierz, King of Poland, 153, 154
Jan of Kolno, 4
Jan of Pilzno, 143
Jefferson, Thomas, 11, 14, 16, 19, 53-4, 123, 124, 132, 220, 222, 227, 228, 229, 230, 231, 241, 245, 249
Jerzy (George) II Rakoczy, Prince of Transylvania, 154
John Sigismund Zanolya, King of Transylvania, 151
Johnson, Lyndon B., President of the United States, 25
Johnson, S., Doctor of Divinity, 168
Justinianus, Spanish translator, 237

Kamphusen, Dirk Rafaelsz, 163
Kant, Emanuel, 192
Karge, Józef, General in the American Civil War, professor at Princeton University, XIII
Kasparek, Franciszek, professor at Jagiellonian University, 58, 61
Katsh, Abraham I., 123
Kazimierz the Great, King of Poland, 28
Kemp, Francis A. van der, 224
Kennedy, John F., President of the United States; original role of the U.S. Senate in the exposition of his, 44, 87; 115
Kepler, Johannes, 126
King, Martin Luther, 145, 235
Klaproth, Heinrich Julius von, 4

Knowles, John, 174, 176, 177, 178, 180, 185
Knox, Henry, American Revolutionary General, 14, 15
Kołłątai, Hugo, Ph.D., D.D., Catholic priest, one of the most important exponents of the Polish Enlightenment, patriot, fighter for social progress branded a Jacobin, writer; 31, 54, 61, 204-6, 210, 211, 231, 241
Konarski, Stanislaw, Catholic priest of great merits for the modernization of the antiquated education system in Poland, 204
Kopernik, Mikołaj (Nicolaus Copernicus), 126, 135, 141, 142, 204, 206, 209, 235
Kościuszko, Tadeusz, General in the American Revolutionary Army, Supreme Leader and Governor of the Uprising in Poland, in 1794, 59, 60, 65, 66
Kościuszko Constitution (1794), 57, 64; kinships with the United States Constitution, 65-7; 225, 232
Kościuszko's Decree of May 10, 1794, 61
Kościuszko Uprising (1794), 63, 64
Kot, Stanisław, professor at Jagiellonian University, politician, writer, 192, 196
Kraków Academy (Jagiellonian University), 135, 141, 237
Kraków Missal, 143
Krzyżanowski, Włodzimierz, General in the American Civil War, XIII
Kucharzewski, Jan, 81
Kukiel, Marian, historian, university professor, General in the Polish Army in WWII, Minister in the Polish Government in London, 64, 83
Kutrzeba, Stanislaw, professor at Jagiellonian University, 58, 64

Lanckoroński, 31
Laplace, Pierre Simon de, 208
Lauchen, Georg Joachim von (known also as Rheticus), professor at the University of Wittenberg, 142
Laud, William, Archbishop of Canterbury, 167
Leibnitz, Gottfried, 126, 204, 228
Lesser Reformed Church (known better as Polish Brethren), precursor of the Socinian and, finally, Unitarian Church, 145, 152
"liberum veto", 41, 73
Limborch, Philip van, 189
Lincoln, Abraham, President of the United States, 223
Lindsey, Theophilus, founder of the first avowedly Unitarian church in London, 218, 219, 224
Linowski, Aleksander, 31
Lismanino, Francisco, 142, 145, 150
Locke, John, M.D., philosopher, 50, 123, 124, 125, 127, 129, 179, 183-4, 185, 187, 189, 190, 191, 192, 193, 204, 207, 208, 215, 217, 231, 241, 245, 248, 249
Logan, James, 128
London press, presenting the political events in Poland on April 14, 1791, 31
Lubieniecki, Stanisław, close relative of Jan Sobieski, astronomer, Socinian minister and historian of the movement, 160
Lublin Government (November, 1918), 82, 229
Lublin Manifesto, 83

Lushington, Thomas, 169
Luther, Martin (Lutherus), 160, 194, 235
Lutherans, in Poland, 143
Łaski, Jan, 237
Łempicki, Zygmunt, 192

Mably, Bonnot de, writings of, 16, 231
Madison, Jámes, President of the United States, 14, 15, 16, 132, 220, 222, 226, 229, 230, 241
Malinowski, Marian, 82
Małachowski, Stanisław, Marshal of the Constitutional Seym, 31, 35
March (1921) Constitution, its basic provisions, 85-6; kinships with the United States Constitution, 86-95; common sources of similar mechanisms, 230; distinct influence of the Enlightenment, 222, 233
Maret, Hugues Bernard, French Minister, 70
Marret, Thomas, 174, 175, 177
Marx, Karl, 249
Mary II, Queen of England, 174, 240
Masson, John, 171
Mather, Cotton, 216
May 3d (1791) Constitution, 30, 35, 40; its chief provisions, 41-2; kinships with the United States Constitution, 41-56; 226, 230, 231, 232
Mayhew, Jonathan, 216, 217
Mersenn, Marin, friend of Pascal and Descartes, 165
Miasta nasze Królewskie wolne (1791), (Free Royal Cities Act), subsequently declared a part of May 3d (1791) Constitution, 31
Mickiewicz, Adam, 160, 241
Middleton, Conyers, 140
Miller, John C., 124
Milton, John, 131, 169, 170, 171, 215, 217
Modrzewski-Frycz (Frycz-Modrzewski), Andrzej, thinker, political writer, King's Secretary, 145, 237, 247
Mohl, Robert von, 41
Moltke, Helmuth von, 29
Montesquieu, Charles Louis Secondat de, 42, 85, 94, 122, 231, 232, 245
Moon, Richard, 171, 172
Moraczewski, Jędrzej, one of the leaders of the Polish Socialist Party, member of the Lublin Government in 1918, prime minister of the Polish government formed in Warsaw, in November, 1918, 82, 83
Moravian Brethren (German Anabaptists), 145
More, L.T., 189
More, Thomas sir (St. Thomas More), 240
Morgan, Thomas, 194
Morison, Samuel Eliot, 4
Morsztyn, Karol Henryk, 160
Moskorzowski, Jarosz Hieronim, thinker and writer, who contributed to the formation of the Polish Brethren's doctrines, 152

Mościcki, Ignacy, President of the Republic of Poland, 116
Mutual Declaration of the Two Peoples (Zaręczenie wzajemne obojga narodów) of October 22, 1791, an affirmation of the unity and indivisibility of Poland and the Grand Duchy of Lithuania, 40
McLachlan, Herbert John, 171, 172, 178, 180, 190, 215
Naeranus, Jan, leader of the Rotterdam Remonstrants, 175
Napoleon Bonaparte, his interests and attitudes toward Poland, 69-70
National Colors Act of February 7, 1831, 73
"Navigation Acts" (of 1660, 1663, 1673, 1696), 5, 6, 8
Necker, Jacques, the writings of, 16
Newman, John Henry, Cardinal, 194
Newton, Isaac, 126, 131, 178, 179, 189, 190, 191, 192, 204, 207, 208, 228, 241
Nicene Council A.D. 325, 150
Nicholas II, Czar of Russia, his January 1, 1917, New Year's Message, 80
Niemcewicz, Julian Ursyn, poet, playwright, political polemist; in the Uprising of 1794 Kościuszko's aid-de-camp; as a Deputy to the Great Seym castigating the privileged nobility and pointing to the example of democracy in America, 33
Niemojewski, thinker and writer, who contributed to the formation of the Polish Brethren's doctrines, 152
Niemojewski, Wacław, leader of Polish monarchists during the First World War, 81
Nixon, Richard M., President of the United States, 22
Nocznicki, Tomasz, 82
no excessive or cruel punishment, 158, 250
"Nonimportation Agreements", 8, 9
Norton, John, 215
November Uprising (1830-1), 72
Novisiltsev, Nicolai N., Russian Senator, member of the Provisional Government of the Congressional Kingdom of Poland, 72

Oath Act of February 8, 1831, 72
oath of office, 72, 77, 89, 106, 247-8, 249
Ochino, Bernardino, 150, 151
Ogonowski, Zbigniew, 187, 190, 192, 193, 195, 196
Opaliński, Krzysztof, cousin of Jan Sobieski, 153
Ossowski, Michał, Catholic priest, thinker, writer, 231
Ostorodt, Krzysztof, sixteenth century Socinian minister, 162

Paine, Thomas, 16, 128, 132, 220, 222, 227, 245
Paleolog, thinker and writer, who contributed to the formation of the Polish Brethren's doctrines, 152
Paleologue, Maurice, French Ambassador to Russia, 80
Parker, Theodore, 223
Pascal, Blaise, 165
Piarist Order, participating in efforts to reform outdated education system in Poland, 204
Piattoli, Scypion, Catholic priest, King's Private Secretary, 31

Piccolomini, Aenas Silvius (later Pope Pius II), 123-4
Piłsudski, Józef, 81, 82, 83, 94, 99, 100, 113-4, 229, 230, 234
Piramowicz, Grzegorz, Catholic priest highly merited for the modernization of the backward education system in Poland, 204
Pisecius, Tomasz, Socinian writer, 175
"Plus ratio quam vis" (More reason than force), 135
Poincaré, Raymond, French statesman and writer, 103
Polish Brethren (Polish Arians, Lesser Reformed Church), 143, 150, 151, 152, 153; their ideas, 154-8; 159, 161, 162, 163, 166; their works popularized their ideas in the West, 169-73; 177, 187, 191; important factor in the development of the world culture, 192; 197, 213, 214
Polish Calvinists, contribution to the banishment of the Polish Brethren, 197
Polish Jacobins, 66
Polish Unitarians, 160
Polish Uprising of 1794, 65
Polonus, Joannes Scolvus (Jan of Kolno), 4
Połaniec Manifesto, of May 7, 1794, 60, 61
Pomian, Krzysztof, 195, 196
Poniatowski, Juliusz, 82
Potocki, Ignacy, 31
Potocki, Wacław, 157
Powers of the Supreme Commander Act of January 24, 1831, 73
Pragier, Adam, 31
Prawo o sejmikach (Regional Seyms Act) (1791), subsequently declared a part of May 3d (1791) Constitution, 31
Price, Richard, 219
Priestley, Joseph, scientist, Unitarian minister, personal friend of Benjamin Franklin, 218, 219, 224, 241
Przypkowski, Samuel, most mature of the thinkers and writers who contributed to the formation of the Polish Brethren's doctrines, 152, 156, 157, 171, 187, 213, 241
Puffendorf, Samuel von, 124
Pułaski, Kazimierz, Polish patriot, General in the American Revolutionary Army, XIII
Pynchon, William, 214-5, 223

Raczkiewicz, Władysław, President of the Polish Republic, 116
Radziwiłł, Mikołaj (Czarny) Prince, 161
Rakoczy, George (Jerzy) II, Prince of Transylvania, 154
Raków Academy ("Sarmatian Athens"), 163, 165, 239
Randolph, Edmund, 15
Reformation, 125; its advent in Poland, and its chief propagators, 142; subsequently done way with, 197
reign of law, 247, 249
Religious freedom in Poland, guaranteed to the Ruthenians, 142; established by law in 1555, reinforced by Warsaw Confederacy, in 1573; 143; Poland — Mecca to fugitives from the West European Inquisition and from Calvin's

tribunals, 150; gradual disappearance of, after a century of nonexistence, religious freedom restored in 1767, 160; religious tolerance in Poland cited by Best, 170; freedom of all rites and religions—a constitutional requirement, 55, 91, 112

Rembrand, Harmenszoon van Rijn, 187

Representation for Lithuania and Volhynia Act of May 11-19, 1831, 73

Rheticus, real name: George Joachim van Lauchen, 142

Ricardo, David, 241, 249

Ries, Hans de, 162

Rittenhouse, David, one of the early American physicists, 128

Rousseau, Jean Jacques, 50, 124, 127, 129, 204, 208, 227, 231, 232, 241, 245, 249

Ruar, Martin, thinker and writer, who contributed to the formation of the Polish Brethren's doctrines, 152; 163, 165, 166, 185

Rutter, Ralph, 165

Rydz-Śmigły, Polish Army colonel, member of the Lublin Government, in November, 1918, 82; General, Chief Inspector of the Polish Armed Forces, officially made "first person in Poland after the President of the Republic", 104-5

Sandius (Sand), Christopher, 172, 181

"Sarmatian Athens" (Rakow Academy of the Polish Brethren), 239

Sazonov, Sergey Dmitrievich, Russian diplomat and statesman, 80

Schlichtyng (Szlichtyng), Jonasz, thinker and writer, who contributed to the formation of the Polish Brethren doctrine, traveled to Holland 163; his book published in Rakow in 1634, subsequently published in English, in London in 1646; 187

Schoepf, Albin, General in the American Civil War, XIII

Scolvus, Johannes Polonus, 4

Second International (1899), Józef Piłsudski took part in, 99

"Second Reformation", 131; the ideas of, 154-8

Segeth, Thomas, 165

separation of church and state, 157

Servetus, Miguel, 143, 145, 241

Sforza, Bona, king Zygmunt I's Italian bride, 135, 142

Shaftesbury, Anthony Ashley Cooper Earl of, 179, 180, 207

Shakespeare, William, 249

Shays, Daniel, 13, 229

Sidney, Algernon, 247

Sierakowski, Karol, Polish General, former Kościuszko's soldier in the Uprising of 1794, 160

Sierakowski, Zygmunt, leader of the Uprising in Lithuania and Samogitia, in 1863, 227

Sieroszewski, Wacław, revolutionary, novelist, ethnographer, 82

Sievers, Jakub Jan, Russian Ambassador in Poland, 58

Sławek, Walery, freedom fighter, Piłsudski's faithful soldier, politician, 100

Smalcius, Walenty, thinker and writer, who contributed to the formation of the Polish Brethren's doctrines, 185

Smith, Adam, 127, 231, 232
Sobieski, Jan, later King of Poland, 153
Socinianism, 162, 166, 168, 169; its attractiveness, 170; "genius of the earlier Socinianism in Poland, 173, 175, 176, 190, 191, 194, 195, 196, 197, 216, 240, 241
Socinians, 152; English speaking, 160; community in London, 174, 177, 176, 178, 183, 189, 191, 192, 193, 194, 196
Socinus (Socyn), Faustus, 151, 152, 157, 158, 162, 163; his writings, 171; criticised by Bidle, 173, 176, 185, 190, 192, 194, 215, 239, 241
Socinus, Laelius (Lelio Sozzini), 150, 151
Sołtyk, Roman, 72
Soner, Ernst, professor in Altdorf, 162, 165
Sosnknowski, Kazimierz, freedom fighter, Polish Army General, WWII politician, 100
Sozzini, Lelio (Laelius Socinus), 150
Spanish Inquisition, 240
Spinowski, Knzysztof (known also as Crellius-Spinowski, Krzysztof), 180
Spinoza, Benedykt, 164, 241
Stanisław August Poniatowski (named also: Stanisław II August), the last King of Poland, 31, 35, 41, 67, 204, 231
Staszic, Stanisław, Catholic priest educated in Poland and abroad, imbued with western ideas strived by means of his writings to contribute to the modernization of his society, 204, 207, 208, 210, 240
Stegman, Joachim, Rector of Raków Academy, thinker and writer, who contributed to the formation of the Polish Brethren's doctrines, English translation of his writings published in 1653, 172, 192, 193, 194
Steuben, Friedrich Wilhelm Ludolf Gerhard Augustine von, former Prussian Army officer, General in the American Revolutionary Army, 229
Stevenson, Adlai, 220
Stolarski, Błażej, 82
Stroński, Stanisław, university professor, Deputy, journalist, politician, 101, 116
Stuartian Divine Right-ology, 247
Stucky, Alice, 178, 179, 181
Suchorzewski, M., 33
Supreme Council's Act of July 1794, 60, 61
Sydenham, Thomas, "the English Hippocrates", 179
Szlichtyng (Schlichtyng), Jonasz, thinker and writer, who contributed to the formation of the Polish Brethren's doctrines, traveled to Holland, 163; his book published in Rakow in 1634, subsequently published in English, in London in 1646, 169; 187
Śmigły-Rydz, Edward, Colonel, member of Lublin Government in November, 1918; Marshal, member of a trinity in the division of power, 105
Śniadecki, Jan, scientist, one of the most important representatives of the Polish Enlightenment, 204, 209, 210, 231, 240
Śniadecki, Jędrzej, Polish scientist of the Enlightenment era, 204, 210, 240
Świtalski, Kazimierz, Colonel, Marshal of the Seym, 101

Taft, William Howard, President of the United States, 220
Tatarkiewicz, Władysław, philosopher, professor of the University of Warsaw, author of a number of highly valued works in philosophy and aesthetics, 161
Taylor, Jeremy, 215
Teslar, J.A., 245, 249
"Tew Circle", 189
Thoreau, Henry David, 145
Thugutt, Stanisław, freedom fighter, politician, 82, 229
Tillich, Paul, theologian, 124
Tillotson, John, Archbishop of Canterbury, 174, 179, 215
Tindal, Matthew, 193, 194
Toland, John, 191, 192, 193, 194, 195, 210
Tolstoy, Lev, 145
Townshend, Charles, 8, 9
Toynbee, Arnold, 53

Union of Utrecht, 236
Unitarianism, 132, 222, 223, 224, 240
United Protestant Religious Society of New York, 224

Vattel, Emmerich, 122
Venator, Adolf, 163
Vidal, Gore, 125
Vladimirus, Paulus (Włodkowic Paweł), 141
Voelkel, 163; cooperated in writing with Jan Crell, 175
Vogler, 165
Voltaire, François Marie Arouet, 16, 131, 208, 228, 235, 241
Vorst, Konrad, 163

Wagner, Wieńczysław, 29
Warsaw Confederacy (1573), increased religious freedom in Poland, 143
Washington, George, 11, 13, 14, 15, 33, 53, 131, 132, 220, 222, 228, 229, 230
Weberly, John, 168
Weigel, Katarzyna, 145
Whitefield, George, 216
Wielhorski, Michał, 231
Wieniawa-Długoszowski, Bolesław, M.D., Cavalry General, diplomat, 116
Wilbur, Earl Morse, 143, 145, 164, 190
Wilson, Woodrof, President of the United States, 80
Winthrop, John, 128
Wiszowaty, Andrzej, one of the leading Polish Socinian writers, 164; grandson of Faust Socyn and his wife born Morsztyn, 165, 166, 185, 192, 193, 194
Wiszowaty, Tobiasz, the last Socinian in the Seym, 154
Władysław Jagiełło, King of Poland, 29
Włodkowic, Pawel (Paulus Vladimirus), 141, 150
Wojdowski, Andrzej, a sixteenth century Socinian minister, 162
Wolf, Jerome, 235
Wolzogen, 185
Wotschke, Theodore, 160

Wytfliet, a Dutch geographer, 4
Yolton, John W., 191
Zamość Academy, 239
Zamoyski, Andrzej, 207
Zamoyski, Jan, 135, 207, 239, 245
Zeltner, G.G., 165
Zenger, John Peter, 129
Ziemięcki, Bronisław, 82
Zwicker, Daniel, 178
Zygmunt II August, King of Poland, 135, 143, 150
Żeleński, Tadeusz /Boy/ (Boy-Żeleński), M.D., translator, author, 153